God's Grace Poured Out on a Man
The Life Story of Merlyn E. Jones

INTRODUCTION

While it is true that God's grace in a general sense reaches down to every man, from my perspective God's grace has been especially and infinitely poured out on me. My life story attests to that. My primary intention for writing down these memories is to encourage my grandkids especially to trust Christ as their Savior and live their lives totally for Him. He really is amazing and so worth living for!! Besides, their eternal destiny depends upon it. But the story of God's grace on my life and ministry can also be an encouragement to others who need to know that a very awesome God really does loves them.

As I look back on my life I believe Satan did everything he could to destroy me and to keep me from becoming a vessel that God could use. Somehow he knew well before I did that God wanted to use me to bring glory to Himself. I know that beyond a shadow of a doubt that if it had not been for God's grace, my physical life would have been taken prematurely or my spiritual life would have ship wrecked and my testimony for God destroyed. Although this story is about **my** life, it is really more about **God**. For some reason known only to God, He chose to preserve and protect me through-out my life. This is a story about what God did!

PHASE   I

GOD'S GRACE POURED OUT ON MY EARLY YEARS

(Age 0-5, 1945-1950)

- Average wage per year: $2400.00
- Average cost per home: $4600.00
- Cost of gasoline: 15 cents per gallon
- TVs: Most homes did not have one (Only 5000)
- Computer: First general purpose computer was made in 1945, but was big enough to fill a whole house.

CHAPTER 1

MY BEGINNINGS AND EARLY MEMORIES

1945 was long before cell phones. Our only phone hung on the wall at our house. To call someone we needed to give the crank on the phone a turn and an operator would ask, "Number please", and we would give her the three digit number we were trying to call. We also had a "party line", which meant that at least three or four other homes on our line could listen in to a conversation at any time. If mom wasn't looking part of our entertainment for my brothers and sister, and me was listening to the conversation of others. Trains were still the chief means of moving goods, although that would soon change. We had a railroad track not far behind our house. Trains came frequently, and I loved to hear their whistles, especially during the night. We still had stream engines that were on the tracks although they were soon replaced by diesel engines. The world was changing rapidly. World War II was coming to a close. Germany surrendered in May of 1945, and Japan did as well in August after the US dropped two atom bombs August 6th and 9th, which seriously got their attention and no doubt saved thousands of American lives. So the general mood of the nation was upbeat and positive.

Into this world I was born on September 28, 1945 in the Edmore, Michigan hospital. I had the distinction of being the first child in our family to be born in a hospital. My six year older sister, Marcia, and four year older brother, Melvin, were born at our home at 729 New Street in Stanton, Michigan. My two year younger brother, Keith, would be born in the Greenville hospital.

My parents, Eldon and Esther Jones were both born in 1913. They had come through the hard times of the Great Depression, so knew how to work hard and value what they had. Dad had experienced working and living on a farm just to survive. He was the first in his family to graduate from high school. After high school he "rode the rails" out to Kansas because he had heard there was work out there, but that work was short lived, so he came back to Stanton.   Mom was also a hard worker and had been able to earn a teaching certificate at a school called County Normal. On June 18, 1939, mom and dad were married and moved into the house he had purchased at 729 New Street in Stanton. Natural gas was just coming into Stanton at that time, so dad went to work for the gas company as a manager. In 1947 he began the Stanton Plumbing and Heating business, which he operated until he sold out in 1969.

Mom and dad had each trusted Christ as their Savior earlier in life and had the blessing of having Christian parents. So it was natural for them to faithfully attend the First Baptist Church of Stanton and to raise their kids to do the same. Church attendance was never optional. If the doors of the church were open, the Jones family would always be there. My first visit to church was no doubt a week after I was born. Though my parent's discipline of us might seem extreme by today's standards, it helped make me what I am today. The usual method for me, at least, was a belt applied to my behind. But I am extremely thankful for that discipline. It was God's grace that gave me the godly, dedicated parents that I had. My parents modeled what it was like to put God first and what a Christian life was like. They read their Bibles every night, treated others with respect, and sacrificed for their children and for others. I was extremely blessed to have Eldon and Esther Jones as my parents.

Dad said that when I was born I was very red in color. So he told Mom after seeing me, "Well, shall we give him back to the Indians?" Mom's roommate in the Edmore Hospital was another new mother, Mrs. Dilno. She had given birth to a daughter just two days before and named her Beverley. Years later mom made a special effort to bring Beverley and her sister to church, which played a key role in their trusting Christ as their Savior.

My earliest memories go back to when I was about 2. I remember going with my older brother Mel down to grandma and grandpa Jones's house to get some fruit jars for mom. We had a red wagon to haul the jars with. I probably rode in the wagon the quarter of a mile or so down to grandma's house, which at that time would have been at the north end of McPherson Street before they moved around the corner to Pine Street. I thought I was 'big stuff" because I was helping my mom. But the happy event went "south" when Mel convinced me that it was my turn to push him and the jars back home, which I was unable to do. He said it would be "fun". He would use that term for years on my younger brother Keith and I. We all laugh about it now.

A couple of other memories include remembering when our dog Max was hit by a car in front of our house. I just remember my sister, Marcia, crying very loudly. I also remember when dad's oldest sister, Marjorie, died suddenly. I don't remember much about it but I remember the crying. I also remember when my dad came into our bedroom to spank either Keith or me for not settling down at night and fainted just before getting to our bedroom door. He apparently had gotten out of bed too quickly. Melvin was the only one with a cool enough head to call the doctor or at least suggest that he be called.

CHAPTER   2

MY SALVATION

My most important memory is when God touched my heart. I was still 4 when I started Kindergarten. I had been to church on a Sunday night. I don't remember who had preached or what had been preached. But I went home troubled at the thought of dying and going to hell. That night I just couldn't sleep. I shared a bedroom with my two brothers. Keith and I slept in a bunk bed – I was on top and he was on the bottom. Mel had his own bed, with a dresser for all three of us between the bunk bed and Mel's bed. The room was small. The ends of the bunk bed touched each wall and the dresser just barely fit between the beds. I remember climbing down out of my top bunk and going out to the living room where mom was. I told her that I didn't want to go to hell, but wanted to go to heaven. She then explained salvation and Christ's death in my place and helped me pray a prayer asking Jesus to save me. I can't begin to explain the peace and joy that came into my little heart and soul. I remember going to school the next day so excited to tell someone that I was now saved! The first person I told was one of my cousins, who came from a family that didn't attend church. I couldn't get over the fact that he didn't seem to care that I was saved.

My salvation began my journey, my life with God. I loved being saved. I would talk with God on my top bunk and could almost see Him, He was so real. I remember in one of those special prayer times saying a prayer that would affect the rest of my life. I think I may have heard my grand dad Chapin say something similar in a testimony at church. But for some reason it stuck with me and meant a lot to me. I prayed with every ounce of sincerity I could have at that age. I asked God to "take hold of the helm of my ship, and steer it the rest of my life." Then I added something because I knew my bent even at that early age. I prayed, "and Lord, please hold on tight and don't let me steer." I am so thankful that He heard and answered that prayer. Even at that early age God's grace was being poured out on me. I was only 5, when I remember gathering the neighbor children and preaching the Gospel to them at our cottage on Dickerson Lake the next summer.

PHASE   II

GOD'S GRACE POURED OUT ON MY GROWING UP YEARS

(Age 6-17, 1951-1963)

- Cost of a new home in 1960: $16,500
- Cost of a gallon of gasoline in 1960: 25 cents
- Rock music began
- Most popular musician: Elvis Presley. He had the most number one hits in 1950s.
- World events: Korean War: 1950-1953, Cuban missile crisis in 1962, Cold War at its peak with bomb shelters common and air raid practices in our school
- Society: Baseball was more popular than football. Girls only wore skirts and blouses or dresses, not pants. Prosperity increased. TVs start to become popular.
- Automobiles: Styles began to change from year to year. The automatic transmission introduced.
- Average cost of a new car: $2752

CHAPTER   3

GOD'S GRACE ALLOWED ME TO HAVE A LOT OF FUN

Fun in the Snow

The next phase of my life was a mixture of both a lot of fun and adventure as well as extreme emotional trauma and struggle. First, I want you to know that I did have a lot of fun while growing up.

 I loved to play in the snow. I would make snow angels with my sister and play "fox and geese" with my bothers. As I recall, a large circle would be made in the snow, and then the circle would be divided to look like slices of a pie. Where the lines intersected in the middle of the pie was the safe zone. One person would be "it" – the "fox", and the others would be the "geese". It was a winter form of "tag".

Of course there were also the usual snowball fights. These lasted until someone got hit in the face and began to cry. These games often include my cousins Marvin and his younger brother Terry. They just lived down the street next to grand ma Jones's house. Our house set up on a small hill that dropped sharply to the gravel road that was called New Street, which ran north and south. Since our house was on the west side of the road, a good west wind always caused a big snow drift across the hill, a natural play ground for a young boy. I loved to make tunnels in that drift that went for several feet along the hillside.

Across the road to the east was a field owned by the Brakes family. About a quarter of a mile across that field was a small pond that was perfect for ice skating. One year the snow was perfect for making snow blocks with the snow shovel. My cousin Marvin and I cut the blocks with the shovel and carried them the short distance next to the pond and made an igloo. We hauled some old boards that were behind the garage on our sled and used them to make the roof by placing them across the blocks of snow and then piling snow on the boards. We used our igloo to keep warm after ice skating. That was neat until the next spring when Mr. Brake asked dad how some boards ended up near his pond.

As a boy I loved to dress up as warm as I could and just walk out in a blizzard. I think it made me feel "tough". I also learned to ski. I think I was around 9 or 10 when I got my first set of snow skis for Christmas. They were cross-country skis not downhill skis, but I didn't know the difference back then. I didn't have poles either and didn't know I was supposed to have them. So I just got on the skis and went down the hills near our house. That was so much fun. A few years later I got some bigger cross-country skis for Christmas. By then I was getting pretty good on them. I made a jump using an old car hood and loved flying over it. At one youth outing at "Thurber's Hill" north of Stanton, the youth leader, Leonard Campbell, pulled me across a field with his Jeep as I hung on to a rope. That was cool and got a lot of laughs. I even walked the mile or so to the Knobs Hill, which was the highest hill around. At that time it had a fire tower on it. There was a two track road that wound its way to the top. As I started down that hill following the two track road, I was really flying. But I didn't quite make the turn to the right and my skis went out from under me. I slid for quite a long ways and then had to walk the whole way home bruised and humbled, but alive. I still have those skis to this day. I haven't been able to part with them.

Fun with Bambi

I was probably 8 or 9 when dad brought home a black cocker spaniel puppy. He was so cute. I think Keith named him. Because the cutest animal he could think of was the baby deer in the new cartoon, we named him Bambi. Bambi was my best friend. I took him hunting with me when I was older. He was great on pheasants. If there was a pheasant around, Bambi would find him. He was also great on "pats" (partridge). One time when I was hunting pats with my friend, Dave Wickes, Bambi put up a pat. Because there was a stump right in front of the pat, it had to fly almost straight up. Bambi jumped up in the air and was able to grab the pat before we could even get a chance to shoot it. He was a great hunter. With his help I got several pheasant on property near our house.

But sometimes Bambi's hunting skill got him into trouble. One day I heard Bambi barking up a storm between our house and the railroad tracks. An awful unbearable smell was also coming from that direction, and I knew, I just knew what was happening. I grabbed my shot gun and some shells and ran in the direction of the barking and the terrible odor. Bambi had cornered a skunk. The skunk had already sprayed Bambi, who was pawing at his nose and then running at the skunk. But Bambi had bitten the skunk and shaken it as well. It was pretty much a stand-off, although the slunk looked like it had gotten the worse end of the deal. I did the only thing I could think of to solve the problem. I managed to get a hold of Bambi's collar and pull him back with one hand. With the other hand I aimed the gun at the skunk and finished him off. With that accomplished Bambi concluded that his job was done. But my job had just begun. Bambi smelled terrible.

Now Bambi usually had the run of the house. He would sit by my chair when we were eating waiting for me to slip him some scraps of meat or anything I really didn't want to eat. But there was no way mom would let him in the house smelling as bad as he did. So I figured that I needed to fix the problem. I took Bambi into our bathroom and put him in the tub, turned on the water and went to work on him with all the soap I could find. Somewhere in that process mom came home. As soon as she entered the door she smelled the skunk smell. Though I tried as hard as I could, I just couldn't get that smell out of Bambi's hair. Mom let out a yell that let me know that I was in trouble again. The dog leaped out of the tub and ran out of the house to safety. I, on the other hand, couldn't run that fast and couldn't live outside. I had to face the "music". I was too old to spank at that point, but she still verbally terrified me. It probably wasn't a good idea to try to clean Bambi up by bringing him into the house.

When we had grown up and gone off to college, Bambi became dad's best friend. He went everywhere with dad. He would ride in his pick-up truck with him in the front seat watching the road like he was human. Sometimes I think he thought he was human and another member of our family. As Bambi got old he developed arthritis and had difficulty getting around. He was across the street in the farmer's field one day, when the farmer, who was mowing hay, accidentally hit Bambi with the mower blade cutting off one of his legs. Dad was called. He took his shot gun out to the field and put Bambi out of his misery. To this day I don't know how dad was able to do that. Dad was sick for several days after losing his best friend.

Fun Camping

I have always enjoyed the out of doors. Whether it was hiking through a woods, climbing hills, fishing, hunting, canoeing, or camping, I loved it all. My earliest campouts began in our yard in an old army pup tent.

Those were usually with Mel or Keith. I remember camping out one early spring night and waking up the next morning with the bucket of water frozen over. Being in the Boy's Brigade at church gave opportunities for campouts as well.

One special campout memory was actually not about my campout. It was about my brother, Mel, and his friend, Steve Hart's campout in our yard. My brothers, Mel and Keith, were always the good guys in our family. I don't remember them ever getting into trouble or getting a spanking, although they probably did once or twice. My sister, Marcia, and I, on the other hand, made up for their "goodness". We were pretty good – at planning mischief.

Marcia's friend, Karen Mitchell (our pastor's daughter), kind of liked Steve Hart at the time. So when they learned that Mel and Steve were planning a campout, they decided to sabotage their peaceful night. For some reason they thought they needed my assistance. I guess I had a reputation at being good at mischief. I was delighted to help. So during the day before the campout I took off the screens to Marcia's and my bedroom windows, so we could get out our windows as quietly as possible. At the appointed time we both snuck out our windows. Keith woke up when I was half way out my window. I think I threatened him with murder in order to keep him silent.

Karen had also snuck out of her house and met us in our driveway. We then crept up on Mel and Steve, who were talking in their tent, and pulled their tent stakes. Unfortunately I could not contain my laughter at seeing these two bumps in the tent (their heads) moving about as they frantically tried to find their way out. Marcia, Karen, and I ran over the hill toward the road. About that time we saw mom and dad's bedroom light go on. We froze in the darkness as we lay tight to the hillside. Soon dad was at the front door hollering. "What's going on out there?" Mom soon joined him.

One of them must have gone to our bedrooms and discovered that we were not there. In the mean time we did the only thing we could think of. Marcia and I decided to run away and stay at Karen's house. We walked nearly a mile and were all the way to where the railroad tracks crossed the road, when Marcia and I decided to go back and take our medicine. This entire time mom was yelling, "You kids get back here, right now!" We could hear her clearly all the way to the tracks. I'm not sure what our punishment was for that escapade, but at the time I think both Marcia and I clearly thought it was worth it.

Another camping experience could have landed me in jail and gotten my picture on the front page of our news paper. I was sixteen and old enough to drive. Keith and I, along with our friends, Phil Hart and Tom Dudenhoffer decided to go camping at Colby. Colby was public property that contained a couple of lakes and a national forest. There was a two track though-out the property. We went all the way to the back of the property and set up camp, which included a pup tent for our supplies and an "umbrella" tent for sleeping.

We gathered wood for a fire, so we could roast hot dogs. In the process of gathering firewood someone turned over an old pine stump which was loaded with ants. Not wanting the ants to get into our food or our tents, we tried everything we could think of to destroy them. We tried poking at them with sticks from our fire and finally found some insect repellent and sprayed them. We finally decided to give up. So we carefully extinguished our camp fire and went swimming. The lakes at Colby were not conducive to swimming, so we

drove out of Colby and went to a beach at Pearl Lake in the nearby town of Sheridan. After a refreshing swim on that hot day we headed back to our camp site.

When we turned off of M66 onto the Colby two track, we saw smoke coming from the back end of the national forest, where we were camping. As we got closer and closer to our campsite the sickening feeling in the pit of our stomachs grew worse and worse.

As we finally rounded the corner and could see our campsite, we were shocked. Our campsite was in a small grassy area right next to the forest. The grass was all black and still smoking. The pup tent and everything in it was consumed. The fire had burned up to the edge of our sleeping tent but had not burned it. Apparently it must have been treated with a fire repellent material. But what socked me the most was that the forest was starting to burn. If that really got going it would be disaster.

We jumped out of my dad's pickup truck, which I was driving. I grabbed a shovel and started throwing dirt on a burning tree. The others grabbed what they could and started beating on anything that was burning. All we could see were our faces on the front page of the newspaper followed by the caption, "Kids Burn Down National Forest". Fortunately by God's grace we were able to put the fire out. Looking back on it, I can say that it had to be with God's help.

After we got the fire out we traced the fire to that pine stump. Apparently the insect repellent had found a spark from one our sticks from the fire. That's all it needed. We all learned a very hard earned lesson that day. Insect repellent is flammable. The only thing that had survived in our pup tent was an axe head and its charred stub of a handle. I can still see the face of its owner as he picked it up, and with a pitiful cry simply said, "My axe, my axe." That seems funny now. It wasn't then. We all went to sleep in our tent that night very tired and a whole lot wiser.

Fun Listening to the Radio

When I was growing up there were no cell phones for texting or computer games. We made our own fun and we were ok with that. Before we had a TV we listened to shows on the radio. I loved listening to the Lone Ranger on the radio. I also loved a show called Amos and Andy. It had mostly black people on the show, and I loved how they talked. (I had no concept of race at an early age. I remember seeing my first black person when I was walking down a street with my mom in Grand Rapids. I remember asking her out loud why "that little boy's skin was so dark"? She just shushed me, and we kept walking.) Another radio show that we listened to every Saturday morning was the Children's Bible Hour. It was produced in Grand Rapids and always had cool stories and children singing. I really loved that show.

Inventing Our Own Fun

For fun we would sometimes take old tin cans and stomp on them with our feet. The can would fold around and adhere to our shoes. We would then walk around with the cans on our feet making lots of noise. We would sometimes take a cloths pin and a piece of card board and fix it in the spokes of our bikes so it would make noise when the wheel went around. I think it made us feel like we were riding motor cycles.

My cousin, Marvin, operated on a stray cat once, using some chloroform, he had somehow gotten from a doctor, to put it to sleep for the surgery. When he opened up the cat he saw that it had kittens inside, so he sewed it back up. The cat survived and later had the kittens.

Marvin and I found the generator part of an old crank telephone. We attached some wires to the poles on the generator and would take turns hanging on to the wires while the other one cranked the generator. We were simply trying to see who could take the most electrical shock and hang on the longest. I think it was a draw. But I remember that my hands and arms were shaking, while I was hanging onto the wires.

Another fun thing we did was to climb down the cloths shoot. There was a small door in the cupboard in our bathroom that led to a shoot that mom used to throw our dirty cloths down to the basement, where the old "ringer" washer was. We would pretend we were getting away from the bad guys and escape down the cloths shoot.

We also made some tunnels, which connected to our old "shed". The "shed" at one time had been a well house, which had a cistern that went down into the ground below the floor of the shed. The cistern had been mostly filled in, but we dug down from the outside of the shed and connected our tunnel to the old cistern so we could start inside of the shed and go down to our tunnel and out, or start at the tunnel entrance and come out through the hole in the floor of the shed. We also made an elaborate tunnel system in the field next to our garage, which dad would later purchase and prepare for grandma Chapin's house trailer. Mel, Keith and I, along with our cousins had a lot of fun playing and imagining all sorts of things in that tunnel. Later I was told that a bull doz-er found our tunnel as he was leveling the ground. I am told that one of the tracks on his bull dozer fell into our tunnel, which caused him a great deal of stress and confusion as to how that tunnel got there. Fortunately I think I was in college at the time.

One summer, while at the cottage, Mel came up with the idea of making a bicycle made for two. We took the front tire off of one bike, and spread the forks a little so it would fit over the rear axle of another bike. We then bolted the two bikes together. It took some practice, but we got so we could ride it pretty well. One day Mel got the idea that he wanted to ride our new invention over to his girl friend's house, which was probably 10-15 miles away. So we took off with Mel riding the front and me on the back bike.

We did fine getting over there. But it came time to go home. His girl friend lived on a gravel road. On the way back we came to a pretty steep hill that went down, but was just as steep going up the other side. So we decided to pick up some speed going down to help us get up the hill on the other side. As we got to the bottom of the hill we were really booking it. Just then, we hit some loose sand and Mel couldn't hold onto the handle bars. The front tire turned a quick 90 degrees which brought the bike to an immediate halt. I went airborne flying right over Mel and landing in the gravel. I had learned to roll in gym, so just did some summer salts until I came to a stop. When we recovered from the shock of it all, we realized that one of the bikes was so messed up that it was not usable. We managed to make one bike out of the two, and Mel rode me most of the way home with me sitting on the handle bars. I think mom got worried about us and went to look for us. She found us somewhere on the way home and gave us a ride the rest of the way home. That was the end of our fun on the bicycle made for two.

Another fun invention was our go cart. The first attempt at making one, used a wood frame and wheels from our wagon and an old lawn mower engine. I don't remember how the drive mechanism worked, but I do remember that Mel had me running behind him as he drove it. My job was to tap wood wedges under the motor which were supposed to tighten the belt that drove the wheels. That system was a complete flop.

But our next try worked great. We took an old push reel type lawn mower apart. That type of lawn mower had gears inside the wheels which turned the mower blade as the wheels turned. We reversed the process so that the turning shaft would turn the wheels. We took the blade part off of its shaft and put two different sized pulleys on the shaft. We then mounted that under the go cart made of pipe frame. We made a steering wheel from an old pulley and made a steering mechanism with dad's help. We made a body using sheet metal from dad's shop. We put two pulleys on the motor with two belts going to the pulleys on the shaft. Using belt tighteners made of electric motor bearings and attached to a shifting rod, we actually had a low and high gear. We also made a gas pedal attached to a cable that went to the motor.

That thing worked great. I drove that all over town. I don't think at that time there were any laws against doing that, at least none that I knew of. It had a top speed of around 25 miles per hour. We drove that go cart until the mower wheels wore completely out. We then welded a bicycle sprocket onto another set of wheels that we found and used direct chain drive. I finally sold it to my cousin Jerry Chapin, when I out grew it and needed to go to college.

Fun Water Skiing

I was always fascinated by speed boats and those who could water ski. I would watch with envy, wishing I could be the one skiing. But our family was not financially able to own a speed boat when we were young, so we just dreamed about it. One day when I was in my early teens, Mel and I were swimming and diving off of the diving dock. One of the speed boats we were watching came by and stopped at our dock. The driver actually asked if we would like to ski. I don't think our yes could get out fast enough. But we had to be honest and say that we had never done it before. That didn't seem to bother him. He just gave us some quick advice and told us to put on the life belt and skis. Mel was the first to try and was successful after a couple of attempts. He did great. It took me longer to get the hang of it, but finally got up. That was awesome. I loved it. I don't know where that man came from. I don't think we ever saw him again. I'm sure he did not know how happy he had made two boys on Dickerson Lake.

A few years later dad was able to purchase a small speed boat. It only had a 40 horse power motor on it, which is certainly small, but it was powerful enough to pull one skier or a surf board. Mel, Keith, and I all skied. I'm not sure if Marcia was ever successful at it. Mel got to be very good on one ski. I could do it, but wasn't as skilled at it as Mel. Because the boat couldn't pull us out of the water on one ski, we learned to stand with one foot in ankle deep water with the other foot in the ski on top of the water holding two loops of rope in our hand.

When the boat took off and the two loops of rope went tight, and we would hop up on the one ski, and off we would go.

I remember one time when my cousin Marvin was skiing on one ski. He had let go of the rope as he was coming in to shore, but came in much too fast. When his ski hit the shore, he flew out of his ski. Instead of falling on his face, he did flips up the shore line until he came to a standing halt on his feet. That was the funniest thing I had ever seen for a long time.

CHAPTER   4

GUNS AND HUNTING

The BB Gun

I loved guns and hunting as long as I can remember. I was probably around 8 when I got my first BB gun. I went everywhere shooting birds with it. I eventually got a BB gun with a scope. Three stories come to mind about my life with my BB gun. The first involves my cousin Darwin. I was out at his house in the country. Darwin's dad was a farmer, so there was lot of land and a lot of birds to shoot. I remember walking across a field, when Darwin challenged me. "I bet you can't shoot that bird", which was flying right to left in front of us. With the gun at my hip I followed the bird and pulled the trigger, and the bird dropped dead. Darwin was so shocked that he fell right on the ground. He never challenged my ability to shoot again.

Another time I and my brother Keith were in the middle of the swamp that was located between our house and town. We often played in the cattails that filled the swamp, and it was a great place to go and shoot birds. For some reason Keith wanted to go back home, and I didn't want him to. But he ran out of the swamp to the road and headed north towards our house. I aimed the gun up in the air and led him as he ran, and pulled the trigger on my BB gun. The BB hit him in one of his fingers. I'm sure that was another time I received a spanking and the loss of my gun for awhile.

But the worse abuse of my BB gun came in the form of BB gun fights, which I would have with my brothers. I remember how it got started. My brother Mel and I and Keith were playing "Cowboys and Indians", an innocent game that we played quite often. We all pretended we had real guns and would shoot at each other. If someone got a clear shot at a person, the person who had been shot had to count to 100 before they could return fire. We called that "taking our deads". I didn't always take my "deads" the way I was supposed to.

On one particular day of playing "Cowboys and Indians" we were using our BB guns and pretending to shoot at each other and just saying the word "bang" when we shot. As usual when Mel shot me, I did not count to 100 but continued to pursue Mel. He had had enough and turned and really shot me in the leg with his BB gun. That really hurt.

Now I was mad. I tore after him and started really shooting at him with my BB gun. What had started as a game had really turned into a gun battle. Mom somehow found out what was going on. Probably our brother Keith squealed on us. She confiscated our guns and … another spanking. We had other BB gun fights after that, but finally decided that was not a good idea after our cousin Marvin got shot just below his eye and had to dig it out using his jack knife.

Home Made Guns

Later I will tell about making a cannon. But we actually made our own guns on two other occasions. One was made using a simple bike spoke. After taking out the spoke, the one end was rolled up to make a handle. The other end had a part that screwed on the spoke and was hollow. We filled that end with match heads and then tapped a small BB into it. We then held a lit match under it until the match heads exploded shooting out the BB. That probably wasn't too safe looking back on it.

The other home-made gun was made by my cousin Marvin with the help of his dad. It was actually a spear gun made to be used under water. He used a dowel rod for the barrel, manufactured a handle and used an old BB gun trigger. He then used the elastic from a sling shot with a paper clip attached at each end. The spear was a welding rod. With one paper clip stretched to a notch in the welding rod and the other paper clip attached to the trigger, the welding rod would be shot forward when the trigger was pulled. Marvin and I had a lot of fun diving using fins on our feet and a face mask trying to shoot fish. I don't remember that we were ever successful in getting any fish, but we had a lot of fun trying.

My First Real Guns

When I turned 13 dad bought me my very first real gun. It was a Remington single shot 22 rifle. I still have that gun. I loved shooting that gun.   It was and is still extremely accurate. Dad had made a squirrel cage out of sheet metal and some fencing material. A few days before pheasant season dad had accidentally hit a pheasant with his truck and knocked it unconscious. Dad brought it home, put it in the squirrel cage, and fed it corn, when it revived. Then on the opening day of pheasant season, dad asked me if I wanted to go out and shoot a pheasant with my 22. Of course, I was very excited to do so. So he took me out back of the house where he had the squirrel cage and the pheasant and said, "There's the pheasant". So I shot it in the head, and we had pheasant for supper.

The next year dad bought me a 20 gage shot gun. Pheasant season was again just opening and dad asked me to go with him. At that time we had lots of pheasant and rabbits around our house, so we could usually kick one up. We were back by the railroad tracks which ran north and south about a quarter of a mile behind our house. (When I was in Junior High and High School I often would walk the rails home from school or run on the railroad bed the two miles or so home from school.)

 As we took a couple steps into the grass beside the railroad, a pheasant flew up startling us both. Dad quickly yelled, "Don't shoot, don't shoot. It's a hen". We both put our guns down. Just then a rooster flew up and we both shot and missed. I had developed a very bad habit while using my BB gun. I couldn't always remember if I had cocked my BB gun, so I would just point my gun at the ground and pull the trigger. If it wasn't cocked, I would simply cock it. If it was cocked, the gun would fire into the ground. No big deal with a BB gun. But it was a big deal when I pointed my shot gun at the ground and pulled the trigger that day. The gun went off leaving a pattern of shot just a few feet away from my dad's foot. He turned white, and I thought that would be the last time dad would ever take me hunting. Instead, he turned to me and simply said, "Don't do that again". That was it. He didn't take my gun away or scolded me or punish me. He didn't have to. I was frightened enough by almost blowing my dad's foot off. I never, ever did that again. That day I learned the best lesson I could have ever learned about gun safety. Guns can kill. You can never be too cautious around guns.

Deer Hunting with Dad

When I turned 14, I was very excited about that fall. An event was about to take place that I had been looking forward to for a very long time. It was my turn to go deer hunting with dad. Deer were very scarce in the Montcalm County area, where I grew up. Dad, Uncle Merton, and some of their friends from church had found a good hunting place up north in the national forest east of Grayling. Before dad had taken Mel with him to hunt up there, dad and mom went together with other couples from the church. They all camped in a big army tent that had a smoke stack going through the tent roof. A wood stove below was used for warmth and for cook-ing. Straw was put on the ground where they would sleep with an old mattress piled on the straw. Another small tent over a whole in the ground formed the "outhouse". It was primitive, but it worked. The hunters would camp there for the first week of deer hunting season, which always began on November 15th. Mel never liked the hunting or killing part, but he loved the camping part and being with dad. I loved it all. Finally it was my turn to go since Mel had gone off to college.

I used mom's 30-30 bolt action rifle. I had shot it a few times, so I knew how to use it. The first day, dad took me out to a spot to hunt. I was so excited! I'm sure he gave me instructions about which direction the camp was, and what to do if I got a deer. But I didn't remember any of it. I was one of the few in the state that had a doe tag that year, which meant that I could shoot a doe or a buck whose horns were less than 3 inches long. In front of me was a deep ravine that dropped probably close to 100 feet. I sat on a log at the top of that ravine. To my right was a plateau that ran into a big hill. I'm not sure what time of day it was, perhaps late morning.

But a deer approached me from my left walking near the edge of the ravine. I could see that it had horns, but they weren't very long. They were close to 3 inches, but I wasn't sure. But knowing that I had a doe tag that I could use if they weren't 3 inches, I decided to shoot it. After all it was my first deer. I took careful aim and fired. The shot hit its front shoulder and broke it. The deer ran to my right on three legs along the edge of the ravine and then fell all the way to the bottom of the ravine.

I was ecstatic and beside myself with excitement. But now I had a problem. I couldn't remember what dad told me to do if I got a deer. And, which direction was it back to camp, and how was I supposed to gut it? I fired a couple shots into the ground hoping that dad would hear them. I then went down to my deer. I had gutted pheasant and rabbit and cleaned fish. How hard could this be? I went to work and gutted it the best I could. Basically I knew that anything loose inside had to come out.

When I got done, dad still hadn't come. I tried to drag the deer up the ravine, but just couldn't do it by myself. I figured the only thing I could do was to go back to camp. But which direction was it? I decided dad had said to go due south from where I was. I so wish I had listened better. He had actually said to go due west.

I had a compass and knew how to use it. I had been part of a boys group at our church called Boys Brigade, which was a Christian form of Boys Scouts. It had similar awards and uniforms. I had been part of that since I was a young boy. One of the badges that I had earned had to do with using a compass. I earned the badge by being dropped off in the middle of a woods at night with only my compass, and told to find a bag of candy two miles away. I found it. Hey, I liked candy. What can I say?

So I lined up my compass to go due south and started off. I walked and walked and walked. Over each hill I thought I would see the camp, but to no avail. Somewhere on my attempt to hike back to camp two very frightening realizations hit me. First, I didn't have my gun. I had apparently set it down somewhere along that hike, when I had taken one of my many compass sightings and forgotten to pick it up again. I was in panic mode. What I did remember was that there were black bear in those woods. In fact, one of the men a few years ago had shot a bear in those very woods. Now all I could think about was a black bear coming after me. The second realization was that I was very lost. By this time in my life I was starting to come back to a closer walk with God. This experience really encouraged that move.

I began to pray very sincerely, "Lord, please just help me get back to where my deer is." I thought that if I could get back there, dad would eventually find me and help me. Dad had told me stories about grown men being lost in those woods and never found. It was possible to walk for miles and not come to a road. So I turned around and used my compass to go due north and fortunately with God's help made it back to my deer.

In the mean time, unbeknownst to me, dad had come to my hunting spot, seen the deer and concluded that I had gone back to camp. When he did not find me at camp, he returned to where I had shot the deer. By that time I had returned and was waiting for dad. Together we managed to haul the deer back to camp. He was so happy for me. He wasn't even mad at me for losing the gun. In fact, after we got back home dad took the hide from that deer and had a pair of buck skin gloves made from them for me. I don't know what ever happened to them. I wish I still had them.

Even though I had gotten my deer and couldn't hunt any more, I still wanted to go back out to my hunting spot the next morning. I wanted to try to retrace some of my steps in hopes that I could find the gun. The next morning dad took me back to the spot where I had shot my deer. I took my 22 just in case I saw a bear, though that size of a bullet would have done about as much harm to a bear as a BB gun. As I sat on the log that morning I tried to mentally retrace my steps. I knew I had the gun when I gutted out the deer. I also remembered having my gun when I took out my compass the first time. I had leaned the gun against a tree.

Once again I prayed. "Lord, please help me to find that gun". I went down to where the deer had fallen and then walked up the hill. I looked over about 20 yards and there was the gun. It was like finding a needle in a hay stack in that big woods. But there it was. I knew God had answered my prayer. There was no other explanation for it. God had used that whole experience just to bring me closer it Him. What amazing grace!
I would deer hunt with dad for two more years before going off the college. Though I never again had a shot at a deer, I always loved being with dad, guns, and camping in the cold for a week – and getting out of school.

Hunting Rabbits

I have several memories of hunting rabbits. Some of those involve my friend, Dave Wickes. But on two occasions I hunted rabbits with my uncle Merton, dad's brother. I always had a very high regard for my uncle Merton. I had him in my mind right up there with Daniel Boone. He was an expert with a bow as well as a gun.

On one occasion I was hunting rabbits on "Pake's Farm" south of Stanton, which was where we usually hunted for rabbits because it had a lot of brush and cover for rabbits. Uncle Merton, his son, Jerry, Delford Golden (who was another Daniel Boone type), and his son, Duane, were also hunting, I believe on that day. Two of us went on one side of a pond, while the others were on the other side. The other group spotted a rabbit and began to shoot at it. They did not realize that we were directly across the pond from them with the rabbit running directly away from them, but straight at us.

When I heard the bullets hitting the brush around me I hit the ground and began to yell. Fortunately no one was hurt. The ones doing the shooting felt bad, but it was not really their fault. We were not clear as to where we were going either.

That same afternoon we went back to the same general area but on the other side of the road. I can't remember where the others were, but I remember uncle Merton finding a fresh rabbit track in the snow and telling me to stand there while he "brought the rabbit around".   He then went off following the tracks barking like a dog.

I could hear his barks fade away in the distance, but then begin to get louder as he came closer to me. Soon he came through the brush and asked why I hadn't shot. He had brought the rabbit around, but I had been looking the wrong way. The rabbit had run behind me, and I never saw it. Uncle Merton then physically turned me and told me to keep looking in "that" direction. He then went off again barking like a dog following the rabbit's new trail.

As I heard his barks begin to get louder again, I readied myself. Sure enough the rabbit came from the exact spot uncle Merton had told me it would. I fired and got the rabbit. Soon uncle Merton appeared and was obviously pleased. I was in awe. I had never seen anything like that before, nor have I since.

CHAPTER   5

LEARNING WISDOM THE HARD WAY

Pretending to Be Tarzan or Superman

I had a bad tendency during my growing up years to make decisions based solely on whether I thought something would be fun. That meant that I often got hurt or in big trouble. This pattern began very early as a child. The first such incident had to do with trying to play Tarzan in a tree. I was probably 6 or 7. I loved to climb trees. At grand ma Jones's house there was a big willow tree, which I climbed with my cousin Marvin. In the process of thinking that I was Tarzan, I jumped from one limb to another. It looked like fun. However, the limb I jumped to apparently wasn't large enough to support my weight and it broke. I fell several feet to the ground. Fortunately another limb broke my fall, and I just got some scrapes and cuts with no broken bones. Aunt Alnora, Marvin's mother, patched me up.

On another occasion Marvin and I played superman and jumped off the roof of the shed which was probably about 8 feet from the ground. I even jumped off the roof of the house on more than one occasion. Funny thing – as often as I tried, I could never seem to fly like superman, even with a towel tied around my neck like a cape.

The Rotten Apple Fight

It is amazing how many of the "fun" things I did ended up poorly – for me. On one occasion Mel and I had gotten into a rotten apple fight. We were not mad at each other. We just thought it would be fun to hit each other with rotten apples. There were two apple trees just south of our property. Dad would later buy that property and move grandma Chapin's (mom's mother) house trailer onto the property after grand dad Chapin died. As boys we thought of that property as ours and played on it all the time. So on the day that Mel and I were throwing rotten apples at each other, I made a tactical and major miscalculation. I thought it would be smart to climb the tree to get above Mel, so I could throw the apples down on him. However, that move only made it easier for Mel to pulverize me with apples – rotten apples. The only ones I could find up in the tree were not rotten, and I was a "sitting duck" for his well aimed throws. I, also, soon ran out of ammunition that was within easy reach. I somehow had not thought things through very well – again. Mel won that fight hands down.

The Cannon

Another no so smart decision had to do with fireworks. I was always fascinated by fireworks. I think it was a combination of loving the big bang and seeing things blow up. That is probably where my son Mark got the fire cracker "bug". He can tell you about blowing up fish, while on vacation in Wisconsin. I graduated from small fire crackers to bigger "cherry bombs" and "silver salutes" (M-80s) when I got older. My cousin Darwin had given me some money to buy the bigger stuff, knowing that I would be coming through Georgia on my way home from a family vacation in Florida. You could legally buy those fireworks in Georgia at that time. I'm not sure how I was able to keep the purchase from mom and dad, but I purchased the heavy duty fireworks for my cousin, and bought a lot of them for myself as well. These were powerful enough to blow your hand off if you weren't careful. I was probably 12 or 13 at the time.

I had learned to weld some, using my dad's acetylene torch welder. So I found a piece of inch and a half pipe, which was about 3 feet long and welded two short legs on the back of it and one longer piece on the front, making a cannon. I then took a coupling and drilled a hole in it for the fuse to stick through. I then put a plug into one end of the coupling and screwed it onto the low end of the cannon. I was really ingenious at planning fun.

Of course I was so excited to try it out in our yard. I think my brother Mel was there for the first firing. After unscrewing the coupling and placing the "silver salute" so the fuse protruded through the hole in the coupling, we stuffed old newspaper down the cannon's barrel and put a rock in after that. I lit the fuse and watched with great delight as that rock went flying out of sight. After seeing that my invention worked great, we tried it at night without newspaper and saw fire shoot out of the end of the barrel at least a foot. I even held it up by the back legs and aimed it like a gun a few times and could hit a telephone pole, which was probably at least 50 yards across the road. Mel thought I was "nuts" when he saw me do that. But I never thought of the possible negative consequences. All I could think about was how much fun it would be. That kind of thinking, or lack thereof, as I said earlier, did get me hurt on occasion. I'm sure God kept me from blowing myself up with that cannon.

Riding My Bike of the Dock

It is amazing how easily I can remember the dumb things I did. Another one of those bad "fun" decisions happened when I was about 10. Several years earlier my dad had purchased some lake frontage property on Dickerson Lake right next to the "fishing site", which was a public area for launching boats. The lake was only about 5 miles west of Stanton so it made it convenient (when we stayed there summers) for dad to get to work, and our continued church attendance. Dad had built a small cottage there which had a hand pump for water and an outhouse for a bathroom. I remember as a small child taking baths on a Saturday night in a metal wash tub. The hot water must have been heated on a stove. Later dad would install a pump, so we had indoor plumbing and hot water. Because of spending our summers at the cottage, I learned to swim when I was very young – probably 5 or 6.

There was a good sized hill that was back from the lake about 40 yards or so. Somehow I got the idea that if I rode my bike fast enough down the hill I would fly off the end of the dock for a ways before hitting the water. I announced my intention to my brother, Mel, who proceeded to warn me not to do such a "stupid" thing. But all I could think about was the fun I would have flying through the air. The part about what happens after hitting the water somehow didn't seem important at the time. Mel wisely positioned himself near the end of the dock somehow knowing what was about to happen. I, on the other hand, was at the top of the hill really excited about the thrill I was about to experience.

I started down the hill going as fast as I could. I was flying. Did I mention that I did not always think things through all that well. Just as I approached the end of the dock, I noticed a gap between the ground at the edge of the lake, and the dock. Somehow I had missed that detail. I slammed on the brakes of my bike as hard as I could, so I would not go flying over the handle bars when I hit that gap. I managed to get over the gap successfully.

Most thinking people would have scrapped the original "fly off the dock" plan. But somehow I just couldn't do that. I still believed I could regain all the speed I had lost and still fly off the end of the dock. So with every ounce of strength I could muster, I began to peddle my bike as fast as I could. As my front tire left the end of the dock I realized for the first time that my great idea wasn't so great. Instead of flying forward off the end of the dock like I had envisioned, my front tire was just going in a downward direction – fast. In fact, my whole bike went in a downward direction, and so did I. When I hit the water head first, the back end of my bike went right over the top of me with the entire bike falling on top of me under water – and I couldn't get it off of me. Fortunately, my brother Mel, who was always the thinking one, had anticipated that very scenario, and pulled the bike off of me saving my life. He still reminds me that he saved my life whenever he has opportunity.

Swimming across Dickerson Lake

By the time I was ten I was a pretty good swimmer. Dad allowed our pastor at the time to move a small house trailer onto our property at the lake. Rev. Buffum loved to fish, and it helped him to unwind from the tensions of the ministry. He and his wife had a son, Dave, that was seven or eight years older than I was, who also had a knack for getting into trouble. Only his kind of trouble was much more serious. Later, he would do time in prison. I thought it was cool that he let me hang around him sometimes, and I thought I could do everything he could do. One hot summer day mom was going to town for some groceries. She explicitly told my brother Mel and me not to go into the water while she was gone. We obeyed her at first. Then Dave Buffum came down in his bathing suit to go swimming. Mel and I could only watch him enjoy the water, and he was enjoying every minute of that. I'm not sure how it happened, but somehow we ended up in the water with him with our bathing suits on. That water felt so good, and we thought surely mom would never find out.

Then Dave got the idea that he wanted to swim across the lake, and asked Mel to row the boat next to him just in case he got a cramp or had to rest. The temptation was just too great for me. I thought, if Dave could swim across the lake, so could I. The lake may have been a half of a mile wide. So off we went with Mel rowing, and Dave and me swimming. The plan was for Dave to swim across the lake and back, with me just swimming across, and Mel swimming on the way back with me rowing the boat back. After successfully swimming across the lake it was Mel's turn to get into the water and for me to get into the boat. I didn't initially want to do that, so I started swimming back. All I could think about was that if Dave could do it, so could I. But Mel finally convinced me that we had made a deal, and that I should keep my word. So I climbed into the boat, and Mel jumped into the water.

We were probably about three fourths of the way back to our side of the lake when we heard a very frightening sound. That sound caused shivers of fear all the way to my toes. It was coming from the end of our boat dock. Mom was home and screaming at the top of her lungs for us to "get back out of the water right now". I panicked. Did I mention that I occasionally did stupid things? This is another one of those times. I turned the boat around and began rowing it as fast as I could for the other shore. I instantly planned to run away from home rather than face my mom in her wrath. That only made it worse for me. I had taken away the "safety net" (the boat) from my brother and left him to fend for himself. But all I could think about was trying to get as far away as I could.

Somewhere in the middle of the lake it dawned on me that my idea of escape wasn't going to work. I knew no one on that side of the lake. I had no place to live, no food, and no way of getting anywhere. So I turned the boat around and headed for our dock. Mom was furious with both of us, but especially with me. She told us to go into the cottage to our bed. Mel and I slept together in the same full sized bed in the lower level of the cottage. So we sat there on the bed waiting for mom to come back with her plan of punishment.

I was not prepared for what I saw next. Mom came into our room holding a big butcher knife. "Oh no," I thought. "Mom really is going to kill us!" But she simply handed the knife to Mel and said, "Go cut your own switch from the willow tree." We had two huge willow trees that grew at the edge of the lake on either side of our property. Usually I loved climbing those trees. Not this time. I remember the words of advice my brother gave me, and I have always held that against him. "Cut a big one", he told me. "It won't hurt as much". He was so wrong. Mom spanked us with our own switches that day. It was a spanking that went down in my memory bank as ranking right up there as one of the hardest and most painful that I can remember. And I have had a lot of spankings for comparison. The only one that topped that spanking was the one I got from dad that I will mention later.

Almost Rolling Over in our Chevy

Somewhere in the early 1950s dad bought a 1950 Chevy. Instead of selling it when it began to show some rust dad bought a station wagon which became the family car. The Chevy became the car that Marcia drove until the motor burned up because "someone" had forgotten, or did not know, to put oil in it. Rather than junk the car, dad put a '55 engine in it. Mel then began to drive the car, when he turned 16. He replaced the floor boards and rocker panels using some of dad's sheet metal from the shop. He put a lot of work into trying to make that car look sharp.

When Mel went off to college and I turned 16, the car became mine to drive. Mel had put a steering knob on the steering wheel so he could drive with one hand. I saw my assignment as trying to see how fast it would go. I think it went 0 to 60 in about a half hour. But I loved that old car. I thought I was hot stuff driving it to school. I took Keith to school with me and picked up some friends (Bev and Cheryl Dilno) on the way.

I had begun driving that car when I was 12. Dad asked me to drive it home from the shop one day. I was very willing to help him out. As I recall mom wasn't all that thrilled about it.

It was the winter after I had turned 13 when I again was asked to drive the car home. There had been a fresh snow fall, and I was excited to see if I could make the back end of the car "fish tail". I waited until New Street turned into the gravel road that our house was on, before I began my fun. I was enjoying my time immensely when the back end of the car came around too far, and I was going sideways down the road. I panicked and slammed on the brakes. That only made the car spin faster out of control and do a 180 into the ditch on the driver's side. When I hit the edge of the road the car rocked up on its side before going into the ditch. I thought for sure it was going to roll over. I could see the snow covered ground through the passenger window. But it settled back down in the upright position.

At that point all I could imagine were "cop" cars coming up the road after me. I saw myself in handcuffs going off to jail. I managed to get the driver's side door open, hop out and hit the road running for home. I ran straight to my room and closed the door.

Fortunately my older, wiser brother was there to try to calm me down. All he could get out of me was, "I'll never drive again. I'm never going to drive again". When I was finally able to tell him what happened, he calmly said, let's just get the truck, and I'll pull you out.

I'm not sure what we told mom. We probably just snuck out. Mel drove one of dad's two pickup trucks down the short ways to where the car was in the ditch and pulled me out. I then turned the car around **carefully** and drove it home. I never, ever did that again. I seemed to learn a lot while I was growing up, but always the hard way.

Skiing at Skyview Ranch

By now you can clearly see that I had a problem thinking ahead.   In spite of my lack of wisdom, God kept me from accidently killing myself or seriously hurting others. I'm amazed that God was so patient with me. I think I didn't start to think ahead about the possible bad consequences until I was about 34 or 35. I remember very well the incident that caused me to wise up. I was asked to be the speaker for a singles winter retreat at Skyview Ranch Youth Camp in Millersburg, Ohio. By this time I was the pastor of the Faith Baptist Church in Mount Vernon, Ohio, which was only about an hour's drive from the camp. I had been married to Nancy for almost 15 years. Her younger sister, Penny, was single at the time, and Becky Durbin from our church in Mount Vernon, was saved by then. Both of them went with me along with some others from our church. There were probably about 50 singles that attended, which included singles from other churches.

I had always wanted to ski down those big hills at Skyview. They were bigger than any of the hills I had ever skied down in Michigan including Knobs Hill. Nancy, on the other hand, was not so excited about me taking my skis. In fact, she was very emphatic about it, saying that I would surely get hurt. I assured her that I would be fine. All I could think about was how fast I would be going down those hills – faster than I had ever gone on skis, and I couldn't wait. I don't remember what I preached on that first night of the retreat. I'm sure it wasn't very Spirit filled. I couldn't wait for the speaker to be done so I could go skiing. And the speaker was me. As soon as the service was over everyone headed out to the hill behind the lodge (an old barn) to go sliding down hill on inner tubes. There was a full moon that night so you could actually see fairly will. I headed to my room to change cloths, and then grabbed my skis.

I found a spot to start my decent quite a ways from where the rest were, so I would not get in their way nor would they get in mine. I was no more than 25 feet down hill when I realized I probably should have checked the hill out before starting out on my skis. I did not know that the spot I chose to go downhill had previously been the spot some "tubers" had used. So underneath the inch or two of powder like snow was basically ice. I was quickly flying faster than I had ever gone before. While that part was fun it did make me a little uncomfortable. But it was what I saw ahead that really opened my eyes very wide. Did I mention that I should have checked that hill out before starting down-hill. But at the time, I could only think of the fun I was about to have. I stared in disbelief at a cliff that was fast approaching. The drop beyond the edge of the cliff appeared to be about 6-8 feet or so. I had never skied over anything like that before. About that time I really got very spiritual. I really started to pray. "Lord, please help me get over this."

I went flying over the edge and finally landed upright on my skis. I was just coming out of my crouch position and feeling pretty proud of myself, when I looked up. Directly in front of me was a wall of earth. Apparently I had jumped over one side of a ditch and was now about to slam into the other side. There was nothing I could do but smack into it. I had just enough time to put out my right hand to partly brace my fall. As my right hand hit the wall, a searing pain shot from my shoulder. No bones seemed to be broken, but it really hurt to move my right arm, and my right leg was very sore. I was too far from any one to yell for help. So I grabbed my skis with my left hand and used them as a crutch to get back up the hill.

I went straight to my room in terrible pain. I was afraid to tell the camp director about the stupid thing I had done. I just hoped and prayed that the pain would go away. It didn't. In fact, it just got worse. Finally I realized I was going to have to tell the camp director and ask him to drive me to the hospital. The x-rays at the hospital revealed that I had separated my shoulder and torn some ligaments, which would require surgery later. They put my arm in a sling and gave me some Tylenol with codeine, which made me a little loopy. Somehow I was able to finish my speaking obligations the next day and to drive home. But I knew that a fate worse than death was awaiting me. I had to face Nancy.

For some reason Penny and Becky thought it would be fun to watch Nancy's reaction, when she found out about what I had done. I tried to warn them. "It won't be funny at all", I said. I remember walking down stairs to our family room where Nancy was sitting on the piano bench with another lady from the church. They apparently had been practicing for a special number at church. I had my coat on over my sling so my right sleeve had no arm in it. Both Penny and Becky (against my advice) had followed me downstairs.

At first Nancy thought I was playing a joke on her when she saw my armless sleeve. But then I unzipped my coat and she saw that my arm was in a very real sling. At that point she began to unleash a lot of "I told you sos" in a tone that was anything but consoling. Penny and Becky for the first time were seeing Nancy in a state they had not observed before. They quickly got out of there. That part **was** funny. I thank the Lord for the poor lady on the piano bench who kept begging Nancy to be merciful to me. I think I might owe her my life.   From that day on I began to be a little wiser about listening to my wife, and secondly, thinking ahead before jumping into something.

CHAPTER   6

GOD'S GRACE BEGINS TO HELP ME GROW UP

Success with Music

I loved music as long as I can remember. I was told that my grandpa Jones predicted that I would be musical.
Mom told me that he came to that conclusion when I was sitting on his knee as a one year old and bounced on
his knee to the music. Music was part of our family life. My mom and dad each came from musical families.
Mom and dad sang together at weddings and both played the piano. Dad also played the mandolin and guitar
very well. One of my fond memories is when the Jones family (dad's brothers and sisters) got together for
Christmas. It was usually out at Uncle Nyle's farm house just north of Stanton. Dad would be playing the guitar or mandolin, Uncle Nyle would be playing the piano, and Uncle Merton would be playing the Hawaiian guitar, and all would be singing. I was only a small child, but I loved it.

Mom made all of us (Marcia, Melvin, Keith, and I) take piano lessons. We started when we were in the second
or third grade. I took piano lessons for six years, but I did not like to practice and never got very good at playing. But I did learn a lot about music, which would help me the rest of my life. Today I regret that I didn't
practice more, and didn't get better at playing the piano.

My brothers, my sister, and I all played band instruments as well. Mel learned to play the trumpet and would go
on to the play in the marching and symphony bands at the University of Michigan. He would become assistant
first chair in the symphony band and earn his master's degree in music, and go back to Stanton as the band director, where he taught for 15 years. Marcia learned to play the clarinet. She went on to Moody Bible Institute,
then to the University of Michigan and Northern Michigan University earning her master's degree in music.
She would teach music most of her adult life in the public school and give private piano lessons in her home.
Keith learned to play the saxophone and guitar. Using his sax he would win second place in the nation in the
newly started Talents for Christ competition sponsored by the General Association of Regular Baptist Churches.
Later in life he would travel with the Liberty men's quartet and make several recordings with them.

I learned to play the trombone. I chose the trombone after going to a band concert that Marcia and Melvin were
in. I was fascinated by the slide and how it gave different sounds. I started playing the trombone when I was in
the 6th grade. By my freshman year in high school I had won the first chair position in the band. That wasn't
too hard since the only other two trombone players that were upper classmen had been kicked out of the band.
That left only Marvin and me as the only two trombone players in the band that year. Marvin and I would battle
throughout our high school years for the first chair position. Since we were the only two trombone players, and
because we also played football, we would have to march with the band in our football uniforms during the
halftime of the football games.

The band director selected me from all the kids in the band to receive a scholarship to the National Music Camp
in Interlochen, Michigan, which I attended the summer before my senior year in high school. That was an awesome experience. During a band rehearsal composed of all the kids at that camp, the band director picked

me out to move up to first chair. It scared me when he pointed at me. Due to some reasons I will mention later I felt very inferior to everyone else. So I told him I would rather stay where I was, which was near the end of the section.

I played my trombone every Sunday night in an orchestra at church and played solos, and often at church in a trio with my brothers, and sometimes with Marvin as a duet. I also played in a school Dixie Land Band with my brother, Mel.

At that stage of my life Mel and I were about the same height and looked enough alike to be twins even though he was almost 4 years older than me. On one occasion Mel was asked to go to the Trinity Church to play a solo on his trumpet. Mel asked me to go with him. After the service a lady came up to me and thought that I was Mel. She said, "Thank you so much for that special number. It was so beautiful". Without missing a beat I simply said, "Thank you so much, mam. I was glad to do it". I told Mel about it later, and we both had a good laugh.

After high school I went on to Cedarville College and majored in music my first year there. I took private trombone lessons (the first I had ever received) and was asked to play my horn in chapel on several occasions. I was also invited to join a trombone trio that traveled for the college to make it a quartet, but again I turned them down saying that I was not good enough.

Singing came so natural for all of us in our family. Harmonizing was not so much something we learned, as something we heard in our heads. So singing or playing our instruments around the piano at home was fun to us. It was a little more scary when we had to do it in front of people at church, but I still enjoyed doing it. I sang in the teen choir at church every Sunday night, and often sang with my brothers in a trio, or sometimes added our sister and made it a quartet.

I was selected from my junior class at high school to go to Boy's State which I attended during the summer before my senior year. Boy's State was composed of boys from all the schools in Michigan and was for the purpose of teaching how our government operated. Boys would campaign in a two party system for different offices starting with governor on down. I remember feeling very intimidated and insecure, and did not run for anything. I think I was appointed assistant dog catcher – seriously. But I was drawn to sing in the choir that week because I loved to sing. In one of the songs during rehearsal there was a need for a solo part. Again the director pointed at me and asked me to do it. I said I didn't think I could do it, so he asked another boy to do it. I honestly did not think I was good enough.

Developing Leadership in School

As I said earlier, I started kindergarten when I was 4, so I was one of the youngest ones in my class. I enjoyed school when I was young, but that wore off as I got older. I would rather be playing. I enjoyed reading at an early age, but that too wore off and later would be a struggle for me. I did well in school but could have done much better if I had worked at it. I graduated seventh in my class. While that sounds like that was amazing, keep in mind that I only had 42 in my graduating class and probably had a B average.

For some reason I was popular at school. I was elected president of both my freshman and senior classes. I think the girls liked me. I never "ran" for office or tried to get elected. I never considered such a thing. I was also elected president of the band and of the Bible Club we had at school. For some reason (God's grace), others saw me as a leader.

During my junior and senior years at high school I did discover something I really enjoyed: drama. The first play I was in was called, "House on the Cliff". It was a murder mystery, and I played the role of a doctor. The way the story was written, I was considered by the audience to be the prime suspect for the murder, initially.

There was a part in the play where I entered from a balcony that had steps that went part way down to the sea. The lights had gone out on the stage just prior to my entrance. There was just enough light for the audience to see a nurse hiding behind a chair, and to see me enter from the balcony. I shuffled with my feet on sand spread on cardboard for sound effects that gave the audience the impression that I had come up the steps prior to my entrance. When I opened the gate that led from the balcony to the living room, one of the prop men (my cousin Darwin) worked a rusty hinge over a microphone. I entered the living room wearing a black slicker and hat, looked around, and started for the chair that the nurse was hiding behind. Just when I was about to turn away a lady screamed to the nurse from the audience, "Get out of there you fool"! It took everything I had to keep from bursting out laughing, but I managed to continue to the hidden entrance – a bookcase. I opened the bookcase, went through the entrance and closed the bookcase behind me. I loved that.

I was in a couple other plays including "Our Town" and "The Miracle Worker", which were plays done during the summer for the community. I did not have big parts, but I learned a lot that would help me later in the ministry.

Learning Teamwork Through Sports

Because Stanton was a small town (about 1000 in population), and our school was small, I had opportunities to play sports that I probably wouldn't have had in a larger setting. I played little league baseball and enjoyed it. At one point I was asked to be a pitcher, but didn't like the pressure. During the summer before I entered the 8th grade I grew six inches. I was only twelve when I started the 8th grade. I was six feet tall and very awkward and uncoordinated. I was asked to play baske ball that fall.

By the time the season began I had turned thirteen and was the tallest kid on the team. I was on the starting five and played every game. I got most of the rebounds both offensively and defensively, but I had a big problem. As hard as I tried, I could not get that ball to go into the basket. Often, during games, I would be playing catch with myself as I got my own rebound time after time until I gave the ball to another teammate.

I would be on the high school basketball team all through high school. I was very good on defense, so during our practice I helped prepare our center for the games, but I did not play that much in real games.

I loved to play baseball with my brothers, cousins, and neighbors, but did not play it in high school. I also played softball on our church team and was pretty good at hitting the ball.

The sport that I would excel at was football. By my freshman year in high school I was six feet tall and weighed maybe 150 pounds soaking wet. I had played football with my brothers, cousins, and neighbors in our yard, but had a lot to learn. Because of a lot of anger issues that had built up inside of me, I really liked hitting people. So football was a natural fit for me, even though I was not built for it. Our high school was so small that if you went out for a sport you usually made the team. There was no junior varsity football team, only varsity. This meant that as a thirteen year old freshman, I was playing against juniors and seniors as well as other freshmen and sophomores. They were well built guys that were a lot older and heavier than I was. I don't think I got to play in one game my freshman year. The freshmen on our team usually made up the practice squad that the starters used as dummies.

My sophomore year was a pivotal year for me. That year we had a very good team. Our quarter back was a good passer and made good decisions. Our half back was fast, although he had a quick temper. Our full back was big, at least for our school. John Bussel was six foot four inches tall and weighed 220 pounds at least. By this time I had grown an inch taller, but was still only 155 pounds.

I was getting tired of only playing during practice and wondering whether it was worth it. My band director wanted Marvin and I to quit football so we could concentrate more on the band. I remember talking with Marvin about it. I think we both had made up our minds to quit football after the next night's practice.

But an event happened that changed my mind. I got knocked out during that practice. John Bussel was leading the interference for our half back on a sweep power play. I was concentrating on the half back and did not see John coming for me. He caught me with his elbow right under my chin and knocked me off of my feet and up into the air. The next thing I knew, I heard coach Helms standing over me asking me how many fingers he was holding up. I don't think I could even see the coach let alone how many fingers he was holding up. But I must have guessed close enough and play resumed.

You would think that that experience would have clinched my decision to quit football. But that was not how I was wired. It had the exact opposite effect on me. I had a score to settle with John Bussel, and I wasn't going to quit until I accomplished my revenge. That opportunity came the very next night in practice. I was playing left tackle in the line on defense. By this time I had learned that because I was smaller in weight compared to almost anyone playing, I had to hit them lower in order to move them backwards or tackle them without hurting myself.

When the ball was snapped, I saw that John was given the ball and was coming right at what we called the two hole on the offense's right side of the center. He was coming my way. With every ounce of energy I had, I dove at his legs and hit him right at the ankles knocking him off his feet. His head hit the ground with a thud, and he didn't get up. I had knocked **him** out. Soon coach Helms was standing over him and asking him how many fingers he was holding up. I absolutely loved it. But it was what the coach said next that really was the frosting on the cake for me: "Get up. It was only Jones."

From that moment on I **loved** football. Not only that, the coach had seen a side of me that he hadn't seen before, and started to put me in the game. I was not starting, but he used me during the game to send in plays. So I was playing on offense about ever other play.

It was in one of those games early in my sophomore year that I had the most embarrassing moment of my life. We were responsible to wash our own football pants and jerseys as well as our practice gear. Only our pads and helmets were kept in our lockers in the shower room at school. So on game night I always took from home all I needed to wear including my cleats (football shoes) in a duffle bag. When I was dressing for the game, I noticed a very important item was missing – my belt. I was really skinny. That belt was a necessity for me. I tried to get a freshman to loan me his belt, but none would. That night it was a home game, and for the first time I was hoping the coach would not put me in.

But not too long after the game was under way the coach yelled, "Jones". I had no choice but to go in and hope for the best. I brought the play in. The ball was snapped. One defensive player hit me on the right and another on the left. The next thing I knew I was laying on the ground with my pants down to my ankles. There was no way I was getting up. Fortunately John Bussel saw my predicament and yelled, "Huddle around Jones. Huddle around Jones." All the players huddled around me laughing, but I was able to quickly get up, pull my pants up, and run back to the sidelines.

By that time the crowd had figured out what had happened and was in hysterics – all except the coach. He was livid with me. "What in the ****do you think you are doing out there?" (Profanity was part of his vocabulary. He spent most of the half time cussing at us.) When I explained that I didn't have a belt, the coach made one of the freshmen loan me his belt. I don't remember who we played that night, or if we won or lost. I think that part has been lost from my memory bank. I wish that that whole night was lost from my memory bank. But unfortunately it seems to be branded in my mind. That may be due in part to the fact that I was the talk of our little town for several weeks after that game, particularly at our barbershop.

But another play during a game that same year would make me a starter for the rest of my high school life, and would cause the whole team and the coaches to be talking about me with respect from that game on. The game was against Vestaburg. It was near the end of the season, and I was playing more than just on offense. I was playing a lot of defense as well. This was a big game for us. In fact, if we won, we would be tied for the league championship.

By this time I was getting a lot of tackles. In fact, my mom said that during the game all the announcer said was "Jones on the bottom of the pile." (Mom often attended my home games, but I don't remember dad ever attending any game in little league, basket ball or football. He was always working.) We would have been able to beat this team with ease, but our great half back had gotten ejected from the game almost after the first play. He slugged a guy right in front of the referee. Not smart. So a lot of pressure had been put on the defense.

The game was almost over, and we were ahead by less than a touchdown. But Vestaburg had the ball and was driving. We had stopped them on 3rd down, but they had decided to go for it on 4th down. If we stopped them we could run out the clock and win the game. If they got the 1st down, they could keep going and possibly beat us.

I was playing my usual spot of left tackle on defense. When Vestaburg came out of their huddle they had made a dramatic change. They had put their biggest player, their fullback across from me. I remember that play like it was in slow motion. Butch Dell who was our right tackle on defense yelled at me, "They're coming your way Jones. They're coming your way. You've got to stop them." He really got me fired up. I started jumping up and down and then got down in my stance. I watched the ball. As soon as I saw it snapped I charged at the big guy across from me with all I had. I hit him with a "forearm shiver", which meant I hit him with both of my forearms underneath his chest and knocked him on his "fanny".

To be honest that wasn't all that hard. For some reason, perhaps because he was not used to playing that position, he was already starting to back up when I hit him. Or perhaps my jumping up and down had scared him. Whatever the reason, I was in the backfield before the quarterback could hand the ball to their half back. I could have, and should have, taken the hand off from their quarterback. For some reason, perhaps because I was just as shocked to be standing there as they were to see me, I just stood there. I can still see the eyes of their halfback. He was a fast running black dude. At that moment his eyes were as big as saucers. He finally, which seemed like an eternity, came forward and took the ball, and I tackled him immediately.

Our team and the crowd went nuts. We had won the game. On the bus I usually sat alone because the guys usually talked dirty, and it made me feel uncomfortable. I could hear Butch Dell talking about that play and telling it over and over. The assistant coach came up and sat with me, and asked me to tell him about it. I was honest and told him that I thought the guy was moving backwards when I hit him. But that didn't seem to matter to him or anyone else. For the first time in my life I was the center of attention for doing something good. It really felt good. And that along with some other things began to change how I saw myself and the world.

Our last game that year was a non conference game against a much bigger school to the north, Edmore. I made a lot tackles in that game against their big fullback, but finally got hurt near the end of the game and had to go to the hospital. I had torn a back muscle that really hurt, but it was not all that serious as injuries go.

I would play the next two seasons and was co-captain of the team my senior year, even though I did not play much that year because of injuries. I played both ways those two years – on defense and offense so did not get any rest during a game. I received a concussion during practice at the beginning of my senior season, when I errantly ducked my head on a tackle against our running back that year, Tom Halleck. His fiber glass thigh pad hit me in the head and knocked me out.

Our first game that senior year was against Carson City. We had not beaten them in several years. The coach got us all fired up. Two weeks had gone by since I had been hurt, and I really wanted to play in that game. I told the coach that I was fine, and he had me start. By this time I was playing linebacker on defense. I loved that position. I got to see better for one thing and could fly to the ball. My job that night was to watch their halfback. He was very fast and had a reputation as an outstanding player. If he made it into our backfield he would be gone for a touchdown.

After the first play one of our players told me, "Watch his feet. He points." What that meant was that every time he was to get the ball he would turn his feet in the direction he was going. So I watched his feet. Sure enough, every time he was to get the ball he would turn his feet. When he turned his feet, I tore after him as soon as the ball was snapped already knowing which direction he was going. I was having a blast. I'm sure their coach was frustrated. Not only was I tackling him, I was tackling him hard. I always spun him around, so he would meet the ground with force.

Somewhere during that first quarter my fun came to a halt. In my attempt to spin him around in the air before he hit the ground, he didn't get all the way around. He came down on my head, not the ground. The next thing I knew the coach was standing over me asking me how many fingers he was holding up. We won that game, but because that was my second head injury, the coach wouldn't let me play anymore until the last game of the season.

The last game was against Sheridan. It would be the last time we would play Sheridan since their school and ours would merge the following year to form and new school called Central Montcalm. There was always a rivalry between our two schools. In fact, every year the winner of that football game could brag that they had won the "Battle of the Red Bull". It was only a statue of a red bull, but the winner got to keep it for a year. It was a pride thing. The coach really wanted to win that game as did we all, and he needed me, so he let me start.

We were losing the game. That year we did not have a passing game. Their defense put players in the holes as well as in front of us and it was almost impossible to open a lane for our running back. We were constantly taking on two players on every play. On offense they had a "Barry Sanders" type running back. Just when you think you had him, he would zig or zag and you would grab air. They were killing us.

I think it was in the fourth quarter. I was playing defense, and I somehow again got into the backfield. However, there was no one there except the ball lying on the ground. I'm not sure to this day what happened.

Apparently there was a bad exchange between their quarterback and running back. I had been taught in a situation like that to just fall on the ball. But I was all by myself. Had I picked up the ball and run with it, I might have made my first and only touchdown. But I fell on the ball. One of their players then slid into my back with his knee in my kidney. I was in a lot of pain. They carried me off of the field, put me in an ambulance, and took me to the Sheridan hospital.

We unfortunately lost that game, but I had fun in the hospital. Tom Halleck was also hurt in that game and taken to the same hospital, where we both underwent therapy for torn muscles. We were confined to wheel chairs, so we raced our wheel chairs up and down the hallways. I think the nurses all cheered when we were released. Tom's son, Ty, went on from playing football at Michigan State, to play in the NFL. I was able to watch him on TV make touch downs on two different teams as a tight end,

One other memory about football brings a smile to my face, only this wasn't in a game. It was in our yard at home. It was the summer after my sophomore year before Mel had gone back to college. Mel suggested that we play some football, so we gathered the usuals, which included our brother Keith, our neighbors, and anyone else in the area. I remember that Mel was playing across from me when the ball was snapped. I simply charged forward as I normally did, and proceeded to knock him over the hill that went down toward our road. I think that ended the game. Mel never wanted to play football with me after that for some reason.

I know that for some, football is a "violent sport", and some mothers don't want their boys to play it. But I have always thought highly of football, and believe that God used it in my life as one of the tools to help me get straightened out and develop my character.

Developing a Healthy Work Ethic

I grew up in a family that honored work. Mom and dad modeled that mindset before us. Work always came before play, and before anything else except church. My siblings and I all had our chores to do, and were given allowances to teach us money management and tithing. At eight years old I had a paper route, which I inherited from Mel. It was difficult at that age and sometimes Mel would help me if there was bad weather. Keith took over that same route later. The best thing I can remember about that paper route was Christmas time. A lot of the customers gave me presents and candy. That seemed to make it all worthwhile.

By the time I was ten years old I was mowing lawns. I not only mowed our lawn at our house in town, but also the lawn at the lake. That lake lawn was huge. Dad had purchased a power lawn mower, but it was not self propelled. It was big and heavy, and took everything I had to push it. But I somehow got it done. I also got the job of mowing for another family at the lake. They were actually relatives on my dad's side. I rather enjoyed mowing their lawn since they had a self propelled mower and gave me all the pop and candy I wanted. I also mowed the lawn for some people in our church by the name of Rasmussen. They had a huge lawn on Main Street just east of the railroad tracks. That job included trimming bushes and raking as well. After Mr. Rasmussen died I continued to take care of that lawn until I went to college.

I was twelve or thirteen when I began to work at dad's plumbing shop. At first the job involved waiting on customers, finding fittings, electrical supplies or, cutting and threading pipe. I thought I was big stuff when I started working at the shop.

Soon dad had me working with Mel making furnace duct, S cleats, and drive cleats upstairs in his sheet metal shop. Dad's "Stanton Plumbing and Heating" business, as it was called, was located in what may have been the oldest building in town. It had once been an old grist mill, where grain had been ground into flour. The big water wheel that was once on the side of the building and powered the mill was long gone, but I remember seeing some of the old tackle that had once been used there. Today, I so wish that the building and its ancient contents had not been destroyed by the new owner when dad sold out.

The sheet metal shop was on the third floor of that old uninsulated building. It was cold but bearable in the winter, but it was very hot up there in the summer. We would have a window fan going full blast trying to circulate the air.

I enjoyed working in the sheet metal shop with Mel and later with Keith. It was fun to see things take shape and to know we were helping dad. Dad also paid us 50 cents an hour, which at the time wasn't too bad. But working with sheet metal could be dangerous. We didn't usually wear gloves, since it made it too hard to grip the metal.

One time I almost cut my brother, Mel's finger off. We were making S cleats at the time. An S cleat is made by first making a quarter inch bend on the brake (a machine used for bending the metal). That bend is then squashed down so that there is not a sharp edge. Next a couple of one inch bends are made in the shape of an s. An S cleat is used usually on ductwork to connect two pieces of duct together.

We were making the S cleats as fast as we could go. That made it fun. I worked one end of the brake and Mel worked the other end. Each of us had a lever we pulled down in order for the heavy brake jaws to close completely. We had made the quarter inch bend, and it was time to close the jaws on it to flatten it. I always closed my end first. I thought Mel said, "Close it." Instead he said, "Hold it". When I had shoved my end of the S cleat inside the jaws, his side had slid back out. I didn't see that. I closed my end with Mel's finger over the quarter inch bend. Fortunately his end was still up, or his finger would have been cut off as well as smashed.

He didn't say anything at first. Because of the pause in our work rhythm, I looked over at Mel and saw him standing there. I soon raised my end, and he grabbed his finger, which was bleeding badly. I followed him half way down the stairs before he collapsed. Mel didn't handle seeing blood very well – especially his own. Somehow we got his finger bandaged and he didn't lose it. From that point on he always used a piece of wood to shove in his side into the brake. I don't think he trusted me.

That wasn't the only time that Mel and I got hurt working together. Dad had told Mel and I to clean out the old shed. There was a lot of junk in that shed including several paint cans that still had old paint in them.   We got a fire going to burn up the stuff that would burn, but the fire seemed to be dying out. It didn't seem to want to burn up the paint cans we had also thrown in the fire.

It really was not a good idea to throw sealed paint cans on a fire. But the next thing we did was even dumber. Mel went and got some gasoline to help the fire get going better. He somehow managed to get the gasoline dumped on the fire without the fire exploding the can that held the gasoline. But it was only seconds later that the paint cans exploded. Mel was standing in front of me, so he got the worse of it. Boiling paint splattered all over both of us. It burnt our faces and hands mostly since the rest of the boiling paint went on our cloths.

We were in a lot of pain. I don't think we went to the hospital. I think we may have gone to the doctor's office. I don't remember that part of it. All I can remember is hurting very badly, and knowing that Mel was hurt much worse than I was. Another lesson was learned the hard way. Don't ever throw gasoline on a fire, and don't try to destroy paint cans in a fire. I can tell you from experience; it isn't a good idea.

The summers between my sophomore through my senior years of high school and my first two years of college I worked out on the job for my dad. My first job out of the shop was back filling a basement by hand. Dad had the plumbing and heating job at a cottage on a lake. The basement walls had caved in when a bull dozer was putting the dirt back next to the walls. So dad apparently told the owner after the walls were repaired that he would back fill the walls so they would not cave in. What dad had in mind was using me to do it. I did get it done.

I remember trying to cut holes in an oak floor by hand in order to put in the furnace "boot", which connected the register to the furnace pipe. I became frustrated with my very slow progress and told dad, "This can't be done". Dad never said a lot, but when he spoke, he always meant what he said. He simply responded, "It has to be done." Somehow I got the job done and learned not to quit. That same lesson was learned over and over as I had to put holes thorough two foot thick stone basement walls for an outside faucet, or notch a floor joist that was made of a huge log in an old house. The lessons and skills I learned from working for my dad have helped me all through my life.

I was working for dad one summer putting in a furnace. I was only a recent graduate from high school, but dad had trusted me with leading the project. My uncle Byrl (Marvin's dad) was helping me that summer, since he had been laid off from his factory job. We had run out of some supplies, so I had sent uncle Byrl back to the shop, which was just down the road from where we were working. In order to get the furnace pipe connected to the "boot" I needed to crawl between some ten inch floor joists. I had done that many times before, so it seemed like no big deal. I got the pipe hooked up to the "boot" and was backing out, when I got the not so smart idea to turn around instead of backing out. I got half way turned around when I got stuck. I was under a house with no one around, and I couldn't move one way or the other.

I was not normally claustrophobic (fear of tight spaces), but that day I had a terrible case of it. I started to panic and freak out. I started to pray like I never had prayed before. And God heard me. To this day I do not know how I got out of there. I just wiggled a little, and out I came. I never forgot how God answered **my** prayer that day.

I had had a similar answer to prayer a few years earlier. Dad had told me to take the car home from the shop. It was winter time and I couldn't get the car to move out of the parking area. The tires just spun. I remember distinctly praying and asking God to help me to get the car out of the snow, so I could go home. As soon as I had finished praying the car moved as if it were on concrete. I was shocked. I knew God had done that. Those answers to prayer helped prepare me for going to Bible College and entering the ministry. I knew God heard **me.**

I Begin to Grow-up in My Attitude Toward Girls

I was a typical boy when it came to girls. I thought they all had "cooties" until I was in the 6th grade. I remember, when I had just started kindergarten, and I was in our family's old 37 Chevy, that one of my little classmates came up to our car, while Mel, Marcia, and I waited for mom who was in a store shopping. My brother and sister kept asking me to stick my head out the window. That particular model had small vent windows for the back seat passengers. I did not know that they had already told my little classmate what to do when I complied. So I stuck my head out the window, and to my utter shock, she kissed me right on the mouth. I remember pulling my head back in quickly as they laughed, and I cried my eyes out in embarrassment.

That attitude toward girls began to change when I was in the 6th grade. I started to see some of them as "cute". One such girl was the girl that I first met when I was two days old in our hospital room – Beverley Dilno. Our mothers had shared the same hospital room, when we were born as I mentioned earlier. I fought a crush on her through most of the rest of our school days, but she saw me as the brother that she never had, so we just remained friends. I don't think we ever had a real date, but we did a lot together and could talk about anything and everything.

My first date was set up by my mom. I think I was in the 8th grade. There was a banquet at our church for our youth group, and mom thought it would be nice for me to take Sue Ann – a new girl in our church. I think dad or mom drove the car to where she lived, so I could properly pick her up. I felt very awkward about the whole deal, but went along with it.

I always felt awkward around most girls. When there was another banquet at a youth camp that our teens attended, I asked my cousin, Janet Chapin, to go, so I wouldn't have to ask anyone else. Her mom thought that was such a nice thing for me to do. I was just trying to take someone with whom I felt "safe". I was attracted to girls, but afraid of a relationship at the same time. I really lacked confidence around them. I had three dates during high school with girls from my school. All of them were by girls who asked me out. I went with them but felt very ill at ease with them.   But that was about to change.

 I was sixteen and a junior in high school when I was told that there was a girl from the Sheridan school that thought I was cute and wanted to meet me. She was on her student council, and so was Ion mine. She had visited our school as part of her student council and apparently saw me in that setting. I was shown a picture of her. She was really cute. I couldn't believe that she was interested in me. I honestly thought that either the person who told me was mistaken, or she had me confused with someone else.

I'm not sure how it came about, but I was introduced to her. Sandy (not her real name) and I hit it off and dated for the next two years. We even talked about getting married someday. But down deep in my heart I knew something wasn't right. Though she said she was a Christian and gave all the right answers, I seriously wondered if she really was saved. I even set up a meeting with her and my pastor. After that meeting pastor Mitchell thought she was saved. But for some reason, I just wasn't sure. As much as I loved being with her, something told me that she wasn't the right one. And by God's grace, He kept us from going too far in our relationship.

I'm so glad God kept me from that relationship. I believe Satan was trying to keep me from God's best and from being used in His service. God had someone so much more perfect for me and for the ministry that He had planned for me. In the middle of my senior year of high school I broke off our relationship. Because every time I saw her I was drawn to her, I knew that it would be best if I never saw her again, and I never did.

CHAPTER   7

GOD'S GRACE THROUGH THE DARKNESS

I mentioned at the beginning of this section of my life that I had a lot of fun growing up. I really did. But I could not tell my story without telling the dark side of my life as well. While this is very painful for me to re-call, and in some ways embarrasses me to tell of the awfully messed up and sinful way that I thought, only by telling this side of me can you understand why I so appreciate and love God's awesome grace poured out on me. I can say with Joseph as he told his brothers in Genesis 50:20, "You (Satan) meant it for evil, but God meant it for good." I was a much better minister for God, a dad, husband, and Christian, because of what I experienced.

Looking back on my life I believe I had wonderful and godly parents. I know they loved me. They disciplined me and taught me Biblical truth not only verbally and through taking us to church, but they modeled godly liv-ing in front of me and my siblings. Dad served faithfully in the church as a deacon and trustee. He served on the Lincoln Lake Camp board and did a lot to help that camp out. He did a lot of work for churches as well.

Mom was a natural leader. She started the Pioneer Girls in our church (Something like a Christian form of Girl Scouts), while dad was a founder of the Boys Brigade. Mom had a heart for people. She took food and clothing to our poor neighbors that lived behind us and brought others to the church. Our home was constantly the place where missionaries or evangelists found a Sunday dinner. I never in my life ever heard my mom or dad ever say a bad word. I think the only time I can remember either of them "losing it" was with me. I guess I really knew how to "push their buttons".

So what I am about to say must be understood from a child's perspective. This is how I saw life at the time that I was growing up, but not necessarily how it really was. I'm sure Satan had a lot to do with how I interpreted my circumstances. I truly believe Satan was out to destroy me and to keep me from ever being used by God.

As I said earlier I was saved when I was almost five. I remember sincerely telling my mom that God wanted me to be a preacher. I was six at the time. I was very serious. I remember where I was standing in the kitchen, when I felt that conviction and told my mom.

But there were some things going on in my head at the same time that, when combined with other events, would royally mess me up. Though it was a small thing, my brother Keith was born less than two years after me. The attention that he got somehow affected me. He got a tricycle on his second birthday. I had never had one. I noticed that Mel and Marcia's pictures were on the wall. I didn't see mine. They had bicycles. I did not have one until I was able to get a used one. I began to think that something was wrong with me. I felt unwanted. This was not true, but this is how I felt at a very early age.

I was probably six or seven when I went to a Sunday School class on Mother's Day. The teacher said some-thing that really caught my attention. She said that if I told my mom that I loved her, she would tell me that she loved me back. I had never heard those words from my mom or my dad. I had never gotten a hug from either of them. That just wasn't how love was expressed in our home. I learned much later, when I was an adult and talking to my mom, that verbal or physical love was never outwardly expressed in the home by her parents. She had never seen her parents kiss for instance. That lack of verbal and physical love was common in other homes as well during the era that I grew up.

But I really needed to hear it. I needed a hug. So I remember hugging my mom after church as she stood over the furnace grate in our dining room and telling her that I loved her. Her response to me was, "That's nice". I was devastated. The pieces were coming together in my mind, and they were not forming a pretty picture. I was not loved. I must be no good. There must be something wrong with me. Satan was laying the ground work in my head to try to destroy me. I was being beguiled. That means I was seeing a set of facts, but I was drawing the wrong conclusion – the conclusion that was the lie of Satan. Unfortunately I was beginning to believe that lie. But it was the following summer at our cottage when something would happen to really mess up my mind and almost destroy me. I was seven years old.

I don't remember the reason, but everyone else in our family needed to go somewhere. Mom had asked a baby sitter to stay with me. That evening the baby sitter wanted to play "doctor and nurse". To do that, we needed to take off our clothes. I didn't think that was right, but I complied. Without giving the details I was sexually abused that night. I remember almost being suffocated by her and crying a lot. That is about all I can remember, except that she told me not to tell anyone, and that it was my fault. (About 20 years later that person called me and asked for forgiveness, which I immediately gave. She had no doubt suffered from guilt for years and had gotten right with God. God's grace reached her and gloriously transformed her. I actually respected her greatly for the courage to make that call. It was certainly part of my own journey on the road to victory over guilt and bitterness.)

After that experience I **knew** that I was bad and no good. For several years after that, I felt I needed to act the way I really was – bad. I displayed a terrible temper. I would beat up my younger brother for no reason other than I didn't like him. I acted up in church and my Sunday School class, and got into fights. I got kicked out of Sunday School. I remember getting spankings every Sunday after church for a month of Sundays. On one occasion I looked up the meaning of my name in a dictionary or encyclopedia and discovered that my name meant, "son of the devil". Somehow that didn't surprise me.

I remember having so much hate inside of me. My relationship with God was nonexistent. I believe I was mad at God. I privately cussed and swore terribly. I once took a rope and threw it over a tree branch and tied my brother, Keith's legs on one side of the branch to our cousin Terry legs on the other side of the branch, and then went off and left them. Somehow they managed to get untied. Terry's mom was not very happy with me when she found that out. There was a point in my life at that young age when I seriously wanted to grow up to be a "hit man". I hated everyone.

I got in fights in school. I didn't care how big the other guy was or how badly I would get beat up. I would tear into anyone when I lost my temper, and that happened frequently. One of our friends at church taught me to box. He was my trainer and coach. He had set up a ring in his town of McBride, and wanted me to fight one of the town kids. I did, and knock him out. I thought that was awesome!

I lost my temper fighting Mel on more than one occasion. It often started with play, but would end in a serious fight. We would watch wrestling on TV and then go downstairs and act it out by throwing each other around the "ring" (old mattresses on the floor). I once lost my temper and grabbed the first thing I could get my hand on, which happened to be a hatchet. Mel took off running as fast as he could up the stairs from our basement. Fortunately mom grabbed me before I could get to Mel. And I calmed down.

When we were at the lake one summer, I disrupted a game of checkers my brother and sister were playing by knocking the board up in the air. I'm not sure why I did that. But dad took off after me as I ran out the front door. I thought I was out running dad, when suddenly he kicked my heel to one side causing that foot to catch on my other leg. I went down flat on my face in a mud puddle. Dad knew exactly what he was doing. He wasn't trying to catch me. He had seen the mud puddle and waited for just the right time to execute his plan. It worked great. I was humiliated. Dad didn't need to spank me that time.

Another time Marvin and I had Mel on the ground at the lake. I had gotten a bloody nose, which was not that unusual for me. We both held Mel on the ground while I bled all over him. He fainted at the sight of blood usually, and I knew he hated what I was doing. I was just being mean. I somehow managed to get away from him by using the boat. Marvin held him, while I ran. That was one of the few times that Mel really was mad at **me**.

Mel saw an order for swords in a catalogue and ordered a pair. They were harmless enough as they were designed. He thought it would be cool to imitate what we saw on TV. They were eighth or quarter inch rods with rubber tips on their ends. The rods were attached to the protective cups and handles. What started usually as something friendly almost always ended poorly. I would lose my temper and take my rubber tip off of my sword, and then Mel would follow suit. It is a wonder we really didn't kill each other: God's grace.

I hated to get my picture taken while I was growing up. I would run and hide when a family picture was to be taken. Pictures were often taken when relatives came to visit or we went to see them. I hated it partly to get negative attention, and partly because I had a problem with feeling part of the family.

By the time I was 9 or 10 I had become very stubborn and rebellious. I was the classic "strong willed child". One summer day, dad asked me to hoe the garden. I didn't feel like hoeing the garden, so didn't do it. When dad got home he asked me why I hadn't hoed the garden.   I told him that I felt I should be paid for doing it. He looked me in the eye and said, "Go hoe the garden". I replied, "I'm not going unless you pay me". Dad really lost it. Only one other time I can remember him losing it like he did that day. He grabbed me and dragged me to the garage. He then took a V-belt and began to spank me with it. A V-belt is the belt that is used to turn pulleys. It is stiff, and believe me, it really hurts when applied by a very angry father. That is without question the hardest spanking I ever received. After the spanking he again asked me to hoe the garden. I still refused. Dad just looked at me in disbelief and sorrow and went back inside.

Another incident will help you to understand how messed up I was. This particular act of rebellion has haunted me. I so wish I could undo it. I particularly felt sorrow about it when mom died. I was at the supper table with the family. I'm not sure what triggered mom's actions other than the fact that I probably sassed her ("talked back"). She came over to me and slapped me in the face. I stood up and slapped her in her face. In a fraction of a second dad flew out of his chair and knocked me to the floor. That was the second and last time that dad lost it with me. I was shocked, but knew I had it coming. I never ever considered doing that again.

Obviously I was also messed up in my mind about sexual matters. This took a sharp turn for the worse when I bought a "Playboy" magazine. I was with a group of boys from church. It was a junior boys Sunday School class that was touring the Lansing airport. In those days there were no security screenings, and one could watch the planes take off and land at a relative close, but safe distance. I loved watching them. The boys noticed the picture of a scantily clothed woman on the cover of a magazine and were pointing and laughing. One of the boys dared me to buy it. That's all I needed. I was the tuff guy – the bad guy. So I bought it.
That magazine started a journey into pornography that would trap me for several years. Mom unknowingly contributed to that lustful journey by subscribing me to a monthly photo magazine. I had purchased an enlarger and for a short time had the hobby of developing my own pictures. Those magazines always had very immoral pictures in them.

To make matters worse the church's Boy's Brigade leader sexually molested several of us boys. At this point in my life this man had become the leader of the group. He was also employed by my dad. It started as sort of sex education, but went "south" rather quickly. It primarily involved "touching" and "demonstrations" that was certainly criminal by today's justice standards. Several years later he was put in prison, and I think he died there. But at this time in my life I was a willing participant in it all, however. Dad and mom never knew any of the things that I have just shared. This is actually the first time that I have ever shared these matters in detail.

I was at a very dark place spiritually and morally. I cannot even mention some of the darkest things I was involved with. Satan had lowered his guns at me. I really thought I was a hopeless case.

CHAPTER 8

GOD'S GRACE AND MY SPIRITUAL REVIVAL

I came out of that darkness purely and totally because of God's grace. The God that I had talked with on my bunk bed still loved me and was pursing me. He had not let go of me. He still had me in His hand even though I was desperately fighting against Him. He heard the prayer I had offered on that bunk bed. He had taken the helm of my ship and was not about to let me crash into the rocks. Words cannot express how thankful I am for my Lord and His grace.

I naturally struggled with the assurance of my salvation during those dark years. Often when an invitation was given at church I felt the need to get saved again. I was never certain that I was saved. I didn't feel saved. I did not understand that God does not give one spiritual peace when he is rebelling against God.

It was during my sophomore year of high school when some light was starting to get through to my soul. It began with another dare. Only this time it was our youth director daring us to start reading our Bibles every day. I certainly wasn't doing that. But for some reason God used that dare to ring a bell in my heart. I never could pass up a dare. I started to read my Bible every day. I remember starting to feel guilty about some of the sinful things I was doing. God's Spirit was working on my heart!!

When I came home at night I would always see mom and dad's bedroom light on, their door open, and see them reading their Bibles. This really socked me in the jaw spiritually. I knew that what they had was real and I needed to get right with God.

About the same time our pastor for some reason (God's grace poured out on me) began to single me out for opportunities for service. The first time was during an evangelistic meeting. During the invitation a young boy raised his hand indicating his need for salvation. Pastor Mitchell pointed at me and asked me to take the boy aside and show him how to be saved. I had no clue how to do that. I remember fumbling around in the Bible and just reading some verses. Finally the guest soloist came through our room, and I asked for his help.   He quickly led the boy to the Lord. That convicted me. I should have been able to do that.

Pastor Mitchell then asked me to teach a junior boy's Sunday School class. They must have really been desperate. I was given no material, and I really didn't know what to do. I think I just started to read the Gospel of John. Our pastor again asked me to go with those boys as their camp counselor to Lincoln Lake Youth Camp. I was only 16 during this time. It was only a few years earlier at that camp that all the boys divided up into two gangs. I'm not sure where the camp counselors were. Somehow Mel and I ended up being the leaders of one of those gangs. When about five or six guys were on top of Mel, I had run into them with all of my strength and took care of them with Mel's help. What in the world was I doing as a camp counselor? I was a terrible camp counselor that year, but God was using all of this to work on my heart.

At the same time my success in football and in music was helping me feel better about myself. I was also feeling totally different about God. I remember going with Mel to pass out flyers about a coming evangelistic meeting. I loved doing that and didn't want to quit. God was preparing me. I'm not sure how it happened, but

God had given me victory over pornography and other sinful ways of life. I had thrown away all the magazines and gotten rid of my photo equipment, so I wouldn't be tempted. I was talking to God again and confessing my sin and asking for strength to do right.

During my senior year of high school it began to hit me that I might not see most of my classmates again. I had never witnessed to any of them. I began to care about their spiritual souls for the first time, but didn't know what to do about it.

Because I loved football, I really wanted to go to a college which had a football team. One Sunday our church had the president of Cedarville College, Dr. James T. Jeremiah, speak at our church. One of the older girls, June Golden, had gone there, but up to then, most of the youth had gone to Baptist Bible College, which was in the state of New York at that time. It would later move to Clarks Summit, Pennsylvania. I remember the first question I asked Dr. Jeremiah: "Do you have a football team?" He said that they could not afford all the expenses and equipment that went with having a football team, but they had a good soccer team. Somehow the fact that they did not have a football team didn't seem to matter as much as I thought it would. What mattered was that I felt very strongly that God wanted me to go there. So I enrolled in Cedarville.

PHASE   III

GOD'S GRACE POURED OUT ON MY CEDARVILLE YEARS

(1963-1967, Age 17-21)

- Average annual income: $6450
- Average cost of home: $13,600
- Cost per gallon of gasoline: 31 cents
- Average cost of a new car: $2650
- Supreme Court prohibits "state sponsored prayer in schools (1963)
- Mini skirt appears
- July 2, 1964 – President Lyndon B. Johnson signs Civil Rights Act into law ending segregation
- March 1965 – Martin Luther King Jr. leads civil rights march from Selma to Montgomery, Alabama
- March 8, 1965 – Marines land in Viet Nam and war escalates
- Hippie and anti Viet Nam War protests explode

(MY FRESHMAN YEAR)

CHAPTER   9

GETTING STARTED

Problems with my Name

I was only 17 when I started at Cedarville College. I had received my room assignment along with my accep-
tance letter. The letter was addressed to Miss Merlyn Jones and my room was in a girl's dormitory. As a
17 year old boy that one was a tuff one for me to correct. But, even though I may have hesitated for a few
seconds, I quickly responded to their registration office and received a new room assignment.

I had had problems like that with my name all my life. Because my name is spelled with a y (Merlyn) many
assume it is to be pronounced like Marilyn. I had that problem repeatedly when a substitute teacher in
elementary school would call the roll. She would always pronounce my name Marilyn, and all the kids would
laugh. I knew it was coming every time we had a substitute. Later in life I received telemarketer calls asking if
Marilyn was there. Of course I could honestly say, "No she's not". I frequently still get mail addressed to Ms.
Merlyn Jones. I once was mailed a card that made me a member of the "National Association of Female Execu-
tives".

My New Friends and Dorm Life

My mom took me to Cedarville that first year. I'm not sure if dad was with her or not. I don't remember. I
found my room and put my stuff on a bunk. It was apparent that I would have two other roommates. I had never been on the campus before, so after mom left I walked around a bit, and then headed to the cafeteria for supper. The line for supper extended outside the cafeteria down one of the narrow campus streets. I struck up a
conversation with a taller than me red headed guy. He looked like he could play football. I later learned that he
had played on a state championship team. I happened to mention that I was staying in Rife Hall and had a
roommate named Paul Jackson. He laughed and said, "I'm Paul Jackson". We both laughed and thought that
was amazing. That began a friendship that has lasted to this day.

Later that evening I met my other roommate, Dale Holms, and many of the others that lived on that second floor
of Rife Hall. Rife Hall was a big old house right on the out skirts of the small town of Cedarville. Directly
across the street was a "Dairy Isle" that served soft ice cream and simple sandwiches. That was convenient.
The house was not insulated, so it was hot in the late spring and early fall, and very cold in the winter. I remember waking up one morning and having a small snow drift that had snuck through a crack in our front window. But none of that seemed to matter to any of us.

Though God was radically changing me, I was still me. For freshman initiation week all the freshman guys had
to wear a shirt backwards, so it buttoned up in the back, and borrow a skirt from a girl to wear. All of us really
didn't want to be seen in public any more than we had to. But that first night in the dorm my roommates dared

me to go across the street in my "outfit" and order some ice cream at the Dairy Isle. Without hesitation I took the dare, went across the street, and ordered some ice cream, while they all watched from our upstairs window. I came back eating my ice cream to words and laughter that went something like, "Jones, you're nuts". I thought to myself, "I think I am too. But I have ice cream and you don't".

We had our share of fun in Rife Hall. This usually took the form of water fights. The college imposed a $10.00 fine if you were caught, but our dorm counselor was gone a lot, so we didn't worry too much about that. A water fight usually began with someone using his sprinkle bottle, when he was ironing. (This was before steam irons.) The fellow who got sprinkled then went and got a larger container and a friend. It would escalate until we were using waste baskets, and the entire floor was involved.

During the last water fight in which I participated, I was in the hall when the shout came, "Dorm Counselor". Everyone ran for their rooms. Unfortunately I wasn't fast enough. Just when I got to my door, my "wonderful" roommates jokingly closed the door and locked it. I was the only one in the hall when Dave Taylor, our dorm counselor, came up the stairs to our floor. He looked at the water dripping from the ceiling; he looked at me and my bucket, and said with a smile, "Humm, must have a leak". I always liked him. Dave would later be used in a marvelous way to start several churches in Brazil and lead hundreds to Christ. He gave his life for the Lord. He ended up dying on that field.

Hitch Hiking

I had never owned a car, so to get home from college, I usually got a ride with a fellow student as far as Ann Arbor, and then hitch hiked the remaining 100 miles or so home. The standard fee to pay a fellow student to help with gas in those days was a penny a mile. From Ann Arbor I would have a sign on the suit case that read "Ionia", face it toward the traffic, put my thumb out, and hope someone would stop. They usually did.

In those days that was a common thing to do. I had been hitch-hiking since I was 12 or 13. I often would hitch-hike to and from our cottage on Dickerson Lake before I had a driver's license. While I was waiting for someone to stop and give me a ride, I would usually walk. Salesmen often wanting someone to talk to would pick me up. Servicemen would often hitch-hike as well. In those days it was not dangerous to do so. Today it can be extremely dangerous to hitch-hike or to pick up a hitch-hiker. On some highways it is now illegal.

One time, while hitch-hiking home between Ann Arbor and Lansing, I was picked up by a salesman for a new yogurt company named Dannon. He was not only the salesman, but apparently the owner of the company. After carrying on a conversation for awhile, he offered me a job in his company. For some reason he liked me. He said his product was going to be big someday, and what he was offering was a great opportunity. I thanked him for his generous offer, but told him that I was called into the ministry and had a job to do for God. I never once regretted turning down his offer.

CHAPTER 10

MY SPIRITUAL GROWTH EXPLOSION

My Renewed Call to the ministry

We developed such a wonderful bond among the young men on that upstairs floor of Rife. On our own we began daily prayer meetings at 7:00 pm that were amazing. God began to work in all of our hearts through those prayer meetings. It was in one of the prayer meetings that I again felt God's call to the ministry. I was overwhelmed that God wanted to use me in His service after all I had done against Him. God also called my friend, Paul, into the ministry. I believe there were 11 guys living on that top floor. Of those, more than half would go into "full time" ministry like missions or the pastorate.

Our Prayer Meeting and God's Miraculous Answer

One day I received an anonymous letter. It was from a girl from my high school. She said she had watched me in high school and knew that I had something that was missing in her life. I was floored by that, but at the same time frustrated. I wanted to respond and share the Gospel with her. I shared the letter with the guys in our prayer group and we began to pray for her salvation, and that I would be able to find out who it was.

A few days later, one of the guys from our prayer group, Tim Duffy, told me that he had an unusual burden for the anonymous writer and had awakened at 1:00 am to pray for her. A couple of days after that, I received another letter from the letter writer. This time she had signed it. I knew who she was: Carolyn Berg. She told in her letter that she had had a dream a couple of nights ago that freaked her out. She dreamed that she was falling into hell. She awoke from her dream and cried out to God to save her.

I immediately wrote her back and told her that we had been praying for her, and gave her some verses to help her with her new found faith. I couldn't wait to share the news in our prayer meeting. I also asked her what day and time this dream occurred. The news of her salvation so electrified the guys. We all rejoiced and praised God. But when I got her letter back that told me what day and time she had had her dream, I couldn't believe it. It was the exact day and time when Tim had awakened to pray for her. I had seen God work in an amazing way. My faith was soaring. Carolyn attended Cedarville the next year and ended up marrying one of my friends from the Stanton area.

My First Preaching Opportunities

My first opportunity to preach came shortly after I started college. Pastor Mitchell from my church learned that I was coming home for a weekend and asked me to preach on a Sunday night. I was scared, but excited at the same time. I think I preached on Jesus healing the man with leprosy from Matthew 8:1-4. I called the message, "The Leper Who Couldn't Change His Spots". I laugh about that title now, but I was dead serious when I preached that evangelistic message. I compared the leprosy to sin. I was still only 17. On another occasion, during that first year of college, I was asked to preach in one of the country churches near my home town, Pine Grove Community Church.

My Classes and my Struggles

After God had renewed my call to the ministry I wasn't sure what to do concerning my major. I had started college as a music major and was enjoying the music classes. I loved music theory but really didn't like music history. I was part of the college choir, taking private piano lessons, and trombone lessons along with the usual load of general courses taken by college freshmen. Every student attending Cedarville also was required to be a Bible minor, so I was taking Bible classes, which I loved.

I discovered that I was far behind most of the other freshmen, especially in my vocabulary. I had a very difficult time even understanding the professors and the textbooks. My whole first semester I was playing catch up. Along with the nightly prayer meetings in our dorm we also studied together. That helped me tremendously to understand what was being said in the classroom and the textbooks. The guys "interpreted" for me.

My First Real Burden for the Lost and Attempt to Witness

Two Bible courses especially would impact me for the rest of my life. The first one was a course on evangelism taught by Dr. Arthur Williams. It was often referred to as Dr. William's memory course, because of the 100s of Bible verses that were required to be memorized. Though I had to really work in that course, God tremendously used that course in my life.

I remember where I stood on Main Street in down town Cedarville, when, for the first time, I had an overwhelming burden for the lost. I had never experienced that before. I saw people walking on the sidewalks, and I wondered if they were headed to hell – and it bothered me terribly.

I remembered my friend, Tom Adams, from high school, and I determined that I would witness to him. Tom played center on our football team in high school, and was my friend. But I had never witnessed to him or even invited him to church. I was determined to change that. Not only was I memorizing verses of Scripture, but I had picked up a little book in the college book store entitled, "Soul Winning Made Easy", by C.S. Lovett. It showed how to steer a conversation into a Gospel presentation. I memorized the steps in the plan. I couldn't wait to try it on Tom.

The first chance I had, when I was home, I invited Tom over to play ping-pong. All of the guys in our family played ping-pong. We started playing on the dining room table when we were young. We finally got a regulation table and had it set up in our basement. Dad was very good at it as well and played up into his 90s.

Tom came over to play some ping-pong not knowing of course about my plan to witness to him. After playing some ping-pong for a while, I asked the first question in the plan. "Tom, are you interested in spiritual things." Tom replied that he didn't think so. So I proceeded to ask the second question. "What do you think a Christian is?" His answer was, "I'm not sure". That's when I thought I had him. I asked the third question. "Would you like for me to show you?" He simply replied, "No". I was devastated. It wasn't supposed to work that way. He was supposed to say "yes" or "ok", and I would then present the Gospel. So that ended my first attempt at witnessing. I had bombed.

After Tom had left that day I got out my book and reviewed the plan. Suddenly I saw what I had done wrong. When I asked the question, "Would you like for me to show you", I was supposed to pull out my little New Testament.

The next break I had from school I invited Tom over to play ping-pong. Once again he came, and once again I started with the exact same questions. This time when I asked, "Would you like for me to show you", I pulled out my New Testament, And Tom replied "ok".

I shared the Gospel with Tom that day. He didn't accept the Lord as His Savior, but it began a commitment to pray for him every day, which I have done since that day. Tom's wife has trusted Christ as her Savior and is a wonderful Christian. She was in our class at school, and was the little girl that Mel and Marcia tricked me into kissing through our car window, when I was in kindergarten. I kept in contact with him and tried to witness to him again, when Nancy and I went to their house for a visit. But Tom shut the conversation off quickly, when he saw the direction I was heading. I was able to share the Gospel with him indirectly when I shared the Gospel with all my high school classmates at our 50th high school class reunion, which I helped plan and lead. I still am praying for him and others in my high school class.

Learning That God Chose Me

The second Bible course that really impacted my life my first year was Old Testament and New Testament Survey taught by Dr. Robert Gromacki. They were actually two courses but tied together over the two semesters of my freshman year. Dr. Gromacki was a nationally known and respected Bible author and teacher. I loved his classes. He really made the Bible come alive to me.

During one of the classes, Dr. Gromacki taught that believers only chose God because He had chosen them. I went up to him immediately after class and tried to argue with him. "What about the verse that says, 'Whosoever will, may come' and 'God is not willing that any should perish but that all should come to repentance'?" "Doesn't the teaching that God chose some to believe and not others, take away the free will of man and make us all robots?" All he would do is smile and say, "Go and read Romans Chapter 9". He had heard what I was saying many times before.

I went back to my dorm and began to argue with the upper classmen. I felt sure I was right. I argued that night until 2:00 in the morning. I finally remembered what Dr. Gromacki had said, "Read Romans chapter 9". I decided that I should probably do that. I read it, and read it again several times. I could not deny what it taught. God was sovereign and in charge of salvation. It finally dawned on me that I had been dead in my sins. I saw other Scripture that taught that no one seeks God. I realized that I had been incapable of seeking God as a corpse. He had to initiate the work of salvation on my heart, or I would not, and could not have been saved.

When it finally got through to me that God chose me to be saved before the foundation of the world, I was brought to tears. God loved me all the while I was growing up, no matter what, even though He hated my sin.

My love and worship of God began to soar. He is so awesome!! Even though God allows us to choose Him, we do so because His Holy Spirit prompts our hearts to do so. Though there **seems** to be a conflict between

God's sovereignty and man's free will, there is no such conflict in God's mind. I decided to let it go and just believe what God's Word said. That truth revolutionized how I saw God, and how I saw myself in relationship to that God. God's grace was being poured out on me.

Meeting Dr. Robert T. Ketcham

One of the courses I was required to take was called English Composition. It focused on writing, which would greatly help me later. I had done well in English grammar, but needed help in the area of composition. One of the course requirements was to write a lengthy paper. I had never done that before, and didn't know what to write about. Finally I decided to write a paper on the history of the General Association of Regular Baptist Churches (GARBC). My home church, the First Baptist Church of Stanton, Michigan, was part of that fellowship of Baptist churches, but the GARBC was not mentioned in the church that I could remember. So I thought I should probably find out what in the world the GARBC was, since Cedarville was also one of its approved colleges.

Someone in my dorm mentioned that a speaker was coming to chapel that had something to do with the GARBC. I thought, "Wow! It would really impress my professor if I could have a personal interview as one of my sources for my paper." So I set up an interview with the chapel speaker for later that day after chapel.

I borrowed my roommate, Paul Jackson's, reel to reel tape recorder, to help me remember what my source said, so I could have accurate quotes. We met backstage where the chapel was held in Alfred Auditorium. I thanked Dr. Ketcham for his willingness to meet with me, and began the interview. I had no idea who he was before that interview. Shortly into the interview, though, I realized that this was "the man". This man was **the** founder of the GARBC – the main man!

He was so gracious as he told how he and others had tried to get rid of the liberalism in what was then called "The Northern Baptist Convention". Because of the way that convention was set up, those who believed in the fundamentals of God's Word, were not able to purge that convention from its liberal element. So a fellowship of churches was formed, the GARBC, in the early 1930s. In the convention the control was at the top – the headquarters of the convention. In the new association of churches the control would be in the local church. So missionaries or colleges or agencies that denied such doctrines as the deity of Christ, the virgin birth, and the substitutionary sacrifice of Christ for sinners, could have their financial support dropped by the churches. Such withdrawal of support would be backed by the fellowship of churches as well.

That interview did much more for me than get an A on a paper. I learned how others before me had stood up for the truths of the Word of God. Many had paid a dear price for it, losing pensions and homes. But I also learned that great men are gracious men. I went to the college library and looked up all I could find about Dr. Ketcham. I discovered that they had several tapes of his messages. I listened to all I could get my hands on. I sat in that library listening to one of the greatest preachers of that day with tears streaming down my cheeks. I heard what great preaching was like. I knew I could never be a Dr. Ketcham, but I wanted to change people's lives through the Word of God like God had changed mine. God was forming me. His grace was being poured out on me.

CHAPTER 11

LEARNING ABOUT THE CHARISMATIC THEOLOGY

One Sunday afternoon Tim Timmons and some other friends said they were planning to attend a Charismatic church that evening and invited me to go along. I had no idea what that was, but they said that these people ran up and down the aisles during church and sometimes leaped over pews. They also "spoke in tongues". I couldn't believe anyone would run up and down an aisle during church or leap over a pew. I know if I had tried that during church, I wouldn't have been able to sit down for a week. But my curiosity peaked, and I was in.

I do not remember the name of the church. But I do remember that it was in Xenia, and had a lot of people attending, especially for a Sunday night. There were probably over five hundred people there. We sat near the back so we could see most of what was going on in the congregation.

The service was very different from anything I had ever seen. The choir loft had at least forty adults behind the pastor and the other musicians. They had two guitar players on the stage as well as a piano and organ and a lady who played the tambourine. They sang a lot of music and usually seven or eight stanzas of each number, it seemed to me. The songs were all very lively and "up-beat", which I actually enjoyed. But what was shocking to me was the behavior of one of the guitar players. He would jump up and down like a rabbit as he played each song. It was though he had springs in his legs. Though I did not see anyone leap over a pew (I was really watching for that one), I did see people run up to the front of the church and then back to their pew.

When the preacher finally got up to preach, the choir members stayed up on the platform behind him. He did refer to a text of Scripture, but what he preached really had nothing to do with that text. As he was preaching I noticed that a lady in the back row of the choir was beginning to jerk. Suddenly she stood up. While she continued to jerk in what looked like uncontrollable spasms, she almost seemed to gracefully float out from her row in the choir and down to the front of the platform.

When she arrived at the front of the platform, the preacher stopped preaching. I assume he saw her out of the corner of his eye. She then began to rattle some sounds that made no sense to me in a very high pitched voice and in rapid succession. When she stopped, she went back to jerking again and "floated" back to her seat and sat down. When she sat down the preacher began to speak in a very rapid succession. I assume he was supposed to be interpreting. He said something about someone being in the audience who hadn't been baptized with the Spirit, and he was looking right at us.

I thought I was pretty tough. But at that moment I wanted out of there. I felt the presence of evil like I had never experienced before. I felt the hair on the back of my neck sticking straight up. I knew what it was like to be near God, and that was not it.

None of us moved. Somehow we made it through the service. We walked to the car in silence. When we got in the car and started down the road, we began to talk and share how we felt. We all felt the same thing. I think we went, thinking it would be fun – almost entertaining. I didn't feel that way when I left. I had witnessed something that was from another realm, and I didn't need to experience that again.

That experience did force me to study the Bible on that subject, which was a good thing. It helped form and solidify my Biblical views on the charismatic movement. Dr. Gromacki had recently published a book on that movement, which I read. I studied the Bible passages pertaining to it, particularly Acts 2 and I Corinthians 12-14. What I discovered was that God's revelation is complete. Before the Bible was completed He did give revelation directly to men. "But when that which is complete is come, then that which is in part shall be done away" (I Cor. 13:8-10). Tongues, prophecy, and supernatural knowledge (I Cor.13:8) are all gifts that have to do with revelation. They would cease when something came that would be "perfect", which is the word for complete. They would no longer have bits and pieces of revelation. They would have it all – all we need for faith and practice of the Christian life – the Bible.

Later when I was in the hospital after having my appendix out, I would come across a lady who believed in "faith healers". This was also new to me, so I did a lot of study on that as well. God was using all of these experiences to prepare me for the ministry.

CHAPTER 12

MEETING NANCY

I first saw Nancy from a distance during our first week at school. There was a freshman talent night, and she sang a solo. I remember thinking, "She has a really nice voice, but sings a little flat sometimes". I had a serious problem being musically critical. But I also noticed that she was pretty good looking.

A few weeks later my cousin, Phil Olsen, came and asked me if I would double date with him and his girl friend, Mary. I met my cousin for the first time at Cedarville shortly after I arrived. He was a couple of years older than I was. I had cousins everywhere I went, it seemed. His mom and my dad were first cousins, but his dad was pastoring a church on the other side of the state of Michigan from where I lived, so we had never met. Mom and dad had told me to make contact with him; he apparently had heard of me as well. So we met and became fast friends with similar interests in guns and music.

Phil told me that they wanted to go to a high school football game that night. Since Nancy, Mary's roommate, would tag along almost everywhere they went, Phil thought this would be a good way to help his situation.

I didn't know Nancy's name at that point or anything about her, so I was reluctant at first. But Phil talked me into it a few minutes before they were planning to leave. He told me that she was in one of the practice rooms playing the piano and was expecting me. The practice rooms were very small rooms big enough for a small pi-ano and piano bench. That's where music students practiced either the piano, voice, or other musical instru-ments. I had probably seen Nancy there before, since I practiced my trombone in one of those rooms, but I did not remember seeing her.

So I went over to her practice room where she was playing and singing. I opened the door and very "romanti-cally" said, "Well, are you ready"? She looked at me and said, "Sure am". And out to the ball game we went. We had a good time that night and did some other things together after that, like going to church together, but I thought we had communication issues, (We are still working on that) so I told her that I thought we should be just friends.

I dated some other girls during that first year of college. But most of those relationships were short lived. Shortly after I had broken it off with Nancy I went to church with a girl named Sandy N. She looked like a model from a magazine. She was extremely beautiful, but had a problem. She couldn't carry on a conversation. She would just look at me and smile. For a short time that seemed to be fine with me, but it got old. When Nancy saw me come into church that day, she said she wanted to throw a hymn book at both of us. But she managed to control herself and give the matter to God.

My Total Lack of Manners

On the way back from church that day with Sandy N., my roommates made it a point to walk on the opposite side of the street from us, so they could annoy me. They succeeded. They were laughing and pointing and having a big time at my expense. When I finally got back to the dorm, I was preparing to give them a piece of my mind, when they started in on **me**. "Jones, don't you know anything?" I was not prepared for that. "What are you talking about?" "Don't you know that the guy is always supposed to walk on the street side of a girl?" "Why in the world is he supposed to do that?" I asked. They went on to explain that that tradition began long ago, and was intended to protect the girl from any splashes from horse drawn carriages or cars that were going by. I responded, "But what if I would rather be the one to stay dry". I was just trying to be difficult. They just said, "Jones, you're hopeless," and dropped the matter.

I really did not know how to treat a girl, or for that matter, how to eat properly. I was used to eating everything with a spoon. I very seldom if ever used a fork. I think Nancy is still trying to teach me how to properly hold one. So academics was not the only area in which I was way behind. But I was learning.

CHAPTER 13

MUSICAL OPPORTUNITIES

The music department of the college always formed the musical groups that represented the school. I don't think my first quartet members realized that. We all just liked to sing and wanted to be used by the Lord. Tim Duffy got that first quartet together. I suggested that my cousin Phil be in it, as well as a new friend, Tim Timmons. Phil had a nice first tenor voice, Tim Timmons sang bass, I sang baritone, and Tim Duffy sang the lead. I still have a recording of one of our practice sessions.

We needed a piano player, so I mentioned that I knew a girl that played well. By this time I had been on that blind date with Nancy, and Phil knew her also. So Nancy became our piano player. We sang locally representing the college on a few occasions and enjoyed it. All of those occasions had been set up by us, not the school.

One weekend, we were informed that the school had set up an opportunity for us to sing up in Michigan. We were excited about the opportunity. It would involve a couple of overnight stays, but the church people at the First Baptist Church of Allegan, Michigan, would house us. After the long drive we finally got to the church. Both Nancy and I were shocked to discover that the church had Nancy and I rooming together. My name had done it again. They thought I was a girl. That correction was quickly made, we sang our numbers, and traveled back to the school tired but blessed.

I also played my trombone in the college band and several times in chapel. I was also in the "pep band" which played for basketball games. I had learned in high school, when I was goofing off, how to make my trombone sound like a hot rod taking off at a drag strip. One of the guys in the pep band dared me to stand up and play the hot rod during a basketball game. I finally got the nerve to do it. When I did the crowd went nuts. They loved it. From then on, when I was in the pep band, my playing the "hot rod" became a regular event at basketball games.

Another opportunity to use my music came in the form of singing in the college choir. I always loved to sing. So when it was required of music majors to sing in the choir, I had no problem with that. I sang second bass in the choir, which is the lowest part. When I auditioned for the choir, the head of the music department was there as well as the professor who directed the choir. They were both amazed at my range. I remember seeing them look at each other and smiling. They said that they needed second basses mostly, so that's the part I would sing.

That first year in the choir we had a girl with absolute perfect pitch. The director never had to use a pitch pipe for our notes. He just asked her for the pitch, and she was always right on. During our spring break that year we traveled all over the Midwest giving concerts. It was while singing in the choir that I got to know a girl named Joan. She was a very good Christian girl, whose father was a pastor in the state of New York. Even though we dated throughout that spring and summer, and I liked Joan, I began to realize that she just wasn't the one God had for me. I didn't realize it at the time, but God's grace was being poured out on me. He had someone He had made just for me. At the beginning of my sophomore year I broke off our relationship.

CHAPTER   14

FALLING IN LOVE WITH NANCY

All the time I was dating Joan and other girls during my first year at college, I continued to be friends with Nancy. That's all it was. We were just friends. But something kept drawing me to her. I would hear her singing and playing the piano in her practice room, and I would put down my trombone and go to her room, so I could sing with her.

Our voices naturally blended together. We could both harmonize, so we could both easily find the notes we needed. There was something about sitting on the piano bench together and singing. I couldn't figure it out. We would go to the Calvary Baptist Church in Xenia in the same car with some of my buddies from Rife, and we would sing on the way over and on the way back. The guys loved it too. But we were just friends.

When I broke off my relationship with Joan, one of the reasons for doing so in my mind was because it felt awkward dating Joan and being friends with Nancy – and I just couldn't bear to lose that friendship. I remember praying about all of it. I did not hear an audible voice, but it might as well have been. God knew I needed all the help I could get.

I was walking toward the campus one night, when I saw Nancy walking across one of the campus sidewalks. The light finally went on. She's the one. She's the one God has for me to partner with for the rest of my life. I did not tell her how I felt. I didn't know how to. I had broken off our dating relationship last year. Now what do I do? God took care of that for me, as well. His grace just kept coming over me.

Our First Kiss

During my first semester of my second year at Cedarville Nancy and I had some music courses together. By this time my cousin Phil was engaged to Mary, Nancy's roommate and friend. The wedding was scheduled during our Christmas break. Mary had asked Nancy to stand up with her, and Phil had asked me to stand up with him. Nancy had initially planned to ride out to New York for the wedding with some other girls. But our music history class exam was scheduled the day those girls were leaving, which made it impossible for Nancy to ride with them.

Nancy was frantic. She went to Mrs. Smith, our professor, and begged her to let her take the exam earlier, but Mrs. Smith wouldn't let her do it. There was only one other way to get out to the New York wedding. She would have to ride with the guys who were going to be in the wedding. She came to me and sheepishly explained the matter to me. She wanted me to know that she had not intentionally planned to ride with me. She did not know that I was actually more than fine with it.

I know that God has a sense of humor. I know He must have chuckled as He orchestrated all these events that threw Nancy and I together. I chuckle too just recalling it all. First, the car we had to ride in was a cloth topped convertible. Second, it was very cold at that time of year. Third, the car heater didn't work. Fourth, there were only two other guys besides myself and Nancy riding in the car, and they chose the front seat. That meant that Nancy and I had to ride in the back seat together. Did I mention that it was very cold in that car?

I'm sure Nancy and I talked, but I don't remember anything about that conversation. Fifth, we were driving all night to get to Mary's home town in the state of New York. But this next piece of work that the Lord certainly orchestrated really is over the top. Sixth, somewhere half way to our destination the guy in the front passenger seat actually turned to me and said, "If you don't put your arm around her, I will." Nancy was shivering. It really was the gentlemanly thing for me to do. I wanted to do it, but I was chicken. God knew that I needed a shove, so He used the guy's words in the front seat to give me the nudge I needed. I looked at her, and put my arm around her. I certainly wasn't about to let the other guy do it.

It was like fireworks going off. What was happening was supposed to be, and I knew it. She put her head on my shoulder, and then looked up at me, and we kissed. Tears filled both of our eyes. We held on to each other the rest of the trip. I think I really helped with her shivering problem. From that moment on until this day we have been a couple.

The news spread fast throughout all those in the wedding party. I think many had thought we should be a couple long before I had thought that. Phil and Mary were ecstatic that their wedding had brought us together. They would later be in our wedding. I don't remember much about their wedding, but I sure remember the ride out to it.

Defending Nancy and My Last Real Temper Flare Up

Nancy and I continued to date the rest of that school year. During that time I had one terrible loss of temper that was very embarrassing. I hadn't lost it in a few years, so this caught me by surprise. I was saying good night to Nancy in the lounge of the girl's dorm, where boys were allowed to be. Guys were never allowed to go to a girl's room. Although holding hands was permitted, public kissing was not allowed. There was also a curfew time, when everyone had to be in their dorms. I always cut that as close as I could.

This particular night two freshmen guys were in the girls lounge of Nancy's dorm getting their "jollies" out of watching guys with girl friends say good night. They thought they were being funny when they said, "After you say good night, we are going down to her room and really tell her good night". With a burst of speed that would make superman proud I grabbed both of them by their shirts under their necks and shoved them up against a brick wall – one guy in my left hand and one in my right. With their eyes as big as saucers, and mine looking straight into theirs, I said through clenched teeth, "Don't you ever talk like that about her again." I felt they were smearing her character, and it really ticked me off.

When I had regained my composure, and let them down from the wall, they took off running out of there. I, then, looked around to see every eye looking at me. I was embarrassed and ashamed. I didn't know that temper was still around. I didn't like it. I went back to my dorm and got on my knees and asked God to take that ugly thing away from me. Looking back over my life I don't think I ever lost it like that again. Later that week one of those freshmen came back and apologized to me. He later became a missionary. I always thought I had something to do with that.

Nancy told me later that year that she had decided that she would not be able to return to Cedarville the next year because of the lack of finances, so she would stay home and get a job to save money. Though I had already met Nancy's parents the previous year when our quartet sang in her dad's church in Findlay, Ohio, I made several weekend trips up to Findlay with Nancy, so she could see her little sister, Penny, and be with her parents. They loved me and I loved and respected them. I immediately felt part of their family. Nancy and I rode with Lyle Culberson who had a car and was dating Nancy's sister Patty, who began to attend Cedarville our second year.

CHAPTER   15

ACADEMICS AND MUSIC

I was taking some difficult courses during my sophomore year. Beginning Greek was very difficult and involved a lot of memorization of vocabulary. I was getting my Greek and Spanish mixed up at times. I had
had a couple years of Spanish in high school, and had used it some in a summer ministry with some missionaries to the migrant workers in the Stanton area. I played my trombone to draw a crowd for the preacher. I also
switched to an English major for the second semester of my sophomore year and was struggling trying to take
Shakespeare at 7:00 am in the morning. What was I thinking!

I continued to sing in the choir my second year and traveled again with them during spring break. We went to
New York City among other places, so I got to go up in the Empire State Building and see the Statue of Liberty,
as well as Niagara Falls in northern New York state.   I was also in a college musical – "The H. M. S. Pinafore".

The quartet that I was singing in the first year folded.   Tim Timmons had his eye on a girl named Carol, who
was singing in a girl's trio. He convinced her that he and I should join the group and make it a mixed quintet,
which we did. I traveled with that school sponsored group singing on a lot of weekends during my sophomore
year. Tim was an outstanding speaker and did most of the preaching. He would later go on to Dallas Theological Seminary, and then become a well known speaker with Campus Crusade for Christ.

CHAPTER   16

GETTING ENGAGED

When our sophomore year of school was over, Nancy got a job working at an RCA factory right across the street from the First Baptist Church in Findlay, where her dad was the pastor. She worked the second shift putting transistors together. Her small piano playing fingers were perfect for the job, and she did well at it. During that summer she bought a little blue Volkswagen that fitted her perfectly – me not so much. She always teased me later that I married her for her car.

In August she drove to northern Ohio and picked up Carol Winner, Tim's girl friend, who accompanied Nancy on her trip up to my brother Mel's wedding in the Detroit area. I met her at the church where the wedding was being held, and was in the wedding as Mel's best man. Carol had made arrangements to get home another way, so I could drive Nancy back to Findlay.

I had purchased a diamond engagement ring through a discount magazine a month earlier. Recently Mel, Keith, and I were exchanging engagement ring stories. Although Keith and I had good stories on how cheap (Dutch) we all were, we all agreed that Mel's story of his diamond ring far surpassed either of ours. He purchased his wife, Carol's, ring from a cousin who had offered it to three girls before. All of them had turned our cousin down. He originally purchased the ring from a pawn shop. We all agreed that we had "married up".

So on the way home from the wedding I was trying to figure out how to give the ring to Nancy. I didn't know what romance was. I had never seen it. Nancy really had a lot of training to do on me. That training actually got started on our trip home to Findlay. I had placed the ring box in my suit coat pocket, and had hung my coat on the coat hook behind my seat in the Volkswagen. As I was driving through Toledo (before there was a by-pass around it) I noticed a drive-in hamburger stand. It was the kind where one could park their car outside, and a girl came to your car (sometimes on roller skates) to take your order. The food tray hooked on to the driver's side window. The girl had not yet come out to take our order, and I had turned around in my seat to try to retrieve the ring box. I just couldn't wait any longer to give it to her. When I turned back around she saw the ring box and began to scream, "Not here! Not here!"

I didn't know what to do. What was the problem? The car was stopped. I had the ring. I didn't know what she meant. So I said, "Where?" "Just drive", she said. So I backed the car out as quickly as possible and took off without a clue as to where I was to go. Finally she said something about it being ok to give it to her on a side road.   Apparently she didn't want anyone around except the two of us. So I turned down the first side road I found, stopped the car, and gave her the ring.

She was happy, kissed me, and couldn't stop talking about it. I'm sure I smiled, but I was still in a total state of shock. "What was that", I thought? I was being introduced for the first time to a lady from a very different world than I had come from. She was all girl, and reacting like most normal girls would. But that was all new to me. I had a lot to learn about romance. Nancy really had her work cut out for her.

CHAPTER   17

A YEAR OF CHANGES AND OPPORTUNITIES

A New Major

I started my junior year at Cedarville as an English major, but that would quickly change. I had to take a litera-ture course entitled "Milton". On the first day of that class the professor had a stack of books on his desk at least a foot high. He began that class by saying that before we completed that semester course we would have read all of those books. I thought to myself, "No. I don't think so."

I knew I needed help as a public speaker if I was going to be in the ministry, so I switched that very day to be-coming a Speech (Communications) major. That was God's grace being poured out on me again. I didn't know what I was doing, but God certainly did.

I had to take some extra course hours to help get caught up on my new major. With having to take second year Greek as well, I had my hands full. One of the speech courses that I took that year was called "Pulpit Speech" (Homiletics). Of all the courses that I took at Cedarville, that course was the most valuable in pre-paring me to be a preacher. I kept that text book and would follow its teaching in preparing and delivering ser-mons throughout my entire ministry. Our professor was outstanding and a great communicator himself, Dr. John Reed. Others that took that class with me would go on and become well know preachers, including Joe Stowell, Tim Timmons, and Paul Jackson. A few years earlier David Jeremiah took that same course and would later have a tremendous ministry both on the radio, television, and in writing.

Being a Dorm Counselor

During this third year of college I became a dorm counselor. That job basically involved making sure the guys in my dorm behaved themselves and followed the school rules. It didn't really involve much counseling. I was gone a lot on weekends singing, which I'm sure the guys in my dorm loved. When I was there I led them in dorm prayer meetings. But looking back on it, I was not a very good dorm counselor. I just wasn't around much. But it did help pay my room and board, which helped greatly, since I was paying my own way through college for the most part.

The New Quartet

At the start on this year the music department contacted Tim Timmons and me. They thought the college need-ed a men's quartet, and wanted Tim and I to be part of it. The music department selected those who would make up this quartet. They selected Dan Boyd to be the bass. He couldn't read music, but he had a fantastic bass voice. Ted Clater was to be the first tenor. His voice was ok, but he was great at keeping us straight on the business end of things. I was to sing the second tenor (lead), and Tim Timmons was to sing baritone. We soon discovered that our voices really worked well together. We practiced every chance we got and memorized all of our music. Our piano player was a new student named John. He was outstanding and could play anything. He also had a flare for southern gospel. We named our quartet, "The Volunteers" based upon one of the songs we sang.

We started to sing in churches almost every weekend. The weekends we weren't singing, I was traveling up to Findlay with Lyle Culberson to see Nancy. We began to travel a lot with the president of the school, Dr. James T. Jeremiah, Dave Jeremiah's father. He really liked us, and it was a great experience to travel with him. I tried to sit in the front seat as he always drove, so I could talk to him. On one trip with him out to the state of New York he hit a deer just before we got to the church. He had just gotten that new car. He was very upset but kept his composer and preached a great message that night.

Before the Christmas break the music department chairman approached us about traveling for the school during the coming summer. The school would pay all of our expenses and provide a semester of schooling free. But they wanted us to make a recording and get matching suits, which would be our responsibility. We quickly accepted their offer, began to prepare for our recording, and got matching suits and ties. The school would set up our concert locations and summer tour itinerary, which would be completed during the second week of August. By this time Nancy and I had set our wedding date for August 27th of that summer. I didn't think that would be a problem. I would be back two weeks before our wedding – plenty of time.

During the spring of that school year we sang at the Cleveland Flower Show in a huge building, something like Van Andel in Grand Rapids. There were thousands of people there. It was a tremendous opportunity, since we could share our testimonies. We also sang on a Columbus television program, which for me was scary but exciting.

When the day came for us to make our recording, I had come down with laryngitis. I could barely talk, let alone sing. But we had a contract with a studio and had to keep it. The technician in charge said he had a very sensitive microphone that he thought would work for me. He put the microphone a fraction of an inch in front of my mouth. We all prayed before we started, and somehow, by God's grace I was able to sing. We recorded every song with one take, and made our recording. We called it, "Without Him", based on one of the songs on the album. It turned out pretty good for the situation. I recently was able to have the one long play record, which I still had, made into a CD, and sent copies to all the quartet members. That recording was made over fifty years ago in 1966.

Our summer tour was to begin in early June. In May the Director of Development for the school called all of us, but our piano player, into his office. He informed us that our piano player, John, would not be allowed to travel with us. He had gotten into some serious trouble of which we were not aware. That was a devastating blow. We didn't know if we would be able to get a piano player that quickly. But the music department somehow found a freshman young man named Cliff, who could play the piano and was willing to go on tour with us at the last minute. Though he did not have John's touch or ear for music, he learned the songs quickly, and did well. He was very shy and made it clear that he never wanted to say anything publically. That was ok with the rest of us, since we all felt called to preach and looked forward to the opportunity of taking turns preaching a short message after each concert.

Our summer tour took us as far west as Missouri and as far east as New Jersey and New York. We were in a different church doing concerts almost every night. After one of those concerts I remember leading a little boy to Christ. That was so awesome! We sold our records after each concert which helped pay for our suits and the recording expenses. I think we ended up selling about 1000 records, which covered our costs and gave us a little spending money.

On a couple of occasions Nancy was able to come to our concert. One of those was in Sandusky, Ohio. She really surprised me that night. I didn't know she was coming. Wow, it was great to see her again, even if it was for a brief time.

The other time Nancy was able to be at one of our concerts was when we sang in my home church in Stanton, Michigan. She and Carol Winner, Tim's girlfriend, drove up together. I remember trying to show off for Nancy on a motorcycle after church. My cousin Darwin had driven up to our house on his Honda and asked me if I wanted to ride it. I still had my quartet suit on, but that didn't deter me or cross my mind. I hopped on and took off up the road. That was so much fun. As I approached the driveway on the way back I was slowing down, but knew I was coming in too fast. I had forgotten to ask Darwin about a minor detail – where the brake was. As I turned into the driveway the motorcycle hit some loose gravel and slid out from under me. I hopped off and hit the ground running. Fortunately I did not fall, so I did not mess up my suit. Again I had done something that looked fun, without thinking everything through very well. I guess I was still growing up. God was so gracious to me that day.

At the end of June we sang at the national convention for the General Association of Regular Baptist Churches, which was held in Grand Rapids that year. Cedarville was associated with that Baptist fellowship of churches. We were scheduled to sing right after their business session, which went way over the allotted time. The "Day-Age" view of creation had become popular in some circles and was being taught in some of the Bible colleges in the GARBC. Cedarville had just fired one of its Biology professors who was teaching that view. We had a "front row seat" for that discussion behind the stage curtain. The association voted to hold only to the "24 Hour" view of creation. Even in my youth that seemed to make sense to me. Later I would see that truth even more clearly, when studying Exodus 20:10&11. God took six days to make everything to set a pattern for man's work week. That wouldn't make sense if the "days" were really ages of thousands of years. No man could follow that work week.

We ministered at two Christian camps that summer. One was in New Jersey where we served also as camp counselors. I had a group of tough guys form an inner city, but I managed to handle them. I understood how they thought and could relate to them better than they knew. I played basketball with several of the guys that summer and accidentally broke one of their noses. That camper's name was Bill Baker. He would later go into the ministry and become a pastor. He currently pastor's the Faith Baptist Church of Greenville, Ohio, where my son-in-law's (Kenny Wall's) brother (Kevin) and his wife attend. Bill and I maintained contact with each other off and on after that summer at camp.

The other camp that we ministered at was the Word of Life camp in Schroon Lake, New York. Jack Wertzen, who founded the Word of Life ministry to youth, had a close relationship with Cedarville College at that time. We were not counselors that week, but sang in every service and gave our testimonies. Jack Wertzen or other men did the preaching. Jack's son, Don, was a wonderful composer and piano player. On one occasion he asked to meet with us and talked with us and heard us sing.

After that summer tour we found out what that meeting was all about. Jack Wertzen and the Word of Life ministry wanted us to come with them full time as their music. We would sing on TV a lot, and travel with Jack Wertzen to his evangelistic crusade meetings. I think we initially responded quickly with excitement, and said yes. But after more thought, we each began to change our minds. We each had been called to preach. Jack would be doing all of the preaching. That just didn't seem to fit in with what God was directing us to do. Though we were sad to do so, we called them back and told them that we did not feel that God wanted us to do that.

CHAPTER 18

OUR WEDDING

Nancy had to do all of the planning for our wedding since I was gone with the quartet. She didn't seem to mind that at all. In fact, when I returned from the quartet tour, and finally met up with Nancy, she had everything planned. Nancy loves to decorated, and she is very good at it. She knows what colors go with one another, and what looks good. I have no clue, and quite frankly don't think much about those things. She had planned our wedding for 8:00 pm., because she wanted it to be dark enough for the candles to show up in the windows. She had the flowers and colors all planned. Basically all I needed to do was to show up and say "I do". That was fine by me.

We didn't have much money and neither did her parents. Nancy's sister, Patty, had married Lyle Culberson in June, and now we were getting married on August 27th. So Nancy had to fund most of the cost. She borrowed her former roommate, Mary's, wedding dress, and I and the men standing up with me simply wore suits. A lady in dad Crown's church made the wedding cake, although we did hire a professional photographer (all black and white photos). Her sister, Patty, was her bridesmaid, and my brother, Keith, was my best man. My brother, Mel, cousin, Phil Olsen, and roommate, Paul Jackson also stood up with me. We had two ministers involved, so dad Crown could walk Nancy down the aisle, and then proceed to the platform to finish performing the ceremony, which was held at his church in Findlay, Ohio.

After our vows we sang a duet to each other: "Whither Thou Goest I Will Go", based on Ruth 1:16&17. It really was a beautiful ceremony. The reception was held in the basement of the church. My sister at that time had a hot car, a Pontiac Lemans with 4 on the floor. She agreed to let me use it for the "get-away car", so it would be decorated and not our V.W. After the reception we made the customary trip through town with lots of cars following us (trying to stay with us), while Keith drove. We ended up at Nancy's parent's home, where we had a change of clothes waiting for us.

I had hidden our V.W. in the garage of some neighbors, who lived right next door to the Crowns. I hadn't told a soul where it was hidden except Nancy. I had our suitcases already in the car as well. I had a couple brothers and some friends from college who would have loved to have messed with that car. I had visions of them putting it up on the roof of the church or the Crown's house. Believe me, they would have. So after Nancy and I had changed our clothes and said our goodbyes, we walked out the front door and down the side walk like we were walking to town. Everyone was watching us and wondering what in the world we were doing. We then walked up the neighbor's driveway and soon drove out in our Volkswagen. That was fun!

The Honeymoon

Our first night was spent in a Holiday Inn motel in Bowling Green, Ohio, which was just up the road north of Findlay. It was midnight by the time we left the Crown residence, which I expected, so we didn't want to travel very far. I was soon very frustrated when we arrived at the motel. I couldn't find our room. It was as though someone was playing a very mean trick on us. The rooms seemed to skip our number. There was room 130 and 132, but no 131. What in the world! I think I went into panic mode. Nancy was the calm one and thought we should go down another direction. Sure enough there was room 131. To this day I don't know why some person numbered those rooms in such an idiotic fashion. That's all I'm going to say about that first night….

I had planned the honeymoon trip, so I thought I would take Nancy to the spots that I thought were beautiful – in Michigan, of course. We traveled to Grand Haven and saw the musical fountain on Sunday evening. We then traveled north across the bridge to Tahquamenon Falls, then to the Pictured Rocks. We ended up at Gitche Gumee Bible Camp in Eagle River, Michigan. I showed her some of the beautiful scenery in that area including Brockway Mountain Drive and Copper Harbor.

At that time there was a place the locals called "The Devil's Washtub", which was a deep opening next to Lake Superior surrounded by steep rock walls. I thought I would show off to Nancy by climbing out on the rock wall. She didn't seem to be impressed, but only could see her new husband falling to his death to the water below. Again I wasn't focused on that part. I knew that if I fell, that I could swim and would probably be ok. Fortunately I didn't fall.

CHAPTER   19

OUR MARRIAGE ADJUSTMENTS

We arrived back in Cedarville a few weeks before school was to start. Nancy had already lined up a place for us to stay. The college had a trailer court next to its soccer field for its married students. There was a small, blue, eight foot wide by thirty eight foot long trailer available for us to rent for $40.00 a month. Our current camper is almost that big. But it was a castle to us. It had two entrance doors, but the one next to the back bedroom did not go outside. Someone had built a storage room off of that door, which came in handy for such a small trailer. Lyle and Patty (Nancy' sister) lived in a trailer directly across the street from us.

As I was bringing our stuff into the trailer I noticed that most of it belonged to Nancy. I also noticed that one of the boxes was quite large, so I peeked inside. I was shocked. It was filled with nothing but shoes. The only shoes I owned were a pair of work shoes, dress shoes, and a pair of tennis shoes. How could one person use all those shoes? I may have made a brief comment, but let it go. I knew I was still new at this. But what she said later that day burst the dam inside. She said she needed to go to nearby Springfield and shop for a pair of shoes. I just couldn't wrap my brain around that. I was raised to only buy what you "needed". It didn't appear to me that she needed any more shoes. When I asked her about why she needed a pair of shoes, she said she didn't have any that went with a particular outfit…. We went to Springfield.

What I soon discovered was that Nancy was a shopper, and she was good at it. She had very small feet, so she could often buy the display shoes that the store couldn't sell. And she bought them for very little money. I, on the other hand, had huge feet. In fact, I often had trouble finding my size. I had to pay a lot more money for my shoes than Nancy paid for hers. I was going through an adjustment.

There was another matter that I'm a bit hesitant to bring up, but it is the elephant in the room. There were certain days in the month that Nancy became someone else. I don't know who that was. All I know is that I wanted to leave earth. I did not know what was happening. I was totally ignorant. I had never seen her like that. It was scary. She tried to explain it to me, and tell me that she just needed a hug, but I wasn't sure I wanted to get that close.

We hadn't been living in our trailer more than a couple of weeks, when I discovered something else about Nancy that rocked my world. She was deathly afraid of cats. I discovered that fact one morning, when I heard the most awful blood curdling scream just outside of our trailer. Nancy had gone outside to go somewhere in our VW. Apparently someone had left the driver's side window down over night, and a cat had crawled in through the window and had curled up on the front seat. When Nancy opened the door, there was the cat.

When I heard the scream I flew out of the trailer expecting to have to deal with a mugger or something worse. When I saw the cat in the front seat, I was shocked, and then made almost a fatal mistake. I laughed, and said, "It's only a cat". That response was not very smart on my part, which I would come to realize over the next few days.

I had grown up with dogs and cats always around. At one time we had ten cats, which was when the mother cat had kittens. My sister Marcia had a cat when Nancy had come up to visit before we were married. She told me later that she was petrified of the cat, but didn't want to offend Marcia. The cat had bitten Nancy when Nancy's mohair sweater gave the cat an electric shock. Nancy had to sleep in the same bed with my sister, Marcia, when she came to stay at my house. Marcia's cat was used to sleeping on Marcia's bed at night, so slept between Marcia and Nancy. Before the cat settled down for the night, it would pace up and down between Nancy and Marcia. I didn't know any of this before the "scream". I thought it was strange to be afraid of a cat. I was not very sympathetic.

I set up an appointment with Dr. Reed, my advisor, to see if I could get some help on how to change Nancy. I was shocked when all he did was talk to me about how I needed to change. I couldn't believe it. I didn't have the problem, at least any problems that I could see. I had a lot of growing up to do.

CHAPTER 20

Our Employment

Working in the Foundry

Mom and dad had a rule that they would help us (me and my siblings) financially on our college costs as long as we were single. But if we got married we were on our own. I knew that, but my schooling was already being paid for by the school my senior year, because I had traveled for the school the previous summer. Besides, I had paid most of my way anyway up to that point, though mom and dad did help some with spending money. Both Mel and Marcia were still in college, when I started, and Keith started in college my junior year.   So I just needed money for living expenses and our personal needs after we were married.

So before classes began, I was able to get a job in a foundry located in the nearby little town of Yellow Springs. Yellow Springs was the home of Antioch College which was extremely liberal politically. Cedarville sent evangelistic teams to Antioch College to share the Gospel. Many of them were "Hippies" with the guys wearing hair down to their hips, and both guys and gals emphasizing "freedom", which meant doing whatever immoral act would come into their mind. But the foundry was a totally separate business from Antioch College.

My job was very physically demanding. I shoveled what looked like chunks of plaster into a big dumpster all night and then took it outside using a fork lift truck. I went to work at 11:00 pm, worked all night, and got off at 7:00 am. I then came home, took a shower, and went to my classes. After classes I studied for a few hours, slept for three or four hours, and went back to work. That was not a great schedule for any married couple, let alone newly-weds. I would get about enough sleep over the week-end to realize I was human, and then go back at it again.

I kept up with that schedule until early November. I came home feeling very ill. I thought I had the flu. I was throwing-up, and feeling very weak. Our family, when I was growing up, seldom went to the doctor. But Nancy thought I should go, so we went to the only doctor in the town of Cedarville at that time. He looked at me but wasn't sure what it was, so sent me back home. Nancy wasn't sure how to help me, but knew a lot of illnesses in her home had been helped by using a hot water bottle. So she borrowed a hot water bottle and put it on my stomach.

It wasn't long before I became violently ill. I barely knew what was going on. We piled back into our V.W. and Nancy drove me back to the doctor's office. He took one look at me and asked Nancy if she could drive me to the hospital in Xenia. He didn't think we should wait for an ambulance. Nancy drove as fast as she dared on the very curvy road between Cedarville and Xenia, and took me straight to the emergency entrance. I was barely able to walk into the hospital. The doctor must have called ahead because they were waiting for us.

I remember getting on the stretcher, but not much more. They took me directly to surgery. I had a severe case of appendicitis. The surgery was a success, but I would have to miss some classes and could not go back to work because of the needed recovery time. I was in very good physical shape during those years, so I recovered quickly.

Nancy and I discussed the work situation. I was against her going to work at first. I believed it was my job to provide for her. She shouldn't have to work. But I looked at my situation, and what she was saying made sense. She quickly got a job as a secretary at a Xenia radio station and later at a nearby black college called Central State. I was able to get a job in the Cedarville College maintenance department.

Working on the Maintenance Department

Students who worked for the college were not paid very well at that time. When the head of the maintenance department told me what I would be getting per hour, he said I was the highest paid student employee because of my maintenance experience.

I'm sure the first job he gave me was both a test and one he really didn't want to do. One of the trailers in the college trailer park, that Nancy and I lived in, had one of its axles settle on the water pipe that was supplying its water. The pipe had broken somewhere beneath the ground and water was bubbling up from where it was broken. Since it was broken before any shut off valve to the trailer, the entire water supply to the trailer court would need to be shut off.

After looking over the situation I shut the main water supply to the trailer court off, and went to work. It was nasty work. I had to lie on my stomach under the trailer and dig down around the pipe until I found where it had broken. I found the break almost three feet below ground, where an elbow was attached to the supply going to the main line. I was able to get the pipe threader onto the pipe, make some new threads, put a new elbow on, and finish the job, and turn the water back on. The head of maintenance seemed pleased.

I did other jobs including help put in a hot water heating system in Alford Auditorium. They had a coal furnace system prior to that. I remember going around one of the tunnels underneath the auditorium and seeing the skeleton of a cat. That was eerie.

A new gym had been built just before my freshman year. Apparently the head of the maintenance department had helped to install the hot water heating system, which was all under concrete. They had not allowed for expansion and contraction, and the pipes had broken under the concrete, so all the pipes needed to be installed above the floors. I was assigned to that job.

The head of maintenance thought he knew everything about plumbing, but he really didn't. I had to be careful not to correct him. But one instance really caused him to stop "watching over my shoulder". The college bookstore had been expanded, and some new heating fin needed to be installed in it. That type of radiant heat used cooper pipe. So the head of the maintenance showed me the project, and then began to show me how to prepare a joint for soldering. I had done that hundreds of times, while working for my dad. But I kept my mouth shut and let him show me.

I had finished the project in a day or two and then went on to another job, when he came to me really upset. He asked me to come with him to the bookstore. He then showed me one of the pipes that had been installed spraying water. He went off on me about how hard it was now to fix a pipe with water in it, and how I really had my hands full now. I let him talk until he was finished. I simply said, "That's the one you did". He looked at the joint, and I could see the light go on. He knew I was right. He never said a word except, "Go back to what you were doing". He never bothered me after that. The only leak in the entire project was the one he did.

CHAPTER 21

MY CLASSES AND ACTIVITIES

Working part time on the maintenance department worked out great for me. I could work my own schedule for the most part. I was given projects and could do them around my classes and studies. I had a much lighter class load my senior year, because of the extra classes I had taken in prior years. I loved my speech classes and did well in them. I also was able to take another Greek class my second semester. I got my best grades my senior year, and ended my final semester with a 3.75, which is an A minus, I think. I should have gotten married sooner.

I continued to travel some weekends with the quartet. After I graduated we talked about getting back together but that really wasn't possible. Both Dan and Ted had another year at Cedarville and Tim and I were going on to seminary. Tim went to Dallas Theological, and I went to Grace in Winona Lake, Indiana.

 Later in life, Nancy secretly had a surprise "This is Your Life" reunion for me on my 50th birthday, and all the quartet members were able to be there except Tim. That was awesome.

Nancy and I also attended the college concerts and sporting events. The soccer field was just a few feet away from our trailer, so we did not have far to go. But I was no longer in the band, choir, or pep band. I was voted to be the class chaplain, for my senior year, which gave me regular opportunities to give devotionals to the class and gain preaching experience. At the end of May I graduated with a B.A. degree in communications with enough hours for several minors including Bible, English, Music, and Greek. God's grace was still being poured out on me.

PHASE   IV

GOD'S GRACE POURED OUT ON MY SEMINARY YEARS

(1967-70, Age 21-24)

- Viet Nam War escalates
- A draft lottery system was instituted to select young men for the Viet Nam War
- Viet Nam War protests reach their peak with the public burning of draft cards
- Attorney General Robert Kennedy was shot on June 6, 1968
- Average cost of house was $23,500
- Average yearly income was $6,186
- Cost of gasoline was 36 cents
- Bell-bottom pants become popular
- Neil Armstrong and Buzz Aldrin land lunar module, Eagle, on the moon on July 20, 1969. Both walk on the moon.

CHAPTER 22

MOVING TO GRACE AND GETTING SETTLED

I believe that God directed me to go to Grace Seminary in Winona Lake, Indiana. In those days men, who went on to seminary from Cedarville, went either to Dallas Theological Seminary in Dallas, Texas, or to Grace. My Cedarville professor, who taught me Greek, received his doctoral degree from Grace. I had the highest love and respect for him. He was patient with me as I struggled to learn the Greek, so I could better teach God's Word. Several of us at Cedarville took Dr. Lawlor out to eat after our last class with him. We had him for three years as our Greek professor. One of the men at that luncheon gave us each a card that had the last word we had studied from II Timothy 4:5. The English translates the word, "fulfill your ministry". It has the idea of filling it up. God has a ministry for each of us, and we are to complete it to the full. The Apostle Paul just a few verses later said he "finished" his race. I have carried that card in my billfold ever since that day.

Though Tim Timmons and some other of my friends were going to Dallas, I felt in my heart that God wanted me to go to Grace. Grace was Biblically sound and had a great reputation among those who had a high regard for God's Word. It also emphasized the role of the local church. So Nancy and I made plans to move to Winona Lake. Nancy's dad had been a pastor in Argos, Indiana which was about 25 miles from Winona Lake. So we visited the First Baptist Church in Argos, and Nancy was able to see the people that she knew, when she had been a young teen. While there, one of the couples that had been friends to the Crowns, when he had pastored there, invited us over to their home to stay, while we searched for a place to live.

Paul and Jo Ann Horn had a chicken farm with about 12,000 chickens. The farm was totally automated. I had never seen anything like it. The chickens were in cages. The eggs that they laid rolled onto a conveyor belt, which brought the eggs into a place where they were washed and sorted by size. I enjoyed helping them to do the work. Even the manure was removed from the chicken house by automation. But boy did it ever stink.

The Horns took us in and treated us as though we were there own kids. They found a 10 X 44 foot house trailer, which we bought and had moved to the Uphouse Trailer Court, which was just south of the Seminary in Winona Lake. I had to do quite a bit of work on the lot to get it ready for the trailer. Mr. Uphouse was a professor at Grace College, which was associated with the seminary, so the trailer court sometimes didn't get his undivided attention. The lot was cut into a pretty steep hill. The trailer itself sat on a concrete slab, but I put in a concrete patio in front of the trailer, and dug out a driveway on the other side of the trailer. I also built a stone retaining wall to keep the hill from caving in on the driveway and trailer.

Our Employment

Because of Nancy's experience, she got a job right away working as a secretary in a public school. Those she worked for were very difficult, so when a job opened up at the seminary she took it. She was the secretary for the vice president of the seminary and worked as the school receptionist. That worked out great for us for a couple of reasons. First, we got to see each other throughout the day. Second, even though she took a pay cut to work there, I received a scholarship of half tuition, because she worked there, which more than made up for the pay cut. She also loved her boss, Dr. Homer Kent Sr. I was able to get a job working for the Kroger grocery store in nearby Warsaw, Indiana. That job eventually involved overseeing the night crew, which stocked the shelves, and sometimes sacking groceries. Several of the men attending the college or seminary worked there. It helped us with groceries at times, because the manager let us take home outdated bread and also milk that leaked. That job worked out great with my class schedule as well.

But another job opened up for me that we were not expecting. The pastor of the First Baptist Church of Argos asked me to serve as the paid youth director of the church. They would pay me $10.00 a week, which would basically cover my gasoline expenses. I would do the job of a youth pastor and help with the music. Nancy and I felt that was a great opportunity to serve, so we accepted their offer. I began that ministry in the fall of 1967 and date the beginning of my ministry from that time.

CHAPTER 23

MY CLASSES AND INVOLVEMENT IN SEMINARY LIFE

I loved every one of my classes, even though they were so much harder than college. Most of the theology classes demanded that the notes including supporting Scripture verses had to be memorized. The reading that was required was ridiculously demanding. But I loved those theology classes too. I was learning so much, and getting some of my deep questions answered. I was well prepared at Cedarville for the Greek classes, and was able to test out of the Greek grammar class. I loved the classes where we translated a New Testament book and then broke every verse apart in the Greek language.

My favorite professor was Dr. John Whitcomb. He taught the theology classes as well as some other classes. He had co-authored a book with Dr. Henry Morris a few years earlier on the "Genesis Flood". It was the book that formed the foundation for another Genesis movement called "Answers in Genesis".

There was no time for socializing while I went to seminary. If I wasn't going to classes, or working, I was studying, or preparing a lesson for the teens at church.

There was a get acquainted reception for the seminary students soon after we began classes. It was led by the homiletics professor, Dr. Fink (his real name, really). Each new student was allowed two minutes to give their testimony. Dr. Fink kept the future preachers in check by using an alarm clock that he set each time to two minutes. If the alarm went off, the speaker knew he needed to sit down. The testimonies were interspersed with some of the new men doing special music. Somehow the ones who planned the service found out that I played the trombone, so I was asked to do special music.

When it came time for me to play my trombone, I went up on the platform. Nancy played the introduction to the number. Just as I lifted my horn to begin to play, the alarm clock went off. The man just before me had given a very short testimony, and Dr. Fink had forgotten to shut the alarm off. When it went off, I lowered my trombone and walked off the stage. The place erupted with laughter. Dr. Fink embarrassingly waved me back to the stage where I completed my solo.

For some reason my classmates elected me as their president of our senior class. There really wasn't much responsibility with that position. But I was honored that they chose me for that position. Paul Jackson, who was also attending Grace, was elected president of the student body during our senior year.

In order to complete the requirements for the Master of Divinity degree each student had to write a very lengthy paper. The paper had to take an apparent Biblical problem and then solve that problem using Scripture. I chose to write my paper about Psalm 139:8. The question I sought to answer concerned God being in hell. The latter part of the verse states, "if I make my bed in hell, Thou art there." I used several verses to show that God is everywhere, even in hell making sure His justice and righteousness is being carried out on those who are lost. Though the problem was not really that difficult, I learned a lot about that Psalm and about God, which would help me much in the future. I did fairly well with my grades in seminary and graduated from Grace in May of 1970.

CHAPTER   24

THE YOUTH MINISTRY AT ARGOS

While I attended Grace Seminary, Nancy and I drove to Argos every Sunday morning to minister at the First Baptist Church. We usually made a day of it. The Horns always provided dinner for us after church and a place for us to rest during the afternoon. In addition to teaching the teen Sunday School class in the morning, I led the youth meeting in the evening before the evening service. Nancy and I often provided special music in the services as well.

During this time I also was on a planning committee for the monthly youth rallies sponsored by the Baptist fellowship of churches in the area.

Nancy and I also planned activities for the church teens. One of these was a campout that turned out to be a disaster. We had planned the campout during the summer when the teens were out of school.   I thought they would enjoy going to one of the state parks along Lake Michigan, since I had always loved climbing the sand dunes, when I was their age. One of the closest Michigan state parks to the Indiana border was Warren Dunes State Park. It had a place to tent camp as well as plenty of sand dunes to climb. The only problem was that the camping area was about a mile from the lake with some very large sand dunes in between.

The first night of camping was not good. Nancy slept in the tent with the girls, and I was in the tent with the boys. It rained very hard that night. I had not prepared properly for that, so all of the water ran into both of the tents. Everyone and everything got soaked with very little sleep. No problem. There is always fun on the sand dunes, right?

The next day to my surprise I discovered that not everyone loved to climb sand dunes, especially Nancy. We were about halfway to the lake, when her frustration finally surfaced. I was having a great time charging up and down the dunes on my way to the lake. When I finally turned around, I noticed that Nancy and a very heavy set boy (I'll call Allen) were lagging quite a bit behind. So, like a caring husband, I went back to try to help. When she saw me coming she sat down in the sand and simply said, "I can't go on. Just leave me here to die".

I was shocked. I did not know what to say. Looking back on it, I really should have put my arm around her and said nothing. Unfortunately my mouth opened and words came out – the wrong words – very wrong words. "You are not like any of the girls I knew growing up." That only brought a flood of tears and sobs and fired her determination to stay in her new home in the sand. She wasn't going forward that was for sure. I could also see that Allen had really had it as well.

I figured Allen could get back to camp, so I wouldn't worry about him. But I didn't think it was a good idea to let Nancy try to live (or die) in the valley of a Michigan sand dune. So even though she wasn't in a mood to cooperate, I said the obvious, to me at least, "You can't stay here. That just isn't going to work. I'll help you get back to the camp ground." I, then, practically carried her up and down the sand dunes back to the camp ground.

Nancy was very upset with me, and rightly so. My only comfort was knowing that she would be in another tent for the weekend. I'm not sure what my devotions were about during that outing, and I really can't remember any details other than the fact that Allen eventually made it back to the tents. But I will forever remember to never ever compare Nancy to any other girls that I have ever known. I'm so glad that Nancy has a very good "forgiver". That has so saved our marriage.

CHAPTER   25

ATTEMPTING TO MAKE AN IMPRESSION IN STANTON

Shortly after graduation from seminary I was asked again to preach at my home church in Stanton. I was excited to have the opportunity, but somewhat nervous at the same time. I had now been through four years of Bible college and three years of seminary. I wanted to make a good impression. I somehow thought more would be expected of me.

I seem to always mess up when I try to make an impression. I had actually really messed up several years earlier when I came home from Cedarville and was asked to lead the singing in the morning service. I was really getting into the leading of a song, when I left the protection of the pulpit and walked to one side. While continuing to energetically lead the song, I was holding the hymn book with my left hand and leading with my right. Suddenly when my right hand went up on the up-beat, it hit the hymn book in my left hand sending it flying across the entire platform. I was humbled. I had to go over and pick it up and keep going amidst the snickers. God was still working on me. But apparently I had not been humbled enough. God still had more work to do on me.

So when I was asked to preach after graduating from seminary I tried to make sure I would not goof up again. Nancy typed up my sermon notes on the best typing paper available at the time. It was a new product called onion skinned paper. It made it easier to erase mistakes, and was a very light weight paper.

The day that I preached was one of those very hot summer days. The ushers had opened the windows on both sides of the auditorium to let any breeze in. Not too long into my message one of the ushers walked down the center aisle towards me. He walked right up to the pulpit. I wasn't sure what was going on. He then got up on the platform beside me and tapped on the microphone, while I tried to keep preaching. He then blew into it. The only thing he didn't do was to say "testing, one, two, three." Needless to say, I had some trouble keeping my composure and concentration.

Once he had left, I noticed a commotion towards the back of the auditorium. Apparently a hornet had landed on the head of a bald man. All the people in the vicinity of the bald gentleman had stopped paying any attention to me, and were being entertained by the hornet drama. The only one that seemed oblivious to it all was the man hosting the hornet. I remember as a kid that hornets frequently attended our church. I remember watching them during a service. It was either watch the hornet or count the holes in the ceiling tile in the old auditorium. I really wasn't interested in the sermon at that point in my life.

About the time I thought it couldn't get any worse, it did. A big gust of wind came though one of the side windows and scattered all my notes all over the platform. I'm not sure where that wind came from. It had been a very sultry day. I'm not sure to this day if God was enjoying teaching His lesson on humility, or if the devil had something to do with it. But picking up pieces of paper on the platform, while mumbling through a very bad sermon, was very humbling. I couldn't help but notice that it was many years before they ever asked me to preach in my home church again. And I totally understood.

PHASE   V

OUR MINISTRY AT DEFIANCE

(1970-1978, Age 24-33)

- The Viet Nam War expands with the invasion of Cambodia in 1970.
- The U.S. Supreme Court rules that busing students may be ordered to achieve racial desegregation of schools.
- Anti-war militants attempt to shut down Washington in 1971. 12,000 arrested.
- 1973 – U.S. troops pull out of Viet Nam and the mobile phone is invented.
- 1974 – President Nixon resigns due to the "Watergate" scandal. He is granted a full pardon by Gerald Ford after he is sworn in as president.
- 1975 – Microsoft Corporation is founded and personal computers begin to appear.
- Styles of the 70's: Long hair for men and leisure suits become common.
- Popular songs: "You Light Up My Life" (Debbie Boone) and "Stayin Alive" (Bee Gees).
- The cost of living almost doubles:

	1970	1978
Postage stamp:	6 cents	15 cents
Gasoline.	40 cents	77 cents
Car:	$2500	$4645
House:	$40,000	$64,370

CHAPTER 26

GETTING STARTED

How God Directed Us to Defiance

By January of 1970 I still had not decided on what I was going to do after graduating from seminary at the end of May. I was asked to preach at the Faith Baptist Church of Greenville, Ohio, which was without a pastor. Rev. Harold Green had started that church, before he came on staff at Cedarville College as the campus pastor. I think he may have recommended me to the church. After preaching that Sunday the deacons met with me and asked me to consider becoming a candidate with the possibility of becoming their pastor. I still had several months of seminary left, and it would have meant driving back and forth to Winona Lake, so I told them I didn't think I was the one for them.

But that experience did confirm to me that God wanted me to be a pastor. Prior to that I was considering the possibility of becoming a youth pastor (I loved teens and had worked with them). I also loved to lead music and knew that I could become a music pastor. I was also open to missions if God so directed. After settling the matter about becoming a pastor, I talked to dad Crown about it and told him that I believed God was directing me to become a pastor, but I didn't know how to get connected to a particular church that needed a pastor. He told me to write to Rev. Earl Umbaugh.

Rev. Umbaugh was the state missionary for the Ohio Association of Regular Baptist Churches. He helped churches which were looking for a pastor as well as helping those people who were trying to start a new church. After meeting Dr. Ketchum and writing my paper on the history of the GARBC, I was already convinced that I wanted to be part of that fellowship of churches. I, also, thought it would be nice to be in Ohio, so we wouldn't be too far from Nancy's parents. So I wrote to Rev. Umbaugh and told him about my schooling, working in the Argos church, and my limited preaching experience, and my desire to be a pastor.

Within a few days he called me. He asked me if I had ever considered starting a new church. I told him that I actually had thought about that, and wanted to do so. But I thought I needed to pastor an existing church first to gain some experience before taking on such a difficult task as starting a church. He went on to tell me that he had been meeting with a small group of people in Defiance, Ohio, who planned to start a church. He said they had already decided to call themselves the Faith Baptist Church. I loved the name. He then asked if I would at least lead a Bible study with them and preach to them. He wanted me to come on Easter weekend, when they were having their first Sunday service. But we were already committed to be somewhere else that weekend, so I agreed to come the following weekend after Easter.

I will never forget that first meeting on April 4, 1970, with the dear people from Defiance. We met at the home of Bob and Norma Cunningham on a Saturday night. That was their usual time for their Bible study. There were about ten adults there at that first meeting. They all had their Bibles open and were waiting for me to teach them what it said. I have no idea what I taught on that night, but I will never forget how God spoke to me. There was no audible voice, of course, but there was a very strong conviction in my heart that I was supposed to help those people get to know what God's Word said.

Rev. Umbaugh had filled me in on their history. They had all been members of a Methodist church located about ten miles south of Defiance on State Route 111 at a little place called Junction. There was not much there except a convenience store, a few houses, a lot of junked cars, and the church. Across the street from the church was an old school house that had been taken over by a group of men called the Junction Fox Club. The members of the church had been listening to godly men on the radio, and had learned that the Methodist Church was part of a national organization called the National Council of Churches. That organization was supporting communist causes and advocating the burning of draft cards in protest of the Vietnam War. After learning about the liberal nature of their denomination and its affiliation with the National Council of Churches they voted unanimously as a church to withdraw from the Methodist denomination. The Methodist district superintendent called a meeting at the church along with the pastor and told them that the Methodist denomination owned the building and everything in it. He also said he would "put a lock on the door" if they tried to meet as another church in that building. In that meeting (I was told later) he said "he did not believe in the doctrine of the virgin birth like they did" and denied other major Bible doctrines.

After being told that they could not have the building if they pulled out of the Methodist denomination, some of the people decided to stay in the denomination. They were attached to the building, its new organ, and all the memories in that building over the years. However, others in the church were even more determined than ever to leave, even if it meant not having a place to worship. One of the young couples that had grown up in that church was Mel and Laura Retcher. They had previously attended the Emmanuel Baptist Church of Toledo before moving back to Defiance. So they knew about a group of Baptist Churches called the OARBC that helped people organize Bible teaching churches. So they contacted Rev. Umbaugh and the group that broke away from the Methodist Church began Bible studies with him.

I preached the next day after that first meeting with them, which was a Sunday, April 5, 1970. They had begun to rent what used to be a Nazarene Church building, which had been purchased by the Disabled Veterans located on the south side of Defiance on State Route 111. The only problem with that location was that they could not meet there in the evenings. So they were renting the Junction Fox Club building ten miles south of Defiance, which was directly across from their old church. About a year later the church was able to rent the Slocum Elementary School and have all their services in one place.

I'm sure Nancy and I sang that Sunday morning. I was shocked when we went to the evening service at the Fox Club. There was one light bulb hanging from the ceiling, and it was not very clean. But that didn't seem to bother the people. They just wanted to hear the Word. I knew that very first Sunday without a doubt that God wanted me to help them and be their pastor. God must have communicated that to them as well because on April 25th they extended a unanimous call for us to come as their pastor. My first official Sunday as their pastor was May 3, 1970.

Settling into Defiance

Defiance had a population of around 15,000 and is located in the north western corner of Ohio. It was founded as Fort Defiance by General "Mad" Anthony Wayne who was largely responsible for bringing peace to that area. Fort Defiance had a very strategic military location during its founding. Rivers were the main means of travel in those days, and three rivers met where Fort Defiance was placed: the Maumee, Auglaize, and Tiffin Rivers. Those who controlled the rivers controlled the area. General Wayne was so convinced of its invincibility that he said, "I defy all the French, and the Indians, and all the demons of hell to take this place." Later I would say, "I don't know about the French and the Indians, but the demons are certainly here."

Defiance in the 1970s was a very nice place to live for the most part. It was home to Defiance College, which was a Church of God School. Religiously the people were largely Catholic or Lutheran. It was large enough to have good medical care, schools, and shopping. There were two other Baptist churches in Defiance, but neither were that large. The rivers posed a challenge to getting around. One had to know where the bridges were located. It was a factory town. The largest, a General Motors foundry, employed over 5000 people.

But I would soon discover that Defiance also had a big drug problem. It was part of a drug "pipe line" coming out of Mexico up to Toledo and Detroit. It had a large population of "Latinos", some of whom contributed to the drug trafficking. I will talk about that later.

We rented our first home, which was out in the area where most of our members lived. It was a nice three bedroom ranch home located about four miles south of Defiance on State Route 111 across from the Auglaize River. We lived there for about two years before buying a home on Harding Street on the northwest side of Defiance. In 1977 we bought a lot from the church, so we could be close to the church, and built a house there. It was located on the corner of State Route 111 and Hammersmith road. We moved into that home in the spring of 1978.

Near Death Experience

During our first winter living in our rental house, I decided to go ice skating on the Auglaize River. I enjoyed ice skating while growing up, but hadn't been able to do so, while going to college and seminary. The river was right across the highway from our house and looked safe enough. So I got my skates and headed to the river totally pumped about having some fun.

I started skating on the ice following a snow mobile track. I hadn't gone more than a hundred yards, when I looked ahead a couple feet and saw water. I immediately turned around and headed back to shore, and went home. I had never seen ice do that before. Either it was frozen or it wasn't. Then, again, I had never skated on a river before, only lakes.

The first chance I got, I told the locals from the church about what I had seen, and asked them about it. They gave me a rather peculiar look and then explained. "No one skates on the river. There are whirlpools that do not allow the ice to freeze in those locations." I was apparently very fortunate that I did not break through the ice. Had I done so, the current would have pulled me under the ice and I would have drowned. Once again God's grace was watching out for me.

My First Baptismal Service

Many of those from the Methodist church had not been baptized by immersion. So on July 12th of my first year we had a baptism at the Cunningham's pond. There were eleven scheduled for baptism that Sunday evening.

The first one to be baptized was Dorothy G., who was rather large in size. I had never baptized before, but I had seen it done all my life. Yet I did not figure on the problem that I would have that day. I began the service by explaining the Biblical truths about baptism. I then stated Dorothy G.'s full name, and said, "Upon your profession of faith, I baptize you in the name of the Father, the name of the Son, and the name of the Holy Spirit, Amen." With that, I took her backwards under the water with the intention of bringing her right back up again. But her body didn't want to go completely under the water. It wanted to float. I managed to push her down as best I could with my hands and brought her back up again. I don't remember if she was coughing or sputtering, but I probably was. I'm not sure what she thought I was trying to do when I baptized her, but the Lord knows my heart.

Becoming an Organized Official Church

Rev. Umbaugh had gotten the group started down the path of organizing, but there was still a long way to go. We had worked through the Articles of Faith, which states what the church believes the Bible to teach on the major doctrines, but we still needed to write the Constitution. Every week day Bible study we worked on that. Finally on June 6th the Constitution and Articles of Faith were finished and approved unanimously.

The church then voted to call for a recognition council to examine the Constitution and Articles of Faith to see if Faith Baptist was indeed a duly organized Baptist church. The recognition council would be composed of Baptist churches from the North Bethel fellowship of Baptist churches, which was supporting the church financially. Later that summer pastors from the North Bethel fellowship of Baptist Churches met and the council unanimously approved our Constitution. We were already a church before God, but it was great to be recognized as such by other Baptist churches.

We announced that we would give opportunity for those who were saved, scripturally baptized, and in agreement with our Articles of Faith and Constitution, to become charter members by signing the charter document. Soon several began to sign the charter.

Becoming an Ordained Minister

Once the church was recognized as a duly organized Baptist church, I began to concentrate on my ordination. I knew, without any doubt that God had called me to the ministry, and that I had excellent Biblical training. But since I was very young, and most of the people in the church were older than I was, I thought it wise to have other experienced pastors publically acknowledge that I was prepared for the ministry. That's basically what being ordained does. So I prepared a doctrinal paper, which would be the basis for the examination, and a council was called on September 17, 1970 to examine me. After three hours of asking me questions about what

I believed, the council voted to recommend to the Faith Baptist Church of Defiance, that the church ordain me to the Gospel ministry.

The ordination service was held the same evening. I was so honored to have at my ordination the man who was largely responsible for me going into the ministry. My pastor when I was growing up, Rev. Mark Mitchell, spoke at the service. Dad Crown also spoke. He was my "go to" person that I often called, when I did not know what to do. I still have my ordination certificate and a press release about my ordination on file.

My First Real Challenge as a Pastor

We had stated that people could have the opportunity to become charter members until the end of the year (1970). One of the provisions in the Constitution stated that only members of the church could be Sunday School teachers. I noticed that one of the ladies, who was an excellent Sunday School teacher with the children, had not signed the charter. She was part of the original group from the Methodist church. She had been in all the Constitutional planning meetings and must have voted for it, because it had been approved unanimously. She was related to several people in the church.

So I went to visit Martha R. I was shocked to hear why she had not signed the charter and joined the church. She said she was a member of Christ's church, and did not feel she needed to be a member of a local church. I reminded her of what the Constitution said about requiring membership to be a teacher, and if she chose not to join she could not be able to continue to teach. I then left somewhat dazed by it all. I went home and immediately wrote the first article I ever wrote to help the church, "Does the Bible Teach Local Church Membership". I then gave the article to Martha and asked her to read it and look up the Bible passages.

Unfortunately 1970 came to an end and Martha still had not joined the church. Even though it was extremely hard for me to do so, I knew that if we started making exceptions to the statements in our Constitution, that it would soon become a worthless document. I had to trust the Lord for whatever would follow. So I went out to her home, and told her that I sadly had to ask for her teaching material. Her husband Bill came to talk to me and was very upset, and did not understand at all. Martha stopped attending the church after that. But no one else left, for which I was thankful.

Two years later I saw Martha come into the service at the Slocum School and sit in the back. After the message, when the invitation was given, Martha came forward with tears in her eyes. She simply said, "I'm so sorry. I was just being stubborn. I want to be a member." From that moment on Bill and Martha attended faithfully. Martha also became one of our best children's workers. Bill even insisted that I use their motorhome for one of our family vacations, which I reluctantly did. What an awesome trip through Wisconsin.

Struggles Preparing Messages

The ministry was a very difficult adjustment for me. I struggled to find the right routine for me. I tried to be dad Crown, but that did not work for me. He always got up at 6:00 am, did his exercises, his devotions, and his reading, and his study with breakfast somewhere in the mix. I just wasn't wired like him. That was frustrating for me.

I did not know how far to take the ministry thing. Was I supposed to chase an ambulance to the hospital, since I was a pastor, even though I had no idea who was in the ambulance? I had to trust God to show me what to do, and what schedule worked for me.   That first year was a struggle.

I also struggled preparing all the messages. I taught the adult Sunday School class, preached the morning message, the evening message, and taught the mid-week Bible study. All of those required preparation time. I took the task very seriously, knowing that I was handling God's holy Word. I sometimes went down the road from where we lived to a road side rest in order to study and concentrate. Somehow by God's grace, He helped me through it all.

Choosing My Life Verse

It was very clear to me from the very beginning that I could never be a pastor in my own strength. Preparing messages, leading people to the Lord, dealing with the people problems, and making decisions about the direction of the church all was overwhelming. Early in my ministry at Defiance God gave me a verse of Scripture that became my life verse. I'm not so sure that I chose it. It may very well have chosen me in a way. It was tailor made for me. I desperately needed it.

I was preaching through Zechariah on Sunday nights. What was I thinking? I guess I decided to preach on that book for a couple of reasons: I had already translated that book from Hebrew as part of an assignment for my Hebrew language class, when I was in seminary, but there were, also, some awesome verses in the book about the Lord's return. But when I came to Zechariah 4:6, I was brought to tears: "…Not by might, nor by power, but by My Spirit says the LORD of host." The Lord clearly states that any work for God must be done by His Spirit working through me. That's what I wanted. That's what I needed. I can honestly say that that verse of Scripture became the foundation for my ministry and my life. It was just the Biblical expression of the prayer I offered as a child on my bunk bed: "Lord steer my ship".

CHAPTER 27

LORI'S ARRIVAL

Nancy was pregnant when we moved to Defiance. This was a new experience for both of us. Nancy weighed about 105 pounds, when we were married, and was five feet tall. So carrying a baby though the summer was not easy for her. Her belly protruded like a basketball, but she never let that stop her from shopping. Nothing ever stopped her from shopping. She loved to go to garage sales and find a bargain. On one of her garage sale shopping trips she found me an entire set of golf clubs including a bag, balls, tees – everything for $5.00. I couldn't believe it. I never ever complained about her shopping after that.

One Saturday morning in late October about 6:00 am Nancy woke me up.   The bed felt wet. I immediately thought, "Oh no. Nancy has wet the bed." I had no idea what was happening. She quickly told me that she had not wet the bed, but that her water had broken. I still did not understand what that meant, but understood that it had something to do with the baby. So Nancy thought that we should probably go to the hospital. Lori was not due for another month, but apparently decided that she had been cooped up long enough.

I had no idea how long it would take for Lori to arrive. I really didn't know much of anything about it. Saturday evening came and went. Nancy's doctor had asked me if I wanted to be present when Lori was delivered, and I answered with an enthusiastic yes. They finally took Nancy to the delivery room late Saturday night, and I waited anxiously for the word from the doctor to come, so I could watch Lori be born. That word never came.

Then sometime after midnight the doctor came out to me and explained that there had been complications. Lori had not turned properly, so she had to be born feet first instead of the usual head first. He also explained that he had to use forceps on Lori's feet to help pull her out, but the bruises on her feet would heal.

A few minutes later I heard Nancy's voice penetrating down the hall and throughout the entire hospital, "It's a girl, Merlyn, it's a girl." Nancy had just been rolled out on the gurney and was so excited that Lori was a girl. That was before ultra sound, so we had no idea whether the baby was going to be a boy or a girl. I ran down the hall and saw Lori for the first time.

Lori was so tiny. She only weighed four pounds and two ounces and was so short. When I held her for the first time, her head fit in my hand and her feet did not reach to my elbow. She lay next to Nancy with a full head of coal black hair. She was beautiful! I was a daddy!! It was so awesome!

I was glad to pitch in and help Nancy after she came home from the hospital. I helped change and feed Lori and loved to do it even if it meant getting up in the middle of the night. For some reason it didn't seem to bother Lori that she would not let us sleep through the night. But God had given us a healthy baby girl that was extremely bright and learned very quickly. He really had poured His grace out on me.

Nancy shared a room with another new mother, Ruth Barber. The Barber's baby girl was their first baby as well. Nancy and I befriended the Barber's, who soon accepted Christ as their Savior, started coming to church, got baptized, and joined the church. So in a way, Lori had a big part in bringing an entire family to Christ before she could talk.

CHAPTER 28

THE CHURCH GROWS

Kids from the County Children's Home Attend

Due to some unfortunate circumstances in his home, Mel Retcher as well as his siblings had grown up in the Defiance County Children's Home. It was probably the best thing that could have happened to him, since the house parents of the home were genuine believers, and regularly took the children, who were under their care, to a Gospel preaching church. When the house parents learned about our church through the Retcher's, they began to bring the children to our church. This really helped our attendance and gave us an immediate youth group. Mel and Laura began to work with them and were the perfect couple for that ministry.

Lost People were Getting Saved

The church was growing, and souls were being saved. I had counted every house in Defiance and mapped out surveys for every street. I visited a lot of the homes myself, but used students from Cedarville to help on a couple of occasions. We basically tried to find those who were unchurched and were interested in a follow up visit, but we shared the Gospel if the opportunity was present.

Wayne's Story

One of these survey visits led me to a house that had upstairs and downstairs apartments. In the upstairs apartment lived the Lawson family. They seemed somewhat interested, so I visited there on several occasions. I'm sure I shared the Gospel with the husband (Wayne) on more than one occasion. Finally they came out to church. I'll never forget the day Wayne was saved. We were singing "Just As I Am" for the invitation number. On the last stanza Wayne threw his hymn book on the floor. That took me by surprise. I had never had anyone do that before, not an adult anyway. The next thing I knew, Wayne was walking down the aisle in tears. Wayne was gloriously saved that day.

Wayne soon told me about the drug problem in Defiance, and that he was part of it. He was a drug "pusher", which meant that he sold drugs. He now had a tremendous burden for his friends to be saved. Many of them were also "pushers". We started to go together to visit some of his friends. The husband that lived below the Lawson's was Latino and in the drug business. He did not come to church, but his wife began to attend on occasion with her kids.

On one occasion I went to visit one of Wayne's friends who lived in a trailer park. When the door opened I saw a group of men sitting in the living room. They were having some sort of meeting, and they didn't seem to appreciate my being there. I believe they were all in the drug business. I quickly invited the owner of the mobile home to come to church and left.

Not too long after that, Wayne and I were making a call in that same trailer park. I had received a call from a woman who said she needed spiritual help. I made it a point, especially when visiting a woman, to never go alone. I was so glad Wayne was with me that day. When the woman answered the door, she had nothing on. She said, "I did not know you were bringing someone with you". With that she closed the door, and we left. Wayne later told me that I had been set up. Someone in town didn't like me. Soon the couple that lived in the mobile home where the drug "meeting" was being held got saved, baptized, and began attending faithfully.

Randy's Story

A wife of one of Wayne's friends, Carol, also began to attend and came to know the Lord, but I just couldn't get her husband, Randy, to attend or listen to the Gospel, though I visited him on many occasions. After about a year of faithful attendance, Randy's wife, Carol, stopped coming to church. When I asked Wayne if he knew why, he said they had to move quickly to Pennsylvania. Randy and a friend had done some drug business on the side, which was not approved by some "higher ups". Randy got scared and left the area.

Randy had every right to be scared. For such a small town, murders did occur. I actually led two murderers to the Lord when they were in jail. I read of one murder that was done using a crossbow. I would later have my own life threatened. I will say more about that later.

Two years went by. Then one Sunday, Randy and Carol came to church again. I could tell that Randy was very nervous. Before the service he said that he wanted to talk to Wayne. They went to a private room and Wayne led Randy to the Lord. Randy and Carol began attending faithfully after that.

Randy also began attending my new believer's class, which I taught during the Sunday School hour. I had realized that I could not possibly personally disciple everyone that was being saved. So I wrote a thirteen chapter course to give the basics to new believers. After the course they were better prepared to enter a regular Sunday School class. I loved teaching those new baby Christians. Most of them had no clue what the Bible said.

On one Sunday I was reading a passage from I Corinthians 11. When I read verse 14, Randy spoke up and said, "I'm not getting my hair cut for anybody". The verse says, "Does not even nature itself teach you that if a man has long hair, it is a dishonor to him?" I never thought about Randy when I was reading that passage. Randy did have long hair. In fact, his hair went all the way down his back to his waist. But that was not something that was a major concern to me at that point. Randy was a new believer and had other major struggles to work on. So I simply said, "Randy, I'm not telling you to get your haircut. But if Jesus tells you to get your haircut then that's a different matter." The next Sunday when Randy came to church, I did not recognize him. He had gotten a regular haircut. I honestly thought he was a first time visitor. When I finally realized that it was Randy, I said, "Randy, you got your haircut." He replied, "Yah. Jesus wanted me to." God's grace is so awesome!

Leo's Story

One Sunday a man came to church driving a Cadillac. That was unusual for our church. But it was even more unusual, when he got out of his car. He didn't have any legs. Leo told me later that he lost his legs in a train accident, when he was a boy. He and his brother had been playing hide and go seek around some train cars. He had fallen and was knocked unconscious with his legs across the tracks. When the train took off it ran over his legs.

But Leo was very independent. He certainly didn't feel sorry for himself. He drove his car using all hand controls. He got around by using his arms as crutches. He wore gloves on his hands, which he would make into fists, and put them on the ground, sidewalk, or hallway. He would then, with the aid of his arms, swing his torso forward with his rear end hitting forward. He repeated the procedure until he got where he was going. When he came to a chair, he would simply pull himself up into the chair. He was incredibly strong in his upper body. He had artificial legs but rarely used them.

Leo started to attend our services after we had moved into the Slocum Elementary School, and soon came forward one Sunday to receive Christ as his Savior. I always talked to new believers about baptism, but I didn't do that with Leo. I didn't think it was possible for him to be baptized. I knew baptism had nothing to do with his salvation, and thought that God surely would not expect that of him.

My faith was so weak. God obviously had some work to do on me, and He was going to use Leo to accomplish that work. It began on a Sunday evening after the service. I was "walking" out of the school with Leo, when he said out of the blue, "Pastor, I want to be baptized". I responded, "That's great, Leo. But, you know, we don't sprinkle. I would have to put you under the water." "That's ok," he said. "I can swim."

I was embarrassed and ashamed. I had not talked to him about this step of obedience because I didn't know how I was going to be able to do it. He never had a doubt about it. He knew God would make it happen. So I scheduled Leo to be baptized along with some others.

Since we did not have our own building yet, we used another Baptist church's baptistery during the winter months. When I called the pastor of the church in Stryker, Ohio, to request permission to use their baptistery, I explained the unique circumstances pertaining to Leo. I had previously called dad Crown and asked for his ideas on how to baptize Leo. He, of course, had the perfect solution. It was so simple. He said, "Just put an old chair in the baptistery, set Leo on the chair, tip it backwards, and then forwards again." Perfect! So I asked the pastor if he could have an old chair handy that we could use for Leo. He said he would take care of it.

When we got to the church, I checked out the baptistery. To my surprise there was no chair, only a saw horse. After recovering from the shock, I decided that I could still set Leo on the saw horse and tip him backwards and bring him up again. It was a little more risky, but I figured that I could make it work.

I purposely planned to baptize Leo last. When it came time to baptize him, he swung his body up the steps that led up to the baptistery entrance. I had the saw horse nearby ready to use, but Leo wasn't waiting for me to put it in the water. So I said to him, "Leo, I need to get the saw horse in the water first." He just kept on going

down the steps into the water as he said, "I don't need that". I quickly responded, "Maybe you don't need it, but I do". But he simply kept on going into the water. Then holding onto the edge of the baptistery with his hands, he made his way to the opening of the baptistery, where the people could see him. He then began to tell how the Lord saved him, and how he wanted to obey the Lord in baptism. After sharing his testimony he shoved himself away from the opening and let go of the edge, lying flat in the water, and in my arms. He was actually not that heavy in the water. After I baptized him, I shoved his body like a surfboard toward the steps. When his little stubs hit the steps, I pushed his body up, and he did the rest. That was so amazing!

I have often told this story to those who were afraid of the water, or afraid to get in front of people. If God could help Leo to get baptized, He can help anyone with their limitations or fears as well.

CHAPTER 29

THE MODEL GIVER

I had always worked for everything I received. I had to work hard in college and seminary. Good grades didn't come easily for me. I had been taught to tithe since I was a child. But I had never been taught to receive. I had never been in a situation where people wanted to do things for me, just because they wanted to do so. I was about to see what a real giver was, and would have to learn the grace of receiving.

We had moved into our house on Harding Street after living for two years in a rented house on State Route 111. I'm not sure what was wrong with me, but I wasn't feeling well. I don't think it was so much physical, but I was "down". I didn't feel like doing anything. I'm not sure why I was feeling that way, but I was. I had not yet planted any grass in our yard and the weeds were a foot high. It looked terrible. I was lying around inside the house, when I heard a lawn mower in our yard. I looked out the window and saw one of our charter members, Gale Yenser, mowing my weed patch. I had not told anyone about my weed patch, or how I felt. But Gale must have driven by our house, and taken it upon himself to mow my weeds. I was moved to tears that day. I had never had anyone do something like that for me. The next day I was feeling much better and ready to go back to work.

Gale rarely let a Sunday go by without inviting us out to eat. That was such a big help to Nancy especially, since she helped with the music at the church and helped with other areas as well. There were times when he would hand me a 20 dollar bill with some comment about "I thought maybe you could use this." I had never seen such a giving man before.

Gale had a good job at the General Motors foundry, but he and his wife, Jane, lived very simply. They drove an old car, and lived in a very modest home in Junction. His two teenage boys, Mark and Steve, were typical teenage boys: somewhat disinterested in the church at first. They would later become wonderful Christian young men, marry sweet Christian girls, and become helpers in the church. Their younger daughter, Opal, would become a good friend to Lori.

Whenever I think of how I should be as a giver, I think of Gale Yenser.

CHAPTER   30

OUR CHURCH BUILDING

Dr. Ray Hein

There were ten churches from the North Bethel Fellowship of Regular Baptist Churches that supported our church in Defiance financially. One of those churches was Calvary Baptist Church of Findlay. The pastor of that church, Rev. Dick Snavely, recommended a church consultant that they had used for their building program named, Dr. Ray Hein. I knew that I needed help with the whole process of raising funds for a building program and building a church building, so I contacted Dr. Hein.

Dr. Hein was a unique man. He flew his own plane. He took me up in it on more than one occasion, which was so awesome. He had been the director of the Conservative Baptist Convention in Michigan, so he had worked with a lot of churches. He had also been a pastor. In fact, I would learn later that he at one time was the pastor of the First Baptist Church of Plainwell, Michigan, which would be very close to where I would pastor in Otsego, Michigan. After talking to Dr. Hein and having him give his presentation to the church, the church voted to call Dr. Hein as their church consultant. He was a tremendous help to me in preparing the necessary paperwork to present to the banks, securing an architect, and a builder and helping to think through the building plans. He also gave me ideas on church growth. The ground breaking service, the caravan procession from the Slocum school, and the dedication service ideas, were all his. I learned so much from working with him.

Buying the Property for Our New Building

The church was growing. It was obvious that we needed our own building. Though the Slocum Elementary School was a great place to meet, it also had its limitations. Every Sunday required a lot of set up and tear down of chairs and nursery equipment. We were also limited as to what we could do, and when we could do it. I had looked for available land on the south side of Defiance. I wanted to be on a state route so we could be easily found. I also wanted to be located in an area that would eventually have a lot of houses from which we could draw people.

There were two possible properties that could be purchased. One was located just south of town across the bridge on Route 66. The owner was asking $3000.00 an acre for the five acres we needed. The other property was located on State Route 111 about four miles south of town. That property was closer to where many of our people lived at that time. The owners, Hugh and Marie, were asking $2000.00 an acre. It was farther from town than the other property. But I checked with a well know realtor, who informed me that there would probably be a large housing edition going up very close to that location.

At the time the second property seemed like the best choice. Looking back on it, I wish I had gone with the other property. Hind sight is always 20/20. That housing edition was never built, but the city did grow out Route 66. I think the church would have done even better had it been built on the first location. But everyone in the church including myself thought the best choice was the property on State Route 111. So we made the purchase and began to prepare for our building program.

Financing for Our New Building

I had no idea how hard it was going to be to get our new building financed. With Dr. Hein's help we had properly prepared. We had a banquet with our church members to tell them what we would need from them financially. They responded by giving promises of monthly support towards the building payments. We had all the paper work the bank would require. Dr. Hein had done this many times and knew what the banks needed and would be looking for.

We took the attractively prepared material to all three banks in town. Every bank refused to loan us any money, even though we could show that we could afford the payments. I was devastated. I didn't know what to do. Dr. Hein suggested that only God could solve this problem and recommended that we make a prayer clock. The prayer clock was simply a clock drawn on a poster board with each hour divided between am. and pm. We then asked the people to commit to pray during one of the hours on the clock and to sign the clock if they were willing to do so. We had people literally praying around the clock to change the banker's minds, so we could get the needed financing for our building. We needed $200,000 for our building project, but we only needed $150,000 from a bank. God had already marvelously provided $50,000 in loans from individuals.

I remember the day that Dr. Hein and I went to pick up the material from the three banks. The first two bank presidents were apologetic, but said pretty much the same thing. They thought our people were all from the "south" and would soon head back "south" if the church got into trouble. The third bank president was very courteous and did not use that excuse. Instead he began to explain that the bank required that we show how we could afford to make the payments. I opened the booklet that we had given him and showed him the page where that had already been done. He simply said, "Oh". He then came up with a couple other things the bank would need, each of which was already in the booklet, which I pointed out. He obviously had not read the booklet. But he was an honest man. He then said, "Let me look this over some more and I will get back to you." A couple days later he called to say they had approved our loan and would be happy to work with us. God had answered our prayers. He had changed the banker's heart. What an exciting blessing and encouragement that was to our people, and to me. God's grace was being poured out again.

Moving to Our New Building

After a few months our building was finally completed. I did not work on the building, but one of our men, Larry Bauer, who was a contractor, helped. It was beautiful with a carport and our own baptistery. It could seat around 200 and had sliding doors and curtains between the classrooms, so the entire building could be opened up to seat close to 500. The only downside to our building was that the well water contained sulfur water. This was a normal problem in the area, but Nancy and I were not used to it. It smelled like rotten eggs. That problem would be fixed later when a cistern was installed.
On Sunday, November 4, 1973, all the church people gathered in front of the Slocum Elementary School for the last time, only no one went into the school. We formed a caravan with over forty cars, and were escorted by a police car from the school to our new building. What a sight as I looked behind me down the road and saw cars as far as I could see. 146 gathered for worship that first day in our new building breaking all our old attendance records. God had done all of this in a little over three years.

It was such a blessing to those who had left their old Methodist church building. God had not only given them a brand new building, but He also provided a brand new organ, which someone donated. God just kept pouring out His grace.

Just two weeks later on November 18th we held a Dedication Service in the afternoon, and dedicated our new building to the Lord. Rev. Earl Umbaugh was the main speaker. I'm sure it was a special joy for him to see what God had done as well.

CHAPTER 31

MARK'S ARRIVAL DURING OUR BUILDING PROCESS

We had planned a Ground Breaking Service for our new building on April 22, 1973. Dr. Hein had helped me with the details. I did not have a clue what to do. So we had ordered little plastic shovels with the name of the church and the date printed on them, so all the people could have a keepsake of the special day. We had a brand new fancy looking real shovel ready to go. It was a Sunday, so I was to bring a message. Following the message I, Dr. Hein, and each deacon would turn over some dirt on our property. Pictures were to be taken and put in the paper.

But Mark had his own plans for the day. He apparently didn't think Nancy and I should be part of the Ground Breaking Service, because on that Sunday morning Nancy started to go into labor. I called Dr. Hein from the hospital to tell him what was happening. He told me what I already knew. My place was with Nancy. He would take care of the Ground Breaking Service. I was so thankful he was there to help.

Nancy was in labor all through the day. Mark was actually born around 2:00 am. the next morning. Again I was not called to come into the delivery room. When the doctor came out to talk to me, he said Mark was struggling some, so they were going to monitor him. At the time it didn't sound serious, so I went home to try to get some sleep.

About 7:00 am I was awakened by a phone call from the hospital. Mark was not breathing well and was not getting better, so they were transporting him to a hospital in Fort Wayne, Indiana, that was equipped to handle a small baby's problems. Mark was also three weeks early and weighed only six pounds.

I jumped out of bed, threw some clothes on, and took off for Fort Wayne, which was normally about an hour's drive from Defiance. I'm not sure how fast I was going, but I caught up to an ambulance that had the word Defiance on it, so I figured it was the one transporting Mark. I stayed behind the ambulance all the way to the Fort Wayne hospital.

I parked in the emergency parking area and ran to the ambulance as they were getting Mark out. He was in a glass case and was hooked up to several wires and tubes. The doctor was just inside the door and walked with us to the elevator. I will never forget the look of the doctor and what he said to me. He said, "We will do all we can, but I can't promise you anything". Then they took Mark away.

I went off somewhere to pray. God had given Mark to us, but I knew in my heart that Mark belonged to God. He could do what He wanted with him, but I so wanted Mark to live and grow up to serve God. I stayed at the hospital for some time. They had Mark hooked up to machines that helped him breath, fed him, and also helped his heart to beat. He was on full life support, and would be that way for four weeks.

I finally realized that I needed to go back and be with Nancy, so I went back to the Defiance hospital, and it was a good thing I did. Nancy was very distraught. All the other mothers were having their babies brought to them, but not Nancy. She had not yet been able to hold her baby. She wanted so desperately to be with her baby but couldn't. I tried to comfort her as best I could, but I wasn't doing very well. But I got an idea. I borrowed a Polaroid camera. They were a relatively new thing. They took pictures and printed them right away in the camera. One didn't have to take the film to the drug store to have the pictures developed. I took the camera to the Fort Wayne hospital and took pictures of Mark. I thought if Nancy couldn't get to Mark, that I would bring Mark to her – at least some pictures of him. What a mistake.

By the time I took the pictures, Mark was doing better, but he was still in the glass case and still hooked up to a lot of tubes. When I showed the pictures to Nancy I thought she would be happy. Wrong – again. She stated crying uncontrollably. My pictures made it worse. But it did do one thing for her. She was determined to get out of the hospital and go to her son. In a few hours she was dismissed from the hospital and we were on our way to Fort Wayne.

Nancy continued to gain in strength after that, and so did Mark. After about four weeks, Mark was breathing on his own, and we were able to take him home to meet his sister. God's grace was so abundantly being poured out on me.

CHAPTER 32

GROWTH OF OUR MINISTRIES

Once we were in our own building our ministries had no limit. It was awesome. I had my own office at the church, which was such a blessing. I had always had my office in our home prior to that. It was great being near my family, but it was certainly not good when it came to a quiet area to study, or privacy for counseling.

The Bus Ministry

Before too long we had three buses. Gale Yenser had some mechanical knowledge and maintained our buses. We also had the drivers, those who rode with the driver, and a man who oversaw the entire ministry. He did a lot of the visitation to build up the attendance on the buses. We began to bring a lot of kids on the buses.

But this did present a challenge. Bus kids were not used to being still in church and their attention span seemed to be much shorter than church kids. Our teaching methods had to include a lot of visuals and creativity. But we were reaching kids that otherwise would never have heard the Gospel.

VBS

Nancy and I have always loved kids. We decided to have a Vacation Bible School in our new church building. We did not have enough trained teachers to have the teaching done in the classrooms, and our movable walls were just not conducive to that approach. So I did the teaching from the platform with all of the ages combined.

I wrote puppet plays using cheap store bought puppets, and made a puppet stage using PVC pipe. I used objects I pulled out of a sack to tell Biblical truth and stories. One the most popular puppets was one we called "Stretch". Stretch was made using an ordinary goofy looking puppet, which I duct taped to a shower rod. I then attached a slinky to the bottom of his head, and put a cylinder of cloth, which Nancy made, over the slinky. When I stuck Stretch's head above the opening of the puppet stage, he looked like a normal puppet. But when I pushed on the shower rod his neck would stretch. We used him to teach truths, as well, with the help of someone working me. He could shake his head yes or no to questions, and would show excitement by making his neck stretch out and in quickly.

Another way we used Stretch was in the song time. We told the kids that the louder they sang the further Stretch's neck would stretch. The workers didn't always appreciate the song time, but the kids loved it. I managed to rig up an extension for the shower rod, so I could make Stretch touch his head on the church chandelier. That was so much fun. Kids came to VBS just to see Stretch, but many of them got to meet Jesus as well.

We built the attendance by means of a contest among those who attended and made a big deal over those who won. A couple of years the first place prize was a ride in an airplane. One of our members, Paul Keim, was a pilot. Lori won one year, so he took Lori, Mark, and I up in his plane. In the middle of the week we always had a special guest show up, which we announced in advance. I rented costumes which I found at a costume shop in Columbus. One of the most popular guests was when I rented a Big Bird costume. I remember walking down the middle aisle of the church in the costume with the kids screaming and going nuts, but also feeling some tugs at my behind. What I didn't realize was that some of the kids were getting souvenirs by pulling feathers from my backside. Once I realized what was happening, I quickly got up on the platform. I had purchased several pair of patty hose. Not that I needed them personally. But a particular kind came in something that looked like a very large egg. All I wanted was the egg part. We told the kids that if they answered a Bible question right, Big Bird would give them one of his eggs. Yah, that might have been a bit much, but it was all in fun.

The last night of VBS we had what we called shower day. I bought a lot of candy taffy or candy that was wrapped in paper and threw it off the roof of the church to the kids. We brought the kids out by age groups so the little ones wouldn't be mauled.

We filled the church up with almost 200 kids every VBS. It was a lot of work and the workers came close to pulling their hair out, but we saw a number of kids come to Christ. Nancy and I were asked to do a VBS for her dad's church one summer as well.

Youth Ministry

When Nancy and I first came to Defiance Mel and Laura Retcher headed up the youth ministry. But by the time we got into our own building we had other couples who could take over that ministry, since Mel and Laura had other responsibilities. Because of the excellent material and support system for the leaders, I thought it would be best to use the Word of Life program. It worked very well for us. Mark Yenser had married Terry Kern by this time and they had grown enough spiritually to head up this ministry. I believe his brother, Steve also helped with this ministry along with his new wife, Dorothy. Another couple that helped was Jim and Mary Shaner, who would later go into the full time ministry.

Deaf Ministry

One Sunday we had a couple come to our church and present their unique ministry to the deaf. They were willing to train some of us to use sign language. I was able to attend some of the classes and leaned enough to communicate a little in sign language. But one of our men and his wife learned it well enough to be able to interpret during the service. We began to have deaf people attend. I had no idea that these people lived so close to the church. A person can be deaf and not be noticed like a blind person would. I'm not certain if any deaf people got saved through this ministry, but they "heard" the Gospel.

Visitation Ministry

As I traveled with the Volunteers Quartet for Cedarville, I obviously got into a lot of churches. I took mental note of the churches that were successful and the things they all had in common. One thing they all had in common was a successful visitation program. They all aggressively sought to bring the lost to Christ.

When I first came to Faith Baptist in Defiance, I was the visitation program. I did the canvassing of the homes in the area, and followed up on those that visited the church services. I soon began to take men with me on those visits. Shortly after we got into our own building, I organized our visitation program. I had meetings every Sunday evening before the service, which included training and giving out visitation assignments. I encouraged people to attend who could not go visiting but would be willing to pray for those who did. They were given prayer assignments that matched the visitation assignments, so they were not only praying for the team that was doing the visits, but also for those being visited. We began to have over twenty people involved in our visitation ministry, and God really blessed.   Souls were being saved and the church was growing.

Men's Retreats

In the spring of 1971 we took our first group of men to a men's retreat at Skyview Ranch Youth Camp in Millersburg, Ohio. That may have been the first time Skyview offered a men's retreat. I think we may have only had four men attend that year including me, but we loved it. The speaker was great. The food was great. And the activities, except for golf, were right down my alley. There were competitions in rifle shooting, trap shooting, ping pong, three on three basketball, as well as golf.   The camp had a swimming pool, horseback riding, and took the men on a canoe trip. We went home from that first retreat all excited and told all the men about it.
From that year on our attendance at the men's retreat began to explode. We soon had the largest group of any church attending the retreat. We began to take the men in one of our buses, and had over thirty attend more than once. Total attendance at the retreat was usually around 200 men from all over the state of Ohio.

One of those early years the ranch foreman, "Dutch" Henry Wolfe, had a special event planned. He had hitched one of the horses to what looked like an old door with a rope attached at the front of the door for a rider to hang onto. He then asked if anyone wanted to ride on the door. No one volunteered. It was a barnyard. It was muddy and filled with manure. If a rider fell off, it would not be pretty, but it would be very funny. But to me it looked like fun. So I shot up my hand and said, "I'll give it a try".

I got on the door and took hold of the rope. He gave the horse a swat, and off we went. I was hanging on for dear life, but having a blast. I could hear all the men laughing their heads off, which made it all the more fun for me.   I went to one end of the coral. The horse then made a quick turn to avoid the fence in front of it, and took off in the opposite direction. This made me fly around in a half circle very close to the fence, but I managed to stay on during the entire ride. There was no way I wanted to fall off in all that "yuk".

When the horse finally came to a stop, the men erupted in applause, and I bowed. I think that was the first and last time they ever had that activity. Years later I still had men, who had been at that retreat, remind me of my ride.

I think the men liked the fact that I loved doing all the activities with them. It made them feel that I was one of them, which helped me be a more effective pastor to them. They also loved to try to beat me. That was easy when it came to golf. But not so easy when it came to ping pong, the rifle shoot, or the trap shoot. In fact, I have several trophies to attest to winning in those three areas on several occasions.

Helping Young Men

The GARBC fellowship of churches had an event each year called Talents for Christ. It was a competition for teens in several areas of music as well as public speaking, Bible knowledge, and writing. I was able to help two of our teenager young men at the church prepare for the public speaking category. One young man won the state competition, but disappointed me when he did not want to compete in the national competition. Winning at the state level qualified you to compete at the national level. However, another young man, David Sugg, won the state competition and earned second place in the national competition. First place prize in the nation for winning in any category was a year's tuition scholarship to a GARBC approved college. Second place was a one semester scholarship. So it was a "big deal". I also was a judge a couple of times at the state level, but not the years that I had someone competing, of course.

State Youth Committee

The Ohio fellowship of GARBC churches was called the Ohio Association of Regular Baptist Churches, or OARBC. It had at that time the State Missionary, Earl Umbaugh, whose job was primarily to help churches like our's get started, and also to help existing churches with their needs. The OARBC had a council made up of twelve pastors, who oversaw the OARBC fellowship. The OARBC had three approved camps, one of which was Skyview Ranch. It also had what was called a State Youth Committee. It was chaired by a Council of Twelve member. The State Youth Committee oversaw the state Talents for Christ (TFC) event and an annual statewide youth rally. I can't remember for sure, but I think it was in 1973 that I was asked to serve on the State Youth Committee. I would continue to serve on that committee for the next five years.

One year the chairman of the committee said that he wanted to do something "different" at the state youth rally. They had become pretty much the same every year with the same workshops and a special speaker. He asked if any of us had any different ways that we could communicate the Gospel to teens. I suggested using drama. All the committee members thought that was a great idea, but then they put me in charge of it. Where was I going to get a drama that would relate to teens, and where was I going to get the actors? I felt that God wanted me to write the drama, and that He would help me get the actors.

I went with Dad Crown and another pastor, Bruce Stewart, to a Bible conference, but not to attend the conference. I needed to get away, so I could have absolute quiet. When the men went to the conference, I stayed in our motel room. I remember praying and asking God for His help. I knew I could not do it on my own. I had written another play for teens, when I was serving in Argos, called "Guilty as Charged", but it was very short and simple, and certainly not of the magnitude that was needed at the Youth Rally. Then an idea came to me. The theme of the youth conference was "Purify of Perish". Politically at that time there were many protests among the young people over pollution. Our intention was to capitalize on the political climate, but, also, to put a spiritual meaning to the pollution idea. Polluted lives don't go to heaven. Only Jesus can make us clean.

I had been in a play called "Our Town", when I was in high school. It was a very unique play using simple props, and a "stage manager" as one of the main characters. I used the "stage manager" and the simple props ideas from "Our Town", but I called it "Our World". Of course, the characters and plot were totally different. The story was about some teens in a youth group who were protesting against pollution, but were also taking drugs. In the end one of the characters dies from an overdose, which leads others to trust Christ. I wrote the entire play during that week away in the motel.

After getting the play written I called a friend of mine at Cedarville. Dr. Jim Phipps had been a classmate of mine and a fellow communication major. He had been hired at Cedarville as a speech professor, and had earned his doctorate. When the chairman of the communications department, Dr. John Reed, left to become a professor at Dallas Theological Seminary, Dr. Phipps was promoted to chairman of the department. I told Jim about my play and what it was for. After he read the copy that I sent him, he said he would be glad to help (In fact he actually wanted to hire me as a professor at the college). He said he would get some of the drama students to be the actors. He would play the part of the "stage manager", which had the most lines. I met with the cast only one time at Cedarville, just to give them a "pep talk". I told them about how important it was to try to reach as many for Christ as we could.

The youth rally was held in the Veterans Memorial Auditorium in Columbus, Ohio. We had over 2000 teens attend that year. After some music, my play was presented followed by the speaker. That year it was Dr. Jack Van Impe. When the invitation was given over fifty teens came forward to receive Christ. I believe the play really helped prepare the hearts for the powerful message by Dr. Van Impe. The actors all did an unbelievable job.

When the play was over the cast all received a standing ovation. Then they asked for the author. I had been back stage all this time as part of the youth committee helping to "direct traffic". I was not expecting them to want to introduce the author. But I went out on the stage and took a bow. But what thrilled me the most is that I had been part of a day where over fifty souls had been saved. That was awesome!

The Skyview Ranch Board

During my ministry years at Defiance I was also asked to serve on the Skyview Ranch board. I would be on the board at Skyview for over sixteen years serving as secretary as well as chairman for several years. When I first came on the board Rev. Bill Russell was the Director. I was on the board when we called Bill Roloff to be the next director, and when Bill Roloff resigned. I enjoyed being part of that ministry.

Music

I continued to play my trombone for special music on occasion at the church. Nancy and I also sang often in church. We were also frequently asked to sing and speak at banquets for other churches. Because Mel and Laura Retcher, who were members of our church, had come from Emanuel Baptist Church in Toledo, we were often asked to sing for various events at that church. I once traveled with their youth group on a special trip to Niagara Falls as their speaker and special music.

CHAPTER   33

GETTING HELP

Counseling Training

Though I had excellent training at seminary in knowing the Bible, I had no training in counseling. I was discovering that counseling was an important part of my ministry. So when I heard about an opportunity to take a counseling course, I jumped at the chance. The course was being taught in connection with the Baptist Children's Home in Valparaiso, Indiana. The course was based on the teachings of a man named Jay Adams, who believed that the Bible was the best book about behavior and the basis for all counseling.

I joined a carpool with some pastors in Fort Wayne. So every Monday for thirteen weeks I drove to Fort Wayne to meet the other pastors. Sometimes I drove all the way, and sometimes they drove from Fort Wayne on to Valparaiso.   One of the pastors I rode with was Pastor Randy Patton. Neither of us knew at that time that he would one day become the national director of that counseling ministry. Today that ministry is nationally acclaimed. I am so thankful for the training I received. It was so well worth the special effort even if it took a three hour drive one way every Monday. It revolutionized my counseling and my attitude toward Nancy.

In one of the sessions I learned a revolutionary concept based on Romans 8:28&29. I knew verse 28 well, but I had not paid a lot of attention to verse 29, and I certainly had not connected the verses to marriage. Verse 28 states: "And we know that all things work together for good to those who love God, to those who are called according to His purpose." Verse 29 goes on to say, "For those He foreknew, He also predestined to be conformed to the image of His Son, that He might be the firstborn among many brethren." As it applies to marriage, the spouse God gave must be good for me since all things work together for my good. Since that is true, the good God intends to accomplish in me is to conform me into the image of His Son – make me more like Jesus. I found out that the image of Jesus is seen in the "fruit of the Spirit" found in Galatians 5:22&23.

I could not wait to get home and talk to Nancy that night. I had such a messed up thinking toward her all this time. I had been resentful at times – even bitter, although I had never discussed it with her. What I saw as her flaws were actually God's tools to work on me and make me more like Jesus. I knew one of the firstfruit mentioned in Galatians 5:22 was love. I knew I needed a lot of work on that one. I needed to learn how to love with agape love. God had given me the perfect wife to drive me from my selfishness and teach me how to put her needs first. That one truth changed my whole outlook on my marriage, and began to make me a better husband.

Administrative Training

Another area that I had no training in was administration. Yet I was discovering that the church was not only a ministry, it was a business. I had been around my dad's plumbing and heating business all my life, but I was never involved in the business side of things. I needed help.

Dad Crown told me about a church management course that he planned to take and wanted to know if I wanted to go with him. I again jumped at the chance. The course was called the Howard Hendrix Management Course and was taught by Howard Hendrix himself. That course was very helpful to me. I learned so much that would help me the rest of my life as a pastor. I also thoroughly enjoyed taking the course with Dad Crown.

I always enjoyed going to conferences with him. He and I got along so well, and he was always teaching me things, not only verbally, but primarily by his example. Whenever he went to a conference he always bought something to take home to mom Crown. Not wanting to look bad, I usually did too.

I usually didn't have much money, but on this particular occasion I only had about one dollar left. I spotted a plastic little boy and girl that were kissing with the caption, "When I am away, I miss you". It was less than a dollar, so I bought it, put it in a paper sack and took it home for Nancy. I was shocked when I gave it to her. You would have thought that I had bought her an expensive diamond ring or something. She even teared up and hugged me.

I learned something from that. Pleasing Nancy had nothing to do with how much I spent. It was the fact that I was thinking of her, and that I missed her.

Getting a Secretary

Up to this point Nancy had done all my secretarial work for me, that I could not do. I could type, but not very well. But Nancy was busy with two children to manage. After we got into our building I really needed someone to answer the phone and do the weekly bulletin. I also wanted to publish a monthly newsletter. I felt that a newsletter would help promote special events as well as provide another means of communicating Biblical truth to our members and unsaved attendees.

I received a call from a single missionary lady who lived in Cleveland, Ohio. She had an aunt who lived in Defiance, and wondered if I would be willing to visit her. Her aunt had recently lost her husband, and was struggling emotionally. She also wasn't sure if she was saved. So I paid her aunt a visit.

Athlene Switzer was a dear sweet lady in her sixties. She had attended a Presbyterian church all her life, and was trusting in her works for her salvation, like most people. She was so open to the Gospel. I led her to Christ that day. She began to attend regularly, and I later baptized her.

After a few months she commented that she thought I could use a secretary, and she would love to volunteer for the job. That was so of the Lord. I immediately told her she had the job. I think we paid her a very small amount each week, but she just wanted to help. She did a great job, though she really did not like the mimeograph printer. We were able to begin our monthly newsletter, and I was able to get more done with less frustration. She continued to serve with me until we moved to Mount Vernon.

CHAPTER 34

FAMILY VACATIONS

Dad and mom Crown always went to the same place on their vacations as long as Nancy can remember. They rented a cabin on Big Clam Lake near Spooner, Wisconsin, from a Christian couple who owned the Robins Nest Resort. The resort was a long drive to the northwest corner of Wisconsin, but Nancy and I decided to join them one year. Mark was just a baby when we went up there the first time.

Dad Crown was an expert at catching northern pike. He knew the lake well and knew what to use to catch them. I just watched him and used the same bait and lures. Soon I was catching "northern" almost as well as he was. Our family continued to plan our vacations together for several years after that.

One year Nancy and I arrived at the resort a week before dad and mom Crown did. I had already gotten over some of the excitement of it all, but he hadn't. When we went out fishing together right after he arrived, we went straight for our favorite fishing spot. Within a few minutes he had a strike. We were both standing up in the boat when this happened. When he set the hook with a huge jerk of his fishing rod, he did so with such force that his feet went right out from under him, and he landed on his rear in the bottom of the boat smack dab in the middle of the big landing net that we used when we caught a big one. Like a true fisherman he never missed a beat and never let go of his rod, which at this point was between his legs. His feet were sticking straight up in the air. The only thing he could say was, "I've still got 'em." I've still got 'em." I had to sit down in the boat before I fell into lake, I was laughing so hard. It was the funniest thing I had ever seen while fishing, and still is to this day.

As mentioned earlier, Bill R. insisted that we use his new motor home for our vacation one year. We again went up to Wisconsin and stopped at the Dells. The scenery from the big windows of that motor home seemed so much more beautiful. We saw the Tommy Bartlett Water Show with all the tricks down on the water skis, which was amazing to me. We then drove it up to the fishing camp and met up with mom and dad Crown. It was a wonderful trip.

CHAPTER 35

SET FREE

No one knew how I struggled with guilt, bitterness, and feelings of insecurity and depression during the early years of my ministry. There was not a day that went by that I was not bothered by it. It was hindering and limiting my ministry. I had asked God for forgiveness for past sins. I knew He had forgiven me, but I didn't feel forgiven. Satan kept beating me up by using my past. I know that I never seriously considered suicide, but the thought crossed my mind a few times. I never told anyone about my inner struggles, not even Nancy.

But again, God used Dad Crown indirectly to help me. He was going to another conference. This one was being held in Detroit, and was called "The Institute in Basic Youth Conflicts". It was being taught by a man named Bill Gothard. I had never heard of him or of this strange sounding conference, but it was another chance to be with dad Crown and perhaps learn some more, so I said I would go with him.

It was all of the Lord. His grace was being poured out on me. I had no clue what I was doing, but He knew just what I needed. When I sat in the session on getting free from guilt, I knew that session was just for me. The session on bitterness was just as life changing.

For some reason dad Crown had to go back early from the conference leaving me alone after those sessions. Part of the steps to break the chains of guilt and bitterness was to write down the offenses starting with the most grievous. I had quite a long list.

I went home from that conference determined to have victory, but knowing I would have to do the hardest thing I have ever had to do in my life. I needed to call some people and ask for their forgiveness. I began to make the calls. I sweated and shook with every call. Satan was doing everything he could to keep me from making those calls. One of those calls was to my own brother, Keith, who I had been so mean to while we were growing up. But I made the calls by God's grace. And God totally set me free for the first time in as long as I could remember.

My life had a new happiness, my ministry took on a new freedom, and my preaching took on a new power. God's grace had been poured out on me again.

CHAPTER 36

SATAN'S ATTACK

Our New Record

Our fifth year anniversary as a church was approaching on Easter Sunday 1975. We had set an attendance goal of 200 for this big Sunday. By this time we had three buses bringing in kids. We also had started a branch church in Napoleon, Ohio, which was about twenty miles east of Defiance. Two of the couples that were attending our church were from that area and wanted to be part of the new "church plant". They had begun their own services and were having ten to twenty in attendance. We asked them to join us for the special day. We went over our goal for the day having 205 in attendance, which was a new record. I was thrilled to see our new church building packed that day. But Satan was not happy.

Satan's Attack on Me

At the end of the service I stood near the door as usual thanking the people for coming. Most people say nice things to me when they leave. On this day after most of the people had left, a man with long hair and rather wild looking eyes said something to me that no one has ever said before or since. "You're a liar", he snarled, as he went passed me. That shocked me, so I said, "Excuse me sir. What do you mean?" He responded, "No one has never been sick a day in his life."

I had used an illustration at the end of my message about a rather young man who had died suddenly, and used the expression, "He had not been sick a day in his life". Those were the actual words that were used by the person who told me the story about the untimely death.   I understood that expression to mean that the person who died was very healthy and had no known health problems. So I explained that to the man who had called me a liar. That didn't seem to faze him. He began to verbally "tear into" me.

Earlier that day in the service I had seen this man sitting next to a woman who had been attending our church for a few months. She had told me how she had escaped from her drug addicted husband, who had been physically and verbally abusing her, but I didn't put the pieces together until he began to verbally assault me. They had lived in Lima, so she had gone to live with her parents who lived in the Defiance area. He apparently had somehow found out that she was attending our church, and shocked her by coming to church that day and sitting next to her. I also did not know that while he was busy "talking" to me, she had snuck away from him and was hiding in the women's restroom nearby.

After he had unloaded his "words" on me, he left the building to try to find his wife.   By then all of the people had left except for a couple of our deacons. When he went out the front door, one of the deacons, Jim Sugg, told me that she was hiding in the women's restroom, and that his wife was with her. As soon as Jim had said that, he came back into the building. He had apparently seen that her car was still in the parking lot. He went by me without saying a word and began to look in every room. Jim asked me what we should do. I told him to let him look wherever he wants, but if he went near the ladies restroom, "Take him down". Jim was fully capable of doing just that.

Finally, when he could not find her, the man came back to verbally attack me some more. He then said he wanted to talk to me privately in my office. I could not imagine what more he had to say, but I told him that would be fine. Jim then said, "I'm going in with you, pastor." "No, Jim, I will be fine." Then after a pause I added, "But stay just outside the door". I knew I could handle myself, but this guy was not acting like a normal guy.

When we went into my office he started in again with more of his verbal attacks, but then started towards me to attack me physically. For some reason I did not respond to him physically. The words of Psalm 105:15 popped into my head and out of my mouth, "Do not touch the Lord's anointed". At that, he fell backwards as if I had slugged him. He then got a wild look in his eyes. What he said next made the hair on the back of my head stand straight up. "There is none anointed but Lucifer". I was pretty sure at this point that the man was demon possessed. They didn't tell me how to deal with this in seminary. I just began to pray silently and quoted scripture. The man finally calmed down and left.

While he was in my office, his wife had left and went to her parent's home. I learned later that her dad was waiting for him with a shotgun, but her husband never went after her. I later notified the sheriff's office, because I thought her life might be in danger. I never saw her again or heard any more about her husband. But I was so thankful that the Lord was with me that day.

Satan's Attack on Our Ministries

That same evening I learned the earth shattering news that the head of our bus ministry was having an adulterous relationship with the wife of the head of our deaf ministry. She had openly ridden on his bus that morning. I called each couple separately into my office. Both parties confessed that it was true. They admitted that it was wrong and prayed in front of me to ask for God's forgiveness. They also asked for forgiveness from their spouse. The next Sunday both couples came forward during the invitation time to publically acknowledge that they had sought God's forgiveness, and intended to live for God. As bad as it was, it looked like we were going to "weather the storm".

But I wasn't prepared for what happened next. The Sunday after they had gone forward in church, neither couple was in church. I learned to my horror that they had gone camping together. The "innocent" spouses thought they could all be friends. That only rekindled the sinful flame in the "guilty" spouses, who went back into their sinful relationship.

But this was all beginning to split the church. Church people had learned about it and were starting to take sides. Some thought it was "all his" fault. Others thought it was "all her" fault. I was seeing a wedge going through our church. They never taught me about this in seminary. I called both couples into my office again. After again pointing out from the Bible what God had to say on the matter, I told them what was happening to the church. I then told them that for the sake of their own marriages and the unity of our church they should go to church elsewhere and not at the same church.

That was hard. They were my friends, and I loved them. But I wanted their marriages to survive as well as the church. They complied with my advice. The church was hurt from it all, but survived and recovered. Unfortunately their marriages didn't.

My Life Threatened

I mentioned earlier that the Defiance area had a drug problem. I also told how we had been able to lead some of those who were in the drug business to the Lord. But one Latino drug dealer was not happy with me. His wife and children attended fairly regularly, but he did not.

One night after a Christmas program he came into the church. I was in the front of the church, when he came into the building. Most of the people at that point were gone. But I was told that he had told some of our men that he was going to kill me. I don't know to this day why he wanted to kill me, but I knew that he was very capable of doing so. For some reason he did not come after me in the church, but left.

I did not tell Nancy anything about it. I did not want to upset her. I went to bed that night, but I don't think I slept very much, because I spent most of the night praying. That very week I learned that he had been arrested for possession of marijuana and was in jail. God had protected me.

CHAPTER   37

THE FUNNIEST THING I HAVE EVER SEEN IN THE MINISTRY

The OARBC Baptist churches that were located in northwest Ohio were formed into a fellowship called the North Bethel Fellowship of Regular Baptist Churches. They not only supported our church for its first five years, but helped start at least ten other churches in their area in ten years. It was a wonderful fellowship. We met as pastors every month, which was a great blessing to me as a young pastor.

Often, when a church already had a special speaker scheduled for a Sunday or a week of meetings, the North Bethel meeting was held at that church, so we could use the special speaker. Since we were having evangelistic meetings at our church, the North Bethel pastor's meeting was held at our church that Monday morning. Usually just the pastors came, but this was February, so the wives were invited too. We met in the auditorium, but did not have the preacher stand on the platform, since our group was only about 25-30. The evangelist stood behind a podium.

The speaker had been preaching for about twenty minutes and was really getting into his message. He was one of those fiery evangelists that did not stay behind a pulpit. He had just made another enthusiastic burst, when his pants fell down to his ankles. All I remember is that he was wearing boxers. I haven't been able to erase that picture. Without stopping or missing a beat or changing any expression, he swooped down and pulled up his pants and kept going. I did not dare look at Nancy. In fact, I wasn't sure if I really saw what I think I saw.

When he finished his message, I think we were still all in shock. Not one pastor mentioned it. We knew if we did we would not be able to stop laughing. But I remember that all of their eyes were very wide open, and they had a funny smile. They all could go home. Nancy and I had to take him out to eat.

Nancy was dying inside. She wanted to laugh so badly, but didn't dare. She was miserable, I could tell. Finally, near the end of the meal, the evangelist brought it up, and said something about wearing a nylon shirt and needing to wear his belt tighter. That was all of the excuse Nancy needed to let it all out. If you have known Nancy, you know that when she laughs, she really laughs. When she started, so did I. Fortunately he laughed too.

Somehow we made it through that meal and the rest of the week, but that story swept through our state fellowship of churches like a wildfire. I had pastors calling me and asking if it really happened. For years after that, the pastors that were in that meeting would bring it up to me. It always began the same: "Do you remember when…." It was without question the funniest experience I ever had in the ministry, although I came close to matching it with some of my pulpit bloopers which I will mention later.

CHAPTER 38

EXPERIENCES WITH LORI AND MARK

Three special experiences come to mind concerning Mark and Lori, while we were living in Defiance. The first has to do with the time Mark thought he was old enough to drive. He was only about three at the time. I was getting ready to leave our house on Harding Street, and Lori and Mark were outside playing in the front yard. I had started the car, but just before I backed out of the driveway, Nancy yelled from the house to say that I had a phone call. Instead of shutting the car off, I left it running – big mistake. I also left my door open.

That was all "Mario Andretti Mark" needed. Even though I was in the house less than a minute, Mark had made his way into the driver's seat and somehow had put the car into neutral. Because our driveway was on a slight slope down to the road, the car began to roll backwards toward the road.

I had just hung up when I heard Lori screaming for me. When I ran out the door, I almost panicked. Lori had opened the passenger door of the car and was trying to be super woman by trying to stop the rolling car. Mark was having the time of his life making the steering wheel go back and forth as he stood up in the driver's seat.

As quickly as I could I got Lori out of the way and jumped into the car in time to get it stopped, and ruin Mark's imaginative first driving experience. I have often thought about the tragedy that could have occurred if Lori had slipped under a wheel. I am so thankful to God that no one was hurt.

On another occasion, when we were living on Harding Street, I was carrying Lori into our house along with some silverware that was in a plastic bag. This may have been when we were moving into the Harding Street house, since Lori was very small. I wanted to get Lori into the house as quickly and safely as I could because of the bad weather. Somehow the point of a sharp knife made its way through the plastic bag and into my right hand. I could not put Lori down, so I ran into the house with the knife in my hand, which I was not able to remove until I safely laid Lori down. I still have the scar in my hand from that knife.

The third experience occurred during our first and only winter at our house on Hammersmith Road. The worst blizzard in the history of Ohio hit in January of 1978. Fifty mile an hour winds accompanied about two feet of snow. All of the roads were closed for three days. The snow had drifted up to the eves of our house. Our car was completely buried in our driveway and not visible. There was no way we could get to a store for food or milk for Lori and Mark. None of the roads had been plowed.

In the midst of that storm, someone knocked on our door and asked if we needed anything. We told him we needed milk and some food for the kids, and gave him some money. He went to the store on his snowmobile and brought us what we needed. To this day I have no idea who the kind stranger was – perhaps an angel. He certainly w

CHAPTER 39

SUMMARY OF OUR MINISTRY AT DEFIANCE

God gave us a great ministry at Defiance. He had accomplished much more in me than through me. I had learned a lot and drawn closer to him. The figures through 1977 showed that we had baptized 150 in those seven years, and had 454 professions of faith. That is an average of more than one a week. Though that is amazing by most standards, I don't see it that way. That is the way it is suppose to be. God expects His church to win the lost to Himself, and help those who are saved to grow. That is what the "normal" church is to do.

Obviously not all those who made professions of faith "panned out", and we included all professions of faith including those made by children during VBS. Jesus, in His parable of the four different kinds of soils, indicated that not all who profess salvation would be genuine. But I considered it my job to win as many as I could to Christ, and to disciple those who were willing to be discipled. I would leave the rest to Him.

I made mistakes at Defiance, but God blessed anyway. But we also saw lives changed, and God's name glorified. We counted every one of those dear people as our friends and still do.

PHASE   VI

OUR MINISTRY AT MOUNT VERNON

(1978-2008, Age 33-62)

Economic Changes

	1978	2008
• Cost of gasoline:	65 cents	Peaked at $4.11
• Cost of home:	$54,800	$284,000
• Average annual income:	$17,000	$52,029
• Postage stamp:	13 cents	41 cents

Political Changes

- Jimmy Carter became president in 1976. Inflation grew from 9% to 12%, 8 million people were unemployed, the national debt grew from $620 billion to $1 trillion, Iran Hostage Crisis.
- Ronald Reagan was president from 1981 to 1989. Taxes and inflation are reduced, conservatism rises, brings about the end of the Cold War against Russia, makes a famous speech in 1987, "Mr. Gorbachev, tear down this wall" (referring to the wall dividing East and West Berlin.
- George H.W. Bush became president in 1989. The Gulf War takes place and Saddam Hussein tries to kill Bush.
- Bill Clinton became president in 1993-2001. Economy does well, but the country dives morally with Bill Clinton leading the dive. He lies about his adulterous affair with Monica Lewinsky, but his approval ratings go up.
- George W. Bush was president from 2001-2009. He focuses on the war on terrorism after terrorists fly planes into the World Trade Center towers, the Pentagon, and attempt to fly one potentially into the White House on September 11, 2001.

Social Changes

- Gay marriages become acceptable and AIDS awareness begins. Country is in moral decline.
- Society becomes more self focused and the "Me" generation comes into being.
- Cell phones become popular, and the ability to see as well as hear the person one is talking to becomes a reality.
- Liberals take control of the news reporting and seek to move our country toward socialism.

CHAPTER 40

HOW GOD CALLED US TO MOUNT VERNON

I had been having uneasiness at Defiance for about a year. I loved the people at our church. But I did not know what was bothering me. In the fall of 1987 we moved into our new house on Hammersmith Road near the church. It was a beautiful ranch style home. It was so great to be near the church. So why was I feeling so uneasy?

"Filling in" at Mount Vernon

Then in July of 1978 I received a call from Rev. Umbaugh. He was looking for dad Crown and had not been able to get a hold of him. I told Rev. Umbaugh that the reason he had not been able to reach dad Crown was because they were on vacation up in Wisconsin. He then told me why he wanted to speak to him. He had been meeting with another group of people in the Mount Vernon, Ohio, area who had already started Sunday services and needed someone to preach to them on the first two Sundays of August. He knew that dad Crown had helped to start churches in the past, and thought he might be interested in going to Mount Vernon.

I had been asked to speak at Youth Camp at Skyview Ranch the first week of August, so I had already arranged to have speakers at Defiance those first two Sundays. So I told him that I could help him out if he wanted me to, since I would be available, and Skyview Ranch was not too far from Mount Vernon. But I quickly added that I had no intention of leaving Defiance. That was fine with him, so I planned to speak at Mount Vernon the Sunday before and the Sunday after my week at Skyview.

The group at Mount Vernon had banded together in July of 1977, and begun Sunday services on September 25th of that year.   Though they had a lot of enthusiasm, they lacked direction. Rev. Umbaugh heard of the group through a member of the Fallsburg Baptist Church, and had his first meeting with them in mid October of 1977. The group, which was having a planning meeting at the home of Jeff Zolman, had decided to call themselves the "Mount Vernon Christian Center". Just as the meeting was being dismissed, Rev. Umbaugh arrived and encouraged the group to "be what you are". They, then, adopted the name of Faith Baptist Church at that meeting.

After meeting with the group for several months they approved their constitution on April 28, 1978. A Recognition Council composed of the West Moriah Association of Regular Baptist Churches (Columbus area) recognized the group as a duly organized Baptist Church, and they were received into the GARBC in June of that year.

The people had been holding their Sunday services in the basement of the city community building called The Memorial Building. Sunday School was to start at 9:30 am. That first Sunday when I was scheduled to speak, I thought I was getting there late. But when I arrived at 9:25, there was still no one there. We thought we were at the wrong place at first. But soon a man by the name of Ken Bandy showed up, and some more began to trickle in.

They were a very friendly bunch. They made us feel very much at home. Nancy and I sang, and I preached.
After the service they all came up to us and asked if we were going to be their pastor. I didn't know quite how
to respond. They were acting like we were potentially their new pastor.

After that Sunday Nancy and I went on to Skyview, which was only about an hour's drive from there. I began
my Bible study series of messages with the teens, but I couldn't stop thinking about those people in Mount Vernon. Nancy knew what was going through my mind. She made her feelings very clear, which was not that un-
common: "I'm not leaving Defiance. We just moved into our beautiful new home!"

Using a Horse to Speak to Nancy

Though Nancy has always had a fear of cats and dogs, she has surprisingly always loved horses. She loves to
watch the horse races on television, and any program that has horses (except westerns). So when she had an
opportunity to ride a horse at Skyview Ranch, she was all in. I was elated that she wanted to do it, because, I
had always loved to ride horses as well, although I had only done so a few times. I thought maybe it might be
something we could do together in the future.

Nancy had never ridden before, but she seemed to be so happy up there on her horse as we left the coral. The
horses all were trained to walk in single file, so my horse fell in line several horses behind Nancy's. We came to
a place in the trail where the horses were scheduled to run for a ways. We had been told in advance to expect
the horses to run. That whole ride I was looking forward to getting to that spot.

My previous limited riding experience had been as a teen. One time while going riding with our youth group, I
was told by the man in charge of the horses, that my horse used to be a lead horse and loved to run in the lead.
He had told me to hold him back until the rest had begun to run, so the other horses wouldn't run before they
were supposed to. When we came close to the opening where the horses were to run, my horse wanted to run,
just like the man said. So I held him back as best as I could, while the others took off. My horse was bucking
up in the air and jumping all over the place. As soon as the last horse had gone by me, I turned my horse lose,
and said, "Let's go boy". And did we ever go. We went flying by the other horses in no time. I loved it. So, I
was really looking forward to running my horse. I remember how much fun I had had before.

Soon the horses began to run. But before we had run very far they all stopped ahead of me. I couldn't see what
the problem was, because there were trees all around us. So I asked the riders ahead of me what was going on.
They replied, "Oh, some lady fell off her horse."

I knew that had to be Nancy. I jumped off of my horse and ran on ahead. Sure enough Nancy was sitting on the
ground acting somewhat dazed. After checking her out, it was apparent that she had no injuries. She said
that she didn't hurt anywhere. When I asked her what had happened, she didn't seem to know. It was strange.
After being sure she was ok, I helped her back on her horse, and we all rode back to the barn.

There was a very steep hill that went up from the barn toward the lodge area. It was nick named "Cardiac Hill"
for a good reason. A few years later I would try to ski down that hill only in a different area from where we

were walking. After walking about a fourth of the way up the hill, Nancy stopped and said, "Where are we?" I was puzzled by her question, but answered, "We are at Skyview Ranch". "What are we doing here?" "I'm the speaker for the week." We went a little further up the hill. She asked again using the exact same words: "Where are we?" "We are at Skyview Ranch." "What are we doing here?" "I'm the speaker for the week." This went on several times as we made our way up the hill. I was petrified. She didn't even remember that she had asked the same questions. Something was seriously wrong with my wife, and I didn't know what to do.

I took Nancy up to our room that was in the old camp owned farm house. After suggesting that she lay down for a while, I went to get the camp nurse. She came and checked Nancy over, and said she was going to call a doctor. The doctor told her what I already knew. She had amnesia. He said it could have been caused by the fall off the horse, or by an emotional trauma. Since she had no signs of injury, I suspected that she had become frightened when the horses started to run, and either tried to get off, or fell off. I'll never really know. But the doctor assured us that she would get better in time. There was little to do but keep an eye on her.

I had to continue to preach at my assigned sessions, but I had a hard time focusing. I was worried about Nancy. Someone had to be with her all the time. She could not remember how to get to the bathroom. And once in the bathroom, she couldn't remember how to get back to the bedroom. She remembered who I was, and the kids, fortunately, but not much more. A couple of days after this, she was starting to feel better. She was leaning out our window, which was on the second floor, when all of a sudden the window came crashing down on her head. The director's mother, who was with her at the time, helped her get back into bed. Her head hurt badly, but she began to remember after that.

God Convinces Us to Go to Mount Vernon

I finished speaking at Skyview, and we headed back to Mount Vernon. We stayed that weekend with one of the families in the church, Dennis and Sharon Zolman. That weekend one of the popular boys in high school, a doctor's son, was killed in a tragic auto accident. The Zolman's teenage daughter, Tammy, was distraught over the death of the boy, but also over the fact that she didn't believe she was saved. That weekend Tammy accepted Christ as her Savior. She would be the first of hundreds that were to accept Christ through our ministry in Mount Vernon.

We preached and sang again that Sunday. The people again asked if we were going to be their pastor. They already had three men that formed their deacons. They asked to meet with me on Sunday afternoon. They basically wanted to know if I would consider being their pastor. I told them that I would pray about it.

The next day on our way home to Defiance I just couldn't stop thinking about the people in Mount Vernon. I was excited about the prospect of helping them organize and build their church. They already seemed to have some leadership type men. I saw great potential, but I loved the people at Defiance. I was torn all the rest of the month of August.

By this time Nancy had totally changed her outlook on the matter. She knew she needed to be submissive to whatever God wanted us to do, even if it meant leaving our beautiful new house. What mattered most was doing what God wanted us to do. Later I often would jokingly say to her that God had to knock her off her horse to get us to go to Mount Vernon.

On August 26th the Mount Vernon church, following the morning service, voted to call me to come and be their first pastor. I had not yet made my decision to do so, at least not out loud. Sometime early in the month of September Dick Jessup, one of the deacons from Mount Vernon, called me and asked in his direct manner, "Well, are you coming?" I knew by then what I needed to say, "Yes, we're coming".

I shared the news with our deacons at Defiance, and said that I would stay through October 25th, which was Lori's birthday. My first Sunday as pastor in Mount Vernon would be October 29th, although we did go down to Mount Vernon earlier in the month for a charter signing service, which we had scheduled.

My Resignation and Selling Our House

On a Sunday morning, late in September at the end of the service, I announced my resignation. The people were shocked. It was so hard to do. We loved the people, but believed God had another job for us to do. After the service most of the people told us that they understood and would be praying for us. One of the couples that had been such a help to us at Defiance was Paul and Karen Keim. Paul had graduated from Moody Bible Institute's aviation program. He also played the trombone and had relieved me by taking over the job as choir director. We often sang together or played our horns together. As Karen came up to Nancy, in the midst of her tears she said, "We are so sorry to see you go, but can we buy your house?" God sold our house that same day.

We considered that to be another confirmation of God's direction. I later told Paul that I would have three different realtors appraise the house and would sell it to him for the lowest appraisal. We couldn't think of anyone we would rather have the house than them. Though the plan was for the church to buy the house at some point in the future as a parsonage, I didn't think the church was financially in a position to buy it at that time, because of having to meet their mortgage payment. So I ask Paul to check with the church, when he was ready to sell the house in the future, to see if they wanted to buy it for a parsonage.

Moving to Mount Vernon

October 25 (Lori's birthday), 1978, fell on a Wednesday, so my last official ministry at Faith Baptist in Defiance was leading prayer meeting. I had been visiting a couple in the area and the man had trusted Christ. When he learned that I was leaving, he asked if I would baptize him. I agreed, but since his request came a week before I was to leave, the only time I could baptize him was on the very last night. So I ended my ministry in Defiance with a baptismal service. That was neat. By 9:00 pm the men from Mount Vernon were at our house with their trucks. I also drove down with them that night and came back the next day for the final load, which included Nancy and the kids. We had moved to Mount Vernon.

CHAPTER   41

GETTING STARTED

Our New Home

After announcing our resignation to our people in Defiance, we made several trips to Mount Vernon primarily to search for a house. We worked with one of the most successful real estate ladies in the area, who found us a three bedroom ranch style home at 12 Upland Terrace in Mount Vernon. It had a full basement, was located on a dead end street, and in a nice neighborhood near the main shopping area on the east side of town. It was a brand new home built by one of the contractors from nearby Fredericktown.

Though it was located on a hill, I still had some concerns about the basement leaking. So I met with the contractor and realtor to ask him about it. He assured me that was not a problem. So we bought the house and moved in. I would later discover that he lied, and was unable to get him to do anything about it. I eventually fixed the problem myself, which required a lot of back breaking work. But we loved the house, and it was a great place to raise the family.

Our Neighbors

The Walton's

We had great neighbors on the entire street. The first neighbor that I met was Brad Walton. Brad and Barb Walton lived just below us on the same side of the street. Our house sat quite a bit above his because of the way the street went up a big hill. Our houses were also quite close to one another. So Brad was concerned that water would not run down from my side and run into his house. It was a legitimate concern, so I assured him that I would put a slight valley between our properties. My first impression of Brad was that he was a bit of a "stick in the mud". I would learn later that I was so wrong.

One of the first things I did after we moved into our home was to visit our neighbors. When I visited Brad and Barb, I discovered that they had just accepted Christ as their Savior. They had attended a Businessmen's Association meeting at the invitation of their dentist, and had gotten saved at that meeting. But they continued to attend the local Episcopal Church because Barb's relative was the priest there. They did admit that they were not in agreement with its doctrine and were not getting anything out of the services. But at that time they were not ready to make a change.

I just started to pray for them. About a month after that visit, their youngest son got into some trouble and was in jail. Brad came to me and asked if I would go visit him. I quickly agreed. Their son was messed up on alcohol and drugs. He did pray with me at that visit, but his life later did not show any change. But my willingness to help their son moved Brad and Barb to start coming to our new church. They later were baptized and became faithful members. Brad would eventually become chairman of our deacons and a good friend. Both have passed away now and are in heaven together.

The Gower's

Mr. and Mrs. Gower lived in the house just above us. They were a sweet elderly couple in their nineties. They were fun to watch when they mowed their lawn. They took turns. One would mow a circle around their yard, and then the other would do the same. They seemed to be having fun. You never saw one without the other.

One day Mrs. Gower came over and relayed the funniest story. She and her husband had locked themselves out of their house. They managed to find a back window that was partly open. So Mr. Gower got down on his hands and knees, while Mrs. Gower climbed up on his back, then stood up, and crawled through the window. If there had been a video of that, it certainly would have taken first place in America's Funniest Home Videos. Unfortunately Mr. and Mrs. Gower passed away not too long after we became their neighbors, but I believe they did know the Lord. Another couple bought their home, the Mickley's.

The Mickley's

Mike and Beckie Mickley were a neat couple. I, of course, invited them to church. Mike had a Catholic background, but Beckie did not. Over time I befriended Mike and they began to attend our church. I remember the day when Mike came over to our house and wanted to be saved. Both accepted Christ and became members of our church. They still attend there as far as I know.

Our Income

Unlike Defiance, we had no churches supporting us at Mount Vernon. I never asked for a set amount of money or asked for a raise in any of the churches that I pastored. I always believed that God would take care of us, and He always did. The salary that the people in Mount Vernon said they would pay me was less than I was receiving in Defiance. I remember what the treasure said, when he told me what they would pay me: "We will give you $ X.00 per week. If that doesn't come in (the offering), we will give you what does." They were taking a step of faith just to pay me what they did. I never missed a paycheck.

But because I needed more income to live, I asked God for wisdom and His help. I have heard of God supplying needs by sending surprise gifts of money in the mail. God has not provided that way for me. He has always chosen to give me more work. So God provided a couple of plumbing jobs for me to do. He also provided an opportunity to hold evangelistic meetings for two churches. Their love offerings combined with the fact that the church had grown sufficiently to give us raises, helped to meet our financial need.

The Charter Service

After making the decision to pastor the Faith Baptist Church in Mount Vernon I was really pastoring two churches at the same time. I was living in Defiance and doing all the duties of a pastor there including planning how to announce my resignation, planning to list our house, and planning our move. At the same time I was seeing what organizational steps still needed to be taken for the Mount Vernon church, and trying to find a place for us to live there. This required several trips to Mount Vernon during the months of September and October.

Though the Mount Vernon church had already approved a constitution, had a recognition service, and elected deacons, they had forgotten a very important step. They had not formed their official membership. New churches usually formed their initial membership by having those spiritually qualified for membership and desiring it, to sign a charter. After explaining this to the people they all agreed to have a charter signing service on October 5, 1978.

I composed a letter announcing the service and sent it to all who had been attending the new group. In the letter I explained, "In signing the charter one is saying in effect, 'I stand with this church in its doctrinal position as stated in the articles of faith. I agree with the purpose of its formation to win the lost and build the saints. I purpose to give my support to it as my signature indicates.'"

Nancy and I, of course, made the three hour trip down to Mount Vernon for this special occasion. Since they had no church building, and the Memorial Building (a community building), which was their usual meeting place, was not available, the service was held at the YMCA building. They had brought in food for the occasion, which was common for this group. Nancy and I sang, and I again explained what the Biblical requirements for membership were, and what it meant to sign the charter. We also stated that if some were not able to be at that service they would have until the end of the month to sign and become charter members.

There were about forty who attended that service and signed the charter. The church would date its beginning and future anniversaries from that date, and celebrate it on the second Sunday of October.

My First Sunday as Pastor

That first Sunday as their pastor on October 29, 1978, was amazing! When the invitation was given at the close of the service thirteen people came forward. Several of them wanted to be baptized, so that afternoon we all went to Apple Valley Lake at King Beach and baptized ten of them. Apple Valley is restricted to property owners only, but there were enough property owners in the group to allow us to use the area. We had almost seventy in attendance that first Sunday. The people really worked at inviting their friends out to church.

Our First Christmas

The Amish Meal

The people at Mount Vernon, like most Baptists, loved to fellowship and loved to eat. So our first church Christmas "party" was at an Amish home. Knox County, where Mount Vernon is located and is the county seat, has a very large population of Amish. Holmes County, which is adjacent to Knox County, has the largest population of Amish in the United States, next to Lancaster, Pennsylvania. I learned that there are different orders of Amish that seem to be pretty much based on what they regard as sinful or worldly. The most "conservative" do not put any reflectors on their buggies, yet they might use tobacco. The more progressive Amish drive cars. These usually have a better understanding of salvation by grace and are called Mennonites. The Amish home where we were meeting were Mennonite.

I had never had a meal like we had that night. The wonderful Amish lady host had prepared homemade every-thing: raisin bread, butter, cottage cheese, apple butter, mashed potatoes, gravy, roast beef, chicken, pies, just to name a few items. Yes I still remember every item. It was amazing! Did I mention that I like to eat. Unfortu-nately our church was too big to meet in her home after that. But we continued to have a great relationship with that sect of Amish. They often used our building for their weddings (which were an all day event), to which I was invited.

The First Christmas Gift

The Sunday before Christmas the people asked Nancy and I to come to the front of the congregation. They then presented us with a box wrapped in Christmas paper. When we took the wrapping paper off, we discovered that the box had a slot in the top with a dollar bill sticking out of the slot. The dollar had a piece of paper attached with the word "pull" written on it. So we pulled on the dollar bill. As we did we soon discovered that it had another dollar bill taped to it. We kept pulling and pulling and pulling. I think there were about $50.00 dollars taped end to end to one another. The people loved every minute of it, and so did we. They were showing their love toward us. And we loved them. They also gave us a card, which I still have. Inside were written the words, "Pastor, the packaging was from you know who --- (meaning Mel Crown). The contents, however, is from your devoted congregation – from deep in their hearts."

That was the beginning of the church's Christmas tradition of giving us a "bonus" every year at Christmas time. Though they never again taped dollar bills together, they always took up an offering and generously showed their love to us, and in later years, to the rest of the pastoral staff.

CHAPTER 42

PHILIP'S ARRIVAL

Sometime in December of 1978 Nancy became pregnant again. When we discovered that she was pregnant we became concerned since both Lori and Mark's births had complications. Fortunately there were two very good baby doctors in Mount Vernon, who had a practice together, and Nancy was able to become their patient. After Nancy met with her doctor he made it clear that Nancy's build was not conducive to delivering a baby safely, and would need to deliver by means of a cesarean (C-section). That did not come as a surprise to us, and actually gave us some relief. Philip's birth was scheduled for September 23rd ,near my birthday.

Nancy's pregnancy went well with no surprises; none until September 15th. Nancy went into labor. Our babies, for some reason, all had a mind of their own as to when they wanted to make their entrance. And all of them were either born on a Sunday or in connection with a Sunday. Philip would top both Lori and Mark in that department. Nancy's doctor was not available on that Saturday, the 15th. So Nancy was given medicine to slow down her labor, so the doctor could perform the C-section the next day, Sunday.

I had my message all prepared. I have never written out my messages word for word, but I always made very detailed outlines and notes. Since the decision to deliver Philip was made late on Saturday, there was no time to get another minister to fill in for me. So I called one of our deacons, Earl Shirkey, and told him he was on for the next morning. He almost went into shock. But when he recovered, he graciously said he would do it since he understood my predicament. I was able to get my sermon notes to him and went over it with him. He preached my sermon the next day. I was told it was one of my best sermons!! I often kidded Earl about that later.

At the time of Philip's birth, Mount Vernon still had two hospital buildings. They were under one management, but a few blocks apart. The one Nancy was in was called Mercy Hospital, which used to be under the ownership of the Catholic Church. It was located directly across the street from the community building, where our church met.

Philip was born exactly in time for church, 11:00 am. Again, I was not able to be in the room when he was born, but I was right outside. I remember so vividly when the nurse brought him out in the hallway. She let me see him before they cleaned him up. He was a beautiful baby with no physical problems. I was so thankful. And Nancy did well, also. Soon we were able to take both mommy and baby home, and introduce Philip to his brother and sister.

CHAPTER 43

LORI AND MARK BEGIN TO SERVE THE LORD

Mark's First Sermon

I knew that all of our children were a gift from God. They were all special. Each of their unique births emphasized that to me. I knew that God's grace was poured out on me when He allowed me to be their father. I did not deserve them. I also knew that God had a special plan for each of them and would use them in His own way. Shortly after each of them was born, I prayed over them in their bed and gave them to God. I knew full well what that meant. God could do whatever he wanted with them including taking him or her home to heaven if that bought Him glory. Though that was hard for me, deep down I knew that giving them to God was not only the right thing to do, it was the best thing to do for them, as well as for Nancy and me.

God's plan for Mark's life was clear almost from the beginning of his life, if not to him, certainly to me. God had spared his life for a very important mission. When Mark came to me and wanted to preach, I suspected what that mission was. He was only six. At first I was very hesitant to give him that opportunity. I was afraid that if he got up in front of people and had a bad experience, it might hinder any future desires he might have to preach, or do anything for the Lord. But he kept after me, almost begging me to let him preach. Finally I gave in, but I wanted to make it as easy as possible for him.

The Mount Vernon church always had what was called "Opening Exercises" before the Sunday School classes began. Everyone met together for a song or two before going to their classes. That was when birthdays were recognized, and special offerings were taken. There weren't as many people there at that time since the church people were notoriously late for Sunday School. I thought that would be an ideal time for Mark to preach his message.

I asked Mark what he was going to preach about, and he went off about Adam and Eve and Jesus dying on the cross. Then he asked **me** a question: "How am I going to know when to quit". That's when I knew he was going to be a preacher. He wasn't concerned about his message. He already had that down. He didn't want to be too "long winded". I chuckled to myself about that one. So we came up with a signal, which I would give him when his three minutes were up. I would sit in the front and hold out my open hand in front of me, so only he could see it. That would be his signal to wind it down.

I only wish I had recorded Mark that day. I stood him on top of a table, so he could be seen. He stuck to his message plan. He started with Adam and Eve and somehow ended up with Jesus on the cross. He was still going strong when I held out my hand, and Mark soon closed his message. There was no mass revival that broke out, or tons of souls flooding the aisles. We did not have that many people there. But God heard, and He was very pleased. Mark had done what God wanted him to do that day. There was also one very proud papa.

Lori and Mark Singing

Lori always loved to sing almost as soon as she could talk. And when she sang, she always sang with all she had in her. Mark also loved to sing, but, unlike Lori, that was not his favorite thing to do. I'm not sure when Lori started to sing the harmony part, but probably about three or four.

One day one of our members, Earl Shirkey, stopped over at our house and had an unusual request. His wife's birthday was coming up in a few days, and he wanted to give her a unique gift. He wanted to give her a recording of Mark and Lori singing "Jesus Loves Me". When Lori and Mark agreed, He set up his cassette tape recorder, and we made the recording in the living room of our house. Mark sang the melody and Lori harmonized. A few years later Earl gave that recording to me. I still have it. Lori was around eight and Mark was probably six.

CHAPTER 44

HUNTING AGAIN

It had been several years since I had gone hunting. In fact, I had not gone hunting since I was married, thirteen years earlier. It certainly wasn't because I had lost interest. I still loved the outdoors and loved to hunt. But during my seminary days and my years at Defiance, there really weren't any good places to hunt. But there was another very big reason I hadn't hunted. Nancy was deathly afraid of guns. Did I mention that we are opposites? So I left my two guns in my closet, and never really thought that much about it.

But the first fall that we were in Mount Vernon, one of the members, Werely Keen, asked me to go deer hunting with him and some of his relatives. There were plenty of places to hunt in the Mount Vernon area, as I would soon discover, and deer were relatively plentiful. I was so pumped about the opportunity to go hunting again. Ohio only allowed shot guns to be used during the regular gun season, but I had a shotgun – my old faithful 20 gage that I had had since I was thirteen. I had never shot a deer slug through it, but I knew it would work.

Nancy somehow did not share my excitement. In fact, she was dead set against it. She was certain that I would get shot. It was true that I had kind of a reputation for not always choosing the safe way of doing things. But when it came to handling guns, that really was a different matter. I had learned the hard way by almost shooting my dad's foot, that gun safety was no joke, and nothing with which to take chances. But I just could not convince Nancy that I would be ok if I went hunting. I knew she was serious about how she felt, and I loved her, so I had resigned myself to saying no to the invitation.

When Janice Keen heard how Nancy felt, she decided to talk to Nancy. Somehow she accomplished what I could never have done. She convinced Nancy that it was safe, and no one would be hurt. I was going hunting!! Yippee!!

I don't think I even practiced shooting before going hunting. I just bought some 20 gage slugs ahead of time and was ready to go when Werely picked me up early on opening morning. We drove east of Mount Vernon half way toward Coshocton to a property that he had permission on which to hunt. He was a well driller, so he had a lot of contacts with property owners. I followed him into the woods in the darkness with only his flash-light to guide the way along the trail that wound through very thick brush. We kicked out a couple of does on our way in. We finally got to the spot where I was to hunt, which was where the woods met the corner of a field. I stood with my back to a tree, while Werely went on to the back side of the field.

Sometime about 9:00 am a three point buck came running through the woods about thirty yards from me, cross-ing the trail we had taken to get to our hunting spots. I quickly pulled up and shot aiming for his vitals. The deer kept running without any sign of being hit. He just kept running.

I walked over to the opening on the trail where he was when I shot at him, but didn't see any blood. I looked in the direction of where he had run. I could see the leaves kicked up, so I followed as best I could. The kicked up leaves trail that I followed took me into extremely thick brush. I walked into this area probably about fifty yards or so, and still saw no blood. I figured I had missed him, so I went back to my tree and waited until 11:00, when Werely came and got me.

When we went to lunch I told him what had happened, so he suggested that we take the gun some place after lunch, where I could shoot it and see how it shot using slugs. So after lunch we went to a field. I aimed at a rock out in the field (not a good idea) and hit it. After I shot it a few times, I realized that the gun shot just fine. I also knew that I had a clear shot at the deer. I made up my mind that as soon as we went back to our hunting spot, I would look a little harder for that deer, which I thought I had missed.

When I got back to the spot where I had shot at the deer, I again began to follow the kicked up leaves. But this time I went further down into the very thick brush. It was so thick it was almost impossible to make any progress, but I kept going. I had gone approximately fifty yards farther than I had gone that morning, when I spotted something white ahead. Sure enough, there was my deer. I couldn't believe it. After field dressing it, I hauled it out.

I learned a valuable lesson that day. When you shoot at a deer, don't be too quick to give up looking for it. But a bigger lesson than that is this: always shoot your gun before going hunting. It is absolutely essential to be confident in your gun and your ability to shoot it accurately. You owe it the God, Who gives you the opportunity to take one of His created creatures, to make a humane kill and not to waste an animal.

We took the deer to Werely's barn and hung it up before taking it to the processer. Nancy came over to see it and brought Lori and Mark. I don't remember Mark's reaction; he may have stayed in the car. But Lori burst into tears to think that her daddy had done such a mean thing as to kill a deer. I think she finally recovered.

Nancy wasn't too excited about fixing any venison, but she probably felt she had to at least try to do so, since Janice had told her how to fix it in the crock pot. So she prepared it according to her directions. As soon as she tasted it, she loved it. In fact, when the meal was over she looked me in the eye and simply said, "Go get another one." I never had a problem with Nancy not wanting me to go hunting after that. I can confidently say that she has become an expert at preparing venison.

CHAPTER 45

FAMILY FUN

Skiing with Lori and Mark

The city of Mount Vernon is somewhat on a dividing line in Ohio's landscape. Northwestern Ohio is extremely flat. In fact, when coming from the west into Mount Vernon, it is still relatively flat. But on the east side of Mount Vernon is starts to get very hilly. On the south east side of Mount Vernon, where our church was to be located, there is a Country Club Golf Course. It has very large hills. In the winter time it is a favorite spot for sled riders of all kinds. When I heard about it, I knew I had to check it out. So I took Lori, Mark, my skis, and our sled and headed to "Country Club Hill".

While Lori and Mark used the sled, I went down the hill on my skis. That was fun, but I really wanted Lori and Mark to enjoy what I was experiencing. So I came up with the idea of standing them on my feet as I skied. There was a very steep part of the hill, but there was also a gentler slope, which I thought would work for the kids. I'm not sure which one I took with me first, but the plan worked great. We went for a very long ride and didn't fall, fortunately for me. Nancy would have killed me if she knew.

Family Vacations

Nancy and I took the kids on a vacation every year. I thought of vacations as a necessity for our family. I worked hard in the ministry. It was demanding on me. But it was also demanding on our family. I had to be gone a lot of evenings, calling on people, or making emergency calls. Vacations were a time, when Nancy didn't have to worry about someone calling me away to solve their marriage problem, and the kids had dad all to themselves.

Wisconsin

We often continued to go up to Wisconsin fishing with mom and dad Crown. One year we turned our station wagon into a camper and camped at the Wisconsin Dells. Nancy had made curtains for the windows, and I had put a mattress in the back for the kids, while Nancy and I slept in the seats. That idea worked for a while until we had a huge thunder storm and the kids all freaked out, especially Lori.

Florida

When Philip was a few months old, we went down to Florida in our new station wagon during spring break. Our station wagon was a Caprice Estate Chevy, and was one of the nicest vehicles I have ever owned. It had power everything. It even had a built in CB radio, which was big back then. I had a mattress in the back for Lori and Mark, and Philip slept in his car bed. Mom and dad lived in Florida after he sold his plumbing business, so we had a place to stay when we got there.

We had a great time in Florida and were on our way home. I mentioned earlier that the economy was in bad shape in those days. But gas prices had also taken a huge jump in price. Not only that, but gasoline was sometimes limited in availability. I knew I was very low on gas, and had been looking for a gas station for miles, but had not found one that was open. It was a Sunday morning, and we were trying to get back in time to see our people at church, even though I had a pulpit supply for the day.

We were on the north side of Columbus, and had made it to the Westerville exit, where we intended to get off on Route 3, so we could head north to Mount Vernon. When the car began to chug and sputter, I knew we were running out of gas. We had already made it up the off ramp, and I was able to get the car off of the road onto the berm. The off ramp circled like a horse shoe down to Route 3 that ran perpendicular underneath our off ramp. I could look off to my right and see a gas station below us at the end of the off ramp, but I didn't know if it was open. But I knew I had no choice but to walk down there, and hope I could get enough gas to get home.

I was just opening my car door, when Mark said, "Dad, there's a car coming behind us fast". So I lifted my legs back inside and pulled the door towards me but not enough to latch it and waited for the car to go by us. I had no sooner done that, when the car smashed into the back of us going 70 miles an hour. I learned later that the driver was a nurse, who had worked all night and had fallen asleep at the wheel, while driving on the bypass around Columbus. Had she not hit us, she would have gone over the embankment on our right and been killed.

Fortunately I had packed all of the luggage in the very back of the station wagon behind the kids, which absorbed most of the impact. The back of the car had folded up like an accordion. But the kids were close to the back seat. The impact forced the mostly closed door into my left shoulder, which was hurting. After checking with the kids and Nancy, they did not seem to be seriously injured. Lori, who had been sitting up complained that her back hurt. Glass had shattered everywhere including into Philip's car bed, but he was not injured at all. The driver of the other car had apparently broken her leg. Soon an ambulance came and took us all to the hospital, where we were all checked out and released.

I must have gotten in touch with some of our people in Mount Vernon, because one of the couples soon showed up and took us home, sore, but alive and wiser.

Camping in Pennsylvania

Nancy and I thought that we should try taking the kids camping. We knew the tent camping idea would not work. We had found that out when I was a youth pastor at Argos. We rented a pop-up camper once. Although that worked, it was not ideal for us. Then I saw a used camper advertised for a little over $1000.00. I called the owner and made arrangements to meet him at the camp ground where he kept it.

When we finally got to the camp ground and saw it, it was obvious that it really needed work. I made him an offer, which he quickly accepted. I later learned, that I should have offered a lot less for it. I made arrangements with Wes Crum to help me pull it back to our house, since Wes had a powerful pick up. We did not even make it out of the camp ground before one of the tires went flat. We managed to pull it to a nearby gas station, where I bought a new tire and put it on. The rest of the trip home was pretty uneventful.

Once I got the camper home, I began to examine it more closely. I discovered that the roof had leaked at the front of the camper causing much of the wood to rot. The floor was also rotten near the front door. I borrowed a nail gun and air compressor, took out the rotten material, and repaired the damaged areas. I was also able to fix the roof.

Our first adventure with that camper was a trip to Hershey Park Pennsylvania. That was a great place to camp with the kids. There was a nice swimming pool for the kids, and a free trolley car ride to the Hershey factory, which was not the real factory, but a model that showed how the chocolate was made. That tour was all free, so we took it several times. There was also an amusement park nearby which we went to once.

Somehow Nancy heard about some factory outlets that were in Reading, Pennsylvania, about an hour's drive from Hershey. If there is a bargain within 100 miles, Nancy will somehow find it. The factory outlets that were in Reading were located in old factory buildings. Whatever those factories had been producing had gone out of business. So some clothing companies purchased and occupied them, and sold their products at bargain rates. This was probably the beginning of what we now know as "Factory Outlets".

I remember our first trip there. Nancy was able to find school cloths for Lori and Mark at a fraction of the cost elsewhere. She also found some tremendous bargains for herself. After that first year we made several vacation trips to Hershey, which always included a trip to the factory outlets. We also made a trip over to Gettysburg and took a tour of that area. Since Lancaster, Pennsylvania, was also near, we went there as well.

On one of those early trips, Mark broke out in hives all over his body. He must have eaten something that he was allergic to. He was miserable for awhile, but seemed to recover quickly.

Myrtle Beach

When Lori was about Junior High age we began to go to Myrtle Beach. By this time I had sold our camper for more that I paid for it. The kids were no longer interested in camping and wanted to do something different. I had led Bill Drown to the Lord, and he and his family were attending our church at that time. They were the ones who told us about Myrtle Beach. They always went there for their vacations, along with Bill's in-laws, the Pattons.

We rented a condominium there for a week and enjoyed walking in the sand. I always loved getting out in the waves on an air mattress. One time I apparently drifted out too far and got into trouble with a lifeguard, who whistled me in. I also got stung by a jellyfish which hurt like a bee sting. The lifeguard poured vinegar on the bite area which took care of it. Mark liked to body surf or use a boogie board. Philip always wanted to get his picture drawn by the artists in the mall. Nancy, of course, always found places to shop. Lori…I think she may have liked watching the boys, and I don't mean her brothers.

Gatlinburg

Another favorite vacation spot for our family was Gatlinburg, Tennessee. There was, of course, the beauty of the mountains and scenery. And Nancy always found more shopping outlets. But the fun for Phil, Mark, and me was always the go-carts. We loved to race each other. I think Lori got involved in it as well, but not like us guys. We took it seriously and were very competitive. The faster they would go the better. We always tried to get the fastest car by watching the cars for awhile. I have to admit, I may have spun my sons out a few times. And when they got me to spin out, they were on "cloud nine". Sometimes we could find coupons in a local advertising magazine, which gave us a discount at the go-cart track. We would get as many coupons as we could.

On one occasion there was a metal track, which required a driver's license to participate. That was just too tempting for me. As usual we watched to see which car was the fastest. In this case, there was no doubt. One of the cars was clearly the fastest, and I really wanted it. Somehow I managed to get that car. I had so much fun that day. I was passing everybody and lapping some. I held the gas peddle to the floor for most of the ride, which meant that I was going sideways around the curves. What I didn't know was that one of the workers was timing me. After the ride was over, he said in amazement that I had gone around the track in twelve seconds, which was apparently some kind of record.

CHAPTER   46

THORNS AMIDST THE ROSES

The Charismatic Problem

I soon began to discover that all was not rosy in Mount Vernon. Even though their doctrinal statement read that the "sign gifts" had ceased, there were some that believed that speaking in tongues was still something that should be practiced in the church. Though they were in the minority, they still held strongly to their position. I wrote a paper on that subject entitled, "Shall We Speak In Tongues" showing that that particular gift ceased with the completion of the Bible. God had given revelatory gifts to the church, so that when the church met the people could have some revelation from God to teach and exhort them. But when "that which was perfect (complete)" came (I Cor. 13:10), there was no more need for "that which was in part". Those who believed differently either eventually left, or changed their thinking. So this problem was not a major one.

The Dick Jessup Story

I had never met anyone like Dick Jessup. He was one of the leaders of the group. He had a lot of things straight doctrinally. He loved the Bible, especially Bible prophecy. He was an adult Sunday School teacher and chairman of the deacons. He invited many to our new church. But he had a personality that was domineering. I believe he always meant well, but he seemed to think it was his responsibility to point out what I did wrong. I believe, as I look back on it, that he may have been trying to help me to be better. But that was not how it came across to me. It seemed that every Monday Dick would stop by and want to tell me what I did wrong the previous day, or discuss something that would add to my tension. I got to the point where I dreaded to see Dick coming.

On one occasion, I had to disagree with Dick in a deacons meeting. It was hard to do, but I had to replace someone who was heading up the teens at that time, who he didn't want replaced. The parents had come to me complaining about the immaturity of the youth leader. It was imperative that we not lose parents over this issue in our little group. Finally one of the other deacons had the courage to agree with me, and the youth leader was replaced. But that was typical of the difficulty I had working with him. I began to pray seriously that God would change Dick. I wasn't sure how God was going to accomplish it, but something had to give. I was not having a godly attitude towards him.

I was reading the life story of Dr. Robert Ketchum, who I mentioned earlier. The book was entitled, "Portrait of Obedience". There was one chapter in that book that stopped me in my tracks. Dr. Ketchum told how another minister, who was nationally known, had accused Dr. Ketchum's daughter and her husband of taking a vacation at their church's expense. When in reality, they had gone to Brazil as missionaries. His daughter had become deathly ill and had to come home from the field. She had become so weak, that she could not sit in a chair without falling out of it.

Dr. Ketchum told how he felt one day when he was caring for his daughter, and she had fallen out of a chair.

He said that he had such hatred for the man, who had written that false article about his daughter and her husband, that if he had a gun "he would have shot him." This was my spiritual hero saying this. I was shocked. As I read on, he told how his thoughts so troubled him, that he went into his bathroom and told the Lord that he was not coming out until he could pray in love for this man. He told how he would almost get the victory over his hatred, and then fall back into his hatred. He described it like climbing a mountain. Finally he cried out to the Lord, "Lord, I can't do it. If I am ever going to be able to pray for J. Frank Norris in love, you will have to do it through me." Almost immediately, Dr. Ketchum began to pray for this man in love.

After reading that story I knew I needed to pray for Dick in love. I'm not sure when it happened, but I began to pray for Dick in love. I know now that God wasn't as concerned about changing Dick as He was in changing me. I began to see Dick differently. He didn't upset me anymore. As I changed my attitude toward Dick, I noticed that he began to change. Oh, he was still Dick, but he seemed to have a different attitude toward me.

As the church grew and Dick got older, he was no longer in the position of leadership that he once was. He would still come into my office usually unannounced. But now he came into my office to talk about Bible prophecy. We had some great talks together. I so wish that I had changed sooner. It would have saved me from a lot of unnecessary stress.

I will always remember standing with the family around Dick's hospital bed as he breathed his last. I had already become the pastor in Otsego by then, but the church in Mount Vernon had not yet called a pastor, and Nancy and I happened to be in Mount Vernon at the time, checking on our house that was still for sale. I had grown to love Dick, and would truly miss him. God's grace was still working on me.

CHAPTER 47

CONVERSION STORIES

It is impossible for me to record in this book all of the conversion stories that occurred over our thirty year ministry in Mount Vernon, since that would number over 2000. But I have recorded a few to give the reader a taste of the blessings God gave us. God began to bless our ministry in Mount Vernon just as He had in Defiance. We would continue to average more than one soul saved per week over our thirty year ministry. The fact that Tammy Zolman was saved even before I became their pastor was an indication of the fruit that God would harvest. In my first year souls were being saved in almost every home I visited, it seemed. Someone would suggest I make a visit in a particular home and almost invariably someone would be saved.

Bringing a Jew to Jesus

Ironically there was a couple in our church with the same last name as Nancy's maiden name of Crown. That obviously made them special. But what made them even more special to me was that Mel Crown was a Jew. Gladys, his wife, had started to attend shortly after we came to Mount Vernon. She had been married before to a man whose last name was Zolman. So she was Denny Zolman's mother, and the grandmother of Tammy, who was the first one saved under our ministry in Mount Vernon. After divorcing Denny's father she had met Mel while working in a trade show for Pepperidge Farm.

Shortly after Gladys began to attend, Mel started coming with her, mostly out of curiosity. He had no idea what a Baptist was. Everything we did and how we did it was new to him. He had never heard the Gospel before. In fact, he had little knowledge even of the Old Testament. Even though his grand fathers on both his mom and his dad's side of the family had been rabbis, Mel had left home when he was fourteen to become a drummer in a band. So he had little interest in spiritual things. In fact when we first met he wasn't sure there was a God.

I enjoyed visiting with Mel. He told me stories of playing for Perry Como and other stars. I told him about his Jewish heritage – how the Jewish race began with Abraham, and how Jesus was a Jew. I told him about how Jesus brought salvation. Mel was concerned that if he "became a Baptist" he would have to stop being a Jew. I explained that he would always be a Jew, but if he got saved, he would be a child of Abraham twice, once physically and second spiritually.

On December 24, 1978, Gladys came forward to receive Christ as her Savior. I can still see the shocked look on Mel's face when she left her seat. He still didn't understand what was going on. After Gladys got saved she became very concerned about her husband. She wanted to be baptized and join our church, but she wanted to do that with Mel. But she had doubts if Mel would ever come around. But to her utter amazement, Mel stepped forward during an invitation on April 5, 1979, and was gloriously saved. They were both baptized together in Apple Valley Lake at King Beach on May 13, 1979. The water was still extremely cold, and Gladys had had some heart problems, but she was determined not to wait any longer. So she wrapped up in plastic and duct tape under her cloths, wore a bathing cap, and was baptized.

Mel was a natural promoter. He kept talking to me about getting our name in front of the community. Most of his ideas were probably not wise for a church to do. But I loved his enthusiasm. During the late 1970s Jimmy Carter was president. Our nation was going through tough times economically and politically. Inflation was out of control. Interest rates were sky high, and the nations of the world, especially our enemies, had lost respect for us. Iran, which had been one of our allies in the middle-east, had gone though a revolution. Our country in my opinion allowed the revolution to take place. The Muslim Ayatollahs took over the control of the nation. In that upheaval the Muslims had taken over two hundred American hostages, and the leaders of our government seemed paralyzed, and did nothing.

I talked to Mel about having a community wide prayer for the hostages. It could be held at the town square. We would involve the mayor and any other political leaders we could get to come. I would be the one leading in prayer. Mel loved the idea and ran with it. He made all the contacts. He organized everything but the program. We had a very large crowd that day at the square. We had a very well known conservative congressman, who lived in nearby Newark, participate, as well as the mayor of Mount Vernon. The event was a huge success. It wasn't too long after that, that the hostages were released.

Mr. Brown

I visited the Browns during my first year. I'm not sure who suggested that I go to visit the Browns, but it was probably Ken Bandy. He had a passion for the lost and, whether he knew it or not, was always encouraging me to share the Gospel.

Mr. Brown was 91 and very hard of hearing. His wife was a believer but he had never trusted Christ. I had to yell the Gospel to him, and had to be careful at every point to make sure he understood. After reviewing the plan of salvation I asked him if he would like to be saved. I explained that it involved putting his absolute trust in Christ as his personal Savior by asking Jesus to come into his heart. He hesitated. I could tell that there was a battle going on inside of him. The old devil had had him for 91 years and didn't want to let go. Finally his wife yelled at him at the top of her lungs, "Do what the man says, Paw. Do what the man says." I will never forget that as long as I live. That was the shove he needed. He prayed with me and was saved, and has the distinction of being the oldest person I led to Christ.

Brenda (Not her real name)

Ken Bandy had a friend that he used to work with who had moved away, and had gotten saved. His daughters, who were just under eighteen, had moved back to the Mount Vernon area, and their father wanted a pastor to talk to them about the Lord. I did do that, but did not get too far. Both girls had been through a lot of turmoil, and spiritual confusion.

Brenda soon became pregnant at 17. I received a call from her one evening to tell me about her pregnancy. She was distraught and contemplating an abortion, because she did not have the means to care for her baby, and did not want her baby to grow up in the environment in which she was now living. After talking with her and praying with her, she decided to keep her baby.

Several years later Brenda repented of her sinful lifestyle. Her "baby", who by this time was a teenager, also trusted in Christ as her Savior. What a joy it was to baptize the mother and her daughter, knowing that I had played a role in saving the daughter's life, and the mother from a life of misery.

Paul McMains

The first time I met Paul was when he came to church with his wife. When I went to visit them shortly after they came to church, Paul was very open about his life. He had grown up in and out of foster care as a ward of the state. He became a notorious bank robber in Knox County, where Mount Vernon was located. He told me that during one car chase to escape the police, he had his gun on the front seat. Had he been caught, he planned to shoot his way out. But his car went out of control and crashed, rendering him unable to carry out his plan.

After he was arrested he was put in the Knox County jail. But after a few days he broke out. He told me that he simply walked out when the guards were not looking. This was a real embarrassment to the Sheriff, who gave orders to shoot him on sight, according to Paul. Somehow he avoided getting shot, and was arrested a second time. But he broke out again a second time. Again he avoided getting shot, when he was arrested the third time. After this arrest he spent twelve years in prison. He had just gotten out when he came to church.

If I put Paul in a line up and asked you to pick out the bank robber, you would never pick Paul. He was quiet, unassuming, polite, and not the kind of person you would ever suspect of robbing a bank. He blended into a crowd.

He told me that he began to read the Bible when he was in prison, but had questions and had not been saved. He met his wife somehow through correspondence, and they had been married recently. She was a believer, who had been a widow, so a bit older than he was.

Paul and his wife, Earlene, continued to attend for a few months regularly. I was at home on a Saturday after-noon when Paul knocked on the door. When I came to the door, Paul simply said in his quiet manner, "I want to be saved". I led Paul to Christ that day and later baptized him. A year or two later he told his story in front of the whole church, which was one of the most moving services I can remember. It so glorified the grace of God. Paul became a good friend and ended up leading our men's ministry.

Don and Karen

Don Durbin began to attend Faith Baptist with his fiancée, Karen Harry, almost from our first Sunday there. Don came from a Danville Catholic family. If you came from the town of Danville and were Catholic it meant that you were "old school" Catholic. The Catholic Church in Danville was still using Latin in its services at the time, and still taught that it was a mortal sin to attend a protestant church. A mortal sin was a big one – you went straight to hell if you committed a mortal sin. Many of the families attending that church were large fami-lies, including the family that Don came from.

But Karen's mother and father were believers, and were attending Faith. So Don and Karen began to attend.

Don had never heard the Gospel before, so it was all new to him. Karen had heard the Gospel but had rebelled against it. But on April 8, 1979, Don and Karen came forward during an invitation and Ken Bandy led them to Christ. This was a major step especially for Don. They continued to attend and to grow spiritually. A few months later I had the joy of baptizing them in the Kokosing River on June 10, 1979.

None of Don's family attended his baptism – well none except his sister, Becky. Well, I'm not sure if you would call it "attend". She did not come to the service itself, but I saw her hiding behind a tree nearby. Her curiosity made her want to see what this was all about, but she did not want to be a bad Catholic and attend a protestant service. I will never forget that scene. But it was the beginning of the Spirit's work in Becky's heart.

I later had the joy of marrying Don and Karen. I saw the hold of the Danville Catholic Church first hand, when Don's own parents would not attend the wedding because it was not a Catholic wedding. We were able to rent the Lakeholm Church of the Nazarene for their wedding.

Becky

Becky continued to stay away from attending any of our services, but God's grace pursued Becky. She had been engaged to a man, whom she dearly loved. But after going into the army he was unfaithful to her numerous times. When he finally owned up to it, this broke her heart. Earlier that year her mom died at the age of 49. It seemed her life was falling apart. Since she needed a place to stay, she went to live with her brother, Don. Don and his new wife, Karen by this time were believers and attending Faith Baptist. During this time they tried to witness to her as she continued to attend Mass. She thought they were crazy, because they spent all morning at church, and she could be done with Mass in 30 minutes. The rest of Don's family thought the same thing. She also continued her cussing and sinful lifestyle.

One day while working at the Knox County Savings Bank, a Nazarene college student came into the bank to open an account. The receptionist that usually handled such matters had stepped away, so Becky chatted with him. In the conversation she mentioned that she was Catholic. That seemed to get his attention. So several days later he invited her to what he called an "Advent Service" at the college on December 2, 1980. Out of curiosity she went. After the service Becky trusted Christ as her Savior.

But she really did not understand what she had done. She just knew that something was different. So she attended a Bible study using the new Bible she had been given, but continued to attend Mass for about three months. She still did not attend our church right away. During those three months she had moved back to her home in Danville to help take care of her younger siblings, since her mom had died. But one Sunday the priest's "sermon" finally convinced Becky to leave the Catholic Church. His entire message was about a coming event at the church called "Las Vegas Night". From that point on she began to attend Faith Baptist. She also started to come to our home, where I began to disciple her, as I did every new convert, who was willing to do so. After seeing what the Bible said about believer's baptism, Becky was baptized on April 12, 1981.

Becky continued to work at the bank in Mount Vernon. Since our church was doing business at that bank, I always saw her when I entered the bank. Before she was saved she was always pleasant, but distant. That changed after she was saved. Nancy had been doing my secretarial work up to this point, but that had its challenges. Nancy was busy taking care of our three kids. She also didn't like to try to decipher my handwriting and directions. I needed a secretary.

I had been impressed with Becky's friendliness and excellent skills on the phone, so I approached Becky about the possibility of coming to work for the church. She agreed, and Becky became my secretary on a part-time basis. But in August of 1984 she quit her job at the bank and was hired full time at the church. She continued in that position until a few years after I resigned from the church. Becoming a staff member at a Baptist church was unimaginable for a Danville Catholic. Only the grace of God could accomplish the transforming work that He did in Becky.

Charles "Fats" Billman

Charles Billman was about as wide as he was tall, thus his nickname, "Fats", which almost everyone called him. He didn't seem to mind. He was a salesman for a local concrete company. His wife, Nellie, was a believer but he was not. Ken Bandy somehow knew of them and invited them to church. Ken seemed to know everyone in the county. He had a passion for the lost, and was a great encouragement to me because of that.

I will never forget the day that Charles was saved. He and his wife had been attending for several weeks. The reason I am recording his salvation was because of the battle that he went through. In all my years of ministry I have never seen such a struggle during an invitation time. I couldn't help but notice. He was hanging on to the chair in front of him with all his might and shaking like a leaf. He was sweating profusely. That went on through the entire invitation song. Finally, when I announced that "this will be the last stanza", he came forward and was saved. What a battle, but Satan lost.

Wes Crum

Wes Crum was the only salesman for a local cabinet shop called Lenki Brothers. He brought in all of their business. He was a kind hearted man, who would "give you the shirt off of his back". But he was not saved. In fact, I think it is safe to say that Wes had a "reputation" in the sin department, and it was not a good one. That's all I'll say about that.

I'm not sure if Wes had been drinking at the time, though that is highly possible, but he had a very bad accident that could have taken his life. His wife was already a believer and may have even attended our church by this time. They also had some neighbors, the Springers, who were charter members of our church. But I think it was again Ken Bandy who suggested that we pay Wes a visit.

God had already gone before us the night of our visit. Wes had no doubt that if he had died in that accident, he would have gone straight to hell. He was ready to be saved and live a new life. He was gloriously saved that night.

I baptized Wes at King Beach in Apple Valley Lake. I believe he was baptized on May 13, 1979, the same day I baptized the Crowns. I remember Wes coming up to me before he was baptized, and I could see he was troubled about something. He said, "Pastor, do you think it is a sin to gamble?" I could have answered him directly, but did not think that was wise. So I said, "Wes, do you think Jesus would gamble?" That answered his question, and he was baptized. Wes and his family became faithful church members after that. He later would open his own cabinet shop and run a very successful business.

Just a few months ago his son, Wes Jr., called me to tell me that his dad had passed away. I thought that was something that after all these years, Wes Jr. thought to call me to tell me that news. I was so glad I went to visit Wes the night he got saved.

Terry VanHouten

There is no other way to say it. God's grace really went after Terry. I know that everyone who receives Christ as Savior does so because of God's grace. But God did some unique things to bring Terry to Himself. First, Terry was a "car guy." He had raced cars and had been a car parts manager for several car dealers in the area. That's all he had done since he was married in 1970. But in 1981 he went to work for Petro Industries, which had nothing to do with cars. It was a distributor of oil field supplies. One of our members, Denny Zolman was its owner. Denny was also a "car guy", who had raced cars, and purchased parts through Terry, when he worked for the local Chevy dealer.

When Terry went to work at Petro his first day, he was shocked to see that several of Denny's employees would go into Denny's office, close the door, and pray every morning. Denny had hired several men from our church including Mike Sprang, Ken Bandy, and Paul Smith. Another one of our members who was a truck driver, Dick Biggs, also often met with them for prayer. This caught Terry's attention. He thought that you only prayed at church. He had never seen men pray at work before. The men also seemed to always be talking about this new church building being built out on Route 586. They were even welding some hand rails for the church.

But there was a second, even more amazing, circumstance that God used to get a hold of Terry. He used our daughter, Lori, even though Lori didn't know it. Lori was in the 4th grade at Pleasant Street Elementary School. Terry and his wife, Diane, also had a daughter named Angie in the 4th grade at the same school. That year Lori and Angie became best friends. Lori went with Angie to her 4 H meetings and slept over at her house.

At the same time Diane was not happy with the church they had been attending. Terry had gone with his family to that church, but he went "just to keep the peace". When Diane heard that Lori's dad was a pastor of a new church, she decided to try it out. She loved the new church and invited Terry to come with her. It "just happened" to be the same church he had been hearing about at work. It was early in 1982 when the VanHoutens began to attend our church, but Terry remained unsaved. Without Terry knowing about it, Diane got several ladies from the church to pray for Terry's salvation.

On March 26, 1983, I went to visit Terry with the intention of leading him to the Lord. During the visit Terry tried to dodge the issue by saying that he needed to get some answers about where the dinosaurs fit in with the Bible. But that night the Holy Spirit brought Terry under such conviction, that he knew the only thing he really needed was Jesus. Terry told me later, "I will always remember how I felt after I did it (got saved). I had been carrying a lot of guilt – even more than I realized. And it was gone! It's like the Toyota commercials, when they say, 'Oh what a feeling'."

Two years later Terry and Diane became youth leaders along with Nancy and I and Kevin and Barb Kidwell. Terry and Diane would continue to serve as youth workers at Faith for twenty five years. Their lives and service touched hundreds of lives for the Lord. Many of those teens grew up to be faithful Christians, because Terry and Diane faithfully modeled the love of Christ before them and to them.

Thank God that His grace pursued Terry and didn't give him a chance. Terry was pursued by the Living God.

CHAPTER 48

PURCHASING PROPERTY

Shortly after we moved to Mount Vernon I began to look for the best location for our church building. Using maps of the city and driving over the surrounding area, I had made my decision as to where the best location was. I felt that the city was going to grow east out on Route 36. I had my eye on some property on the south side of 36 before coming to the radio station at the top of the hill. I found out that it was owned by some developers. I thought the location would be ideal, even though it would involve a lot of excavation, because it was a big hill.

At the same time I was doing my research, a couple of sisters in the congregation were talking to their uncle about selling the church some of his property. The uncle was Ivan Rockwell, and the sisters were Karen Ashcraft and Sharon Zolman. After I heard about this property I went to check it out. The location actually wasn't too bad. It was also located on a state route (586) and across from the Country Club golf course. The land was part of the Twin Oaks Orchard, which was owned by Ivan and Bessie Rockwell.

But that property had a main transmission gas line that ran across it, which meant that the gas company had a right of way that went with that gas line. That limited how much of the land was really usable for building and parking. The other problem with the property was the very steep way it sloped down. There was a 100 foot drop from the front of the property near the road to the back of the property. All this meant that only about two to three acres of the ten acres in question would be usable for the church.

When I got the news that Ivan was willing to sell us that property, I was not in favor of the idea at first. I was looking ten years ahead for the church, and I thought that that property would cause some limitations for the church. But the more I thought about it, I began to change my mind. I could see that most of the church was in favor of the Rockwell property. I did not think it would be wise to "die on that hill". It might cause disunity. And in a small church, that could be disastrous. So against my better judgment, we purchased the Rockwell property in May of 1979 for thirty thousand dollars.

 Later Bessie Rockwell gave me a picture of that property when it was still part of their orchard and had apple trees all over it in bloom. I have always treasured that picture. The fruit trees on that property spoke to me of the spiritual fruit that God would one day produce on that same ground.

Looking back on that decision, it was the right decision. Even though I was right about the city growing east out Route 36, the property I had in mind would have been way too expensive for us to buy at that time, if the developers would have even sold it to us. That property eventually became a shopping plaza. We would have challenges with the Rockwell property as I foresaw, but by going to two services we were able to have enough parking to make it work. The property below the gas pipe line continues to remain unusable for the church today.

The church people were so excited about having their own property. One of the first things we did was to celebrate by having a picnic on our new property – eating again. We also rented a big tent and held evangelistic meetings. We used a flatbed trailer for the platform. We had several saved in those meetings.

Against Nancy's better judgment we moved her piano from our home to the tent for the meetings. In the process one of the movers slipped and we broke one of its legs. I felt terrible. I thought I was in so much trouble, that I might not be able to go home for awhile. But Nancy was forgiving, and the piano leg was repaired, so it looked almost as good as new.

Our First VBS on Our New Property

With excitement running high we decided to have a VBS out on our property, while we still had the big tent. We borrowed some smaller tents to use for the class rooms, advertised it, and kids came from everywhere. I think the tent idea was actually a draw for the kids. It was different. But it was such a difficult week.

I used "Stretch" as I had in Defiance, as well as some of the other ideas, but I did not count on the difficulty we would have trying to control the kids. The tents did have walls. But the kids would climb underneath the floorless tents or squirt out though the front of them. It was pandemonium. The workers were beside themselves. But somehow we made it through the week without losing any kids or getting any run over on the highway. I'm sure we even had kids saved in spite of it all. But I made up my mind to never again try to have a VBS by using tents.

CHAPTER 49

OUR NEW BUILDING

Style and Location

Because Dr. Ray Hein had been such a big help to me in Defiance, I recommended that we hire him to help us through our building project in Mount Vernon. After Dr. Hein met with the congregation, the congregation voted to hire him to help them secure financing, acquire the architect, and see them through the building process.

But the Mount Vernon people were much more involved than the people in Defiance had been. There were more business type people, and people who had been involved in building projects. So they took a more active interest in the details.

Mount Vernon was known as "The Colonial City", so it seemed that our building would best fit into the community if it were a colonial style building. When the architect, Carl Geiser, presented his concept of our new building, it was immediately accepted. It was beautiful. It was designed to have the platform in one of the corners, so that the seating would be fanned in front of it. It would have a big stained glass window facing the road.

The only problem was where he and Dr. Hein thought the building should be located. They initially had it located back by the gas line far from the road and close to the Rockwell property line. Their reasoning for doing so was so that the future buildings could have a place to be built. But that location would almost hide our beautiful building. That idea did not fly with our people or with me. So the present site location was approved. Dr. Hein wasn't happy about that, but went along with it.

Financing

Dr. Hein helped us prepare the necessary material for the bank. We had the architectural plans, had secured financial commitments from the people to underwrite the loan, and could show the phenomenal growth of the church. Again we had problems getting a loan. Banks really were afraid of giving loans to new churches. One banker jokingly said that if the church couldn't make its payments, about the only thing they could do with it was to "turn it into a dance floor". Only one bank was at all interested in giving us a loan – The BancOhio Savings Bank. Mr. Win Curry was the president of that bank at that time. He was a gracious man who seemed interested in our project. His son, who was a quadriplegic, would later attend our youth group. However, the interest rate on our loan would be a whopping thirteen and a half percent. That was the best we could get during those bad economic times. So we secured the loan.

The Split with Dr. Hein

The original building was designed with no basement. There were to be sliding glass doors in the back of the auditorium to divide it from what was intended to be the only classrooms. These were to be located in what eventually became the "overflow" area of the auditorium. One side of the building would have the offices and restrooms, while the other side would contain the nursery and P.A. room.

But our congregation was growing rapidly. By the end of 1980 we already had nearly 100 members and were averaging well over that in attendance. The auditorium that was planned would seat around 200. We were going to need to forget the glass doors and use the back area for auditorium overflow. If we did that we wouldn't have any classroom space. It was obvious that we needed more room then what was originally planned.

A meeting was called with Dr. Hein to try to resolve the matter. The only possible solution was to put a basement under the main floor. I remember that Gladys Crown felt very strongly about this. When this was proposed by the people, Dr. Hein was very much opposed to the idea. His reason was simple – we couldn't afford it. And on paper he was right. But it also seemed foolish to build a building that would be woefully inadequate. Dr. Hein said he could no longer be our consultant if we did not follow his direction. We understood that. So we paid him his entire fee, even though the building project itself had not begun, and we parted on good terms. Now all we had to do was get enough money to build a basement.

Ground Breaking Service

A Ground Breaking Service was held on our property on September 28, 1980, my birthday. The day before, I had been cutting down some small trees with Mel Crown in an attempt to clear some of the church property. I was not used to using the chain saw and was not being as careful as I should. Suddenly the chain saw jumped off the little tree I was cutting and flew back toward my face. I instinctively put my left hand up toward my face for protection. The chain saw hit my little finger on my left hand and nearly cut it to the bone. Mel took me in his car to the emergency room where a surgeon sewed my finger together. Fortunately it healed well, although I still can't bend the last joint of that finger.

The next day at the Ground Breaking Service the mayor of Mount Vernon attended as well as all the major players in the process. We each took a turn at turning over some dirt, took pictures, and handed out plastic shovels as a memento of the occasion. We all knew that God had made it all happen up to this point, and God would see us through the project. Construction began the next week.

The Construction

I had gone through a church building project in Defiance, but it had been "turn- key". This church did not want to spend the money on a contractor, so we hired a job superintendent by the name of Ken Miller. Ken was a builder and a wonderful Christian man, who was a member of a nearby Baptist church in Fallsburg. Denny Zolman knew him and recommended him. Ken would oversee all the subcontractors and would do a lot of the carpentry work himself. Any of the members could help as well, if they were available. Though there was a lot of talk about helping, it didn't materialize for the most part.

I helped quite a bit throughout the project including bolting some of the steel beams and tarring the exterior of the basement walls, painting, and finish work. One of the men who helped a lot was Gary Fraley. He was the superintendent at a cabinet factory in Mount Vernon called Lenki Brothers. He and his wife were in the process of moving from a church near Wooster. Gary, Mel Crown and I did all the finish work on the doors and trim.

Often we would work until 2:00 am. Gladys Crown and several others helped do the painting. It was looking great.

The Basement

We knew when we started construction that we did not have the funds to complete a basement. But we built in such a way that we could finish a basement eventually. We built the main floor on top of basement walls and poured a basement floor. We also roughed in the plumbing for the restrooms downstairs, but we did not have the funds to finish it.

But we really needed that space. I asked Ken Miller what he thought we needed financially to finish the basement. He thought it would take around $40,000. That was a lot of money in those days. I talked it over with the deacons, and they agreed that we should put the need out to the people. So the next Sunday I told the people that we needed $40,000 to be able to finish our basement – and we prayed. The following Sunday we received the entire $40,000 in the offering designated toward finishing our basement. God had supplied our need. We finished the basement, and I am so glad we did. God is so amazing!

Moving In

The building was finished the first of August in 1981. On August 9th, like we had done in Defiance, we formed a caravan and left the Memorial Building in down town Mount Vernon. We traveled by police escort out to our new church home on Route 586. What a sight it was for me to look back behind me and see cars as far as I could see going to our church. It was awesome!

That first Sunday we were using our overflow area, which we had initially planned to be classrooms. What an exciting day!

Dedication Service

A Dedication Service was held on November 9, 1980, with Rev. Earl Umbaugh as the main speaker. God had once again poured His grace, not only on me, but upon our church.

CHAPTER 50

PHILIP'S EARLY YEARS

Philip the BloodHound

It was so nice to be able to have my office at the church. I had built an office in the basement of our house, but it was not always quiet there, nor was it conducive to counseling. Across the hall from my office in our new church building was another office for the secretary. Nancy continued to do that job until the church hired Becky.

One day when Nancy was working at the church, she had put Philip in the church nursery to sleep. He was probably not even two years old at the time, because he was not yet walking. Somehow Philip had climbed out of his crib, and crawled out of the Nursery rooms, across the entire back of the church, and down the hall, all the way to the secretary's office. I was shocked when I walked out of my office to see him sitting near Nancy's door. To this day I don't know how he got out of his crib, or how he knew how to find where Nancy was. It was almost as if he were some kind of blood hound.

Philip and His Physical Limitations

We noticed that Philip always chose to sit a few feet from the TV. We would put him back at a normal distance, but soon he would be back where he started. We did not know that he could hardly see. I don't think we really knew he could not see well until he began kindergarten. His teacher suggested that perhaps one of the reasons he was struggling was because he had poor eye sight. After taking him to the eye doctor and discovering how bad his eyes really were, Nancy and I felt so bad that we had missed that. After getting his glasses he began to do much better.

I think because of his limited vision Phil did not take that much interest in the ball sports. But he did have a huge interest in art. It always amazed me how he could see images in his mind and transport those images onto paper. I could never do that, so I know he did not get that ability from me. I'm sure he got some of that ability from his mom, and probably from his great grandpa Jones who was a tremendous artist.

Another physical problem Philip had when he was born was with his feet. His pediatrician told us that Phil would have to wear special shoes to correct the way his feet turned in toward one another. So we purchased the specialty shoes from the Stride Rite Company to help Phil learn to walk correctly. He wore that kind of shoe until he was three or four.

Philip and His Little Men

Phil loved to play with little soldiers and men that he could take apart. Sometimes we would see a whole string of men dangling from one of Nancy's plants or nick-knacks. And sometimes we would see parts of one attached to some other toy. He was sort of like the scary kid in the movie Toy Story. But he was showing his creativity.

CHAPTER 51

FAMILY CONCERTS

Nancy and I had sung together almost from the first day that we met. We loved to sing special numbers together in church, and had done so since we were married. We had also sung for other churches at banquets and special occasions. As Lori and Mark grew, they also loved to sing, and seemed to have no problem getting up in front of people. Phil was a different story. He showed no interest in singing and absolutely no interest in getting up in front of people.

Our family concerts began in our church in Mount Vernon. I'm not sure when we did our first Easter concert. That probably began with just Nancy and me. Since Easter Sunday evenings were not too well attended, we thought a concert would help. Soon we added Lori and Mark into the mix and the Easter Concerts began to become a tradition for our church.

In 1988 we decided to make a professional live recording of our concert. We had a special picture taken for the front of the cassette and hired a professional to record our Easter concert. Though Philip was still not all that excited about being in front of people at eight years old, we talked him into doing one number with us. I sat him on my lap and we sang a duet.

We recently had some CDs made of that recording so we could give a copy to some of our friends and the kids. I think we sold about 500 of the original recording. That was fun and will be a memory we will all treasure.

CHAPTER   52

THE NEED FOR ADDITIONAL CHURCH STAFF

Nancy

Our church was growing rapidly. By the beginning of 1979 we had doubled our average attendance from 42 to 83. I needed secretarial help badly, since I was a very poor typist at that time, and very busy with visiting and growing the new church. So at a quarterly business meeting on January 10, 1979, the church voted to hire Nancy as my secretary for $50.00 per month. Her salary was later raised to $50.00 per week on November 1, 1981. She has the distinction of being the first one hired on the staff of Faith Baptist.

Joanie Fraley and Betty Jessup

Next came the need for custodians for our new building. Joanie Fraley and Betty Jessup were hired as a team for that position on October 28, 1981. They were excellent custodians. I called them the "White Tornados" because they really were so conscientious about keeping the new building looking so nice. They continued in that position until just before we moved to Otsego. By that time their physical limitations made it difficult to continue.

Becky Durbin

Becky Durbin was hired to replace Nancy and began her part time job as secretary in December of 1982. By August 1, 1984, her job became full time. Becky had a wonderful phone voice and loved her job. She saw it as a ministry for the Lord. She was very accurate in all her work and relieved me of several tasks. Her job description definitely grew over the years. Since her mother had passed away, and she did not have a good relationship with her father, I think she saw Nancy and me as her mother and father figure. Though Becky sometimes overstepped her bounds, her positive qualities far out-weighed any negatives she might have had. She was always dependable and so helpful to me in my ministry.

Dad Crown

Jumping ahead several years to 1986, membership had grown to 259, and I really needed help doing the pastoral work. By this time dad Crown was finishing his pastoral ministry at a church up near Cleveland in the town of Willowick. Faith Baptist voted to call him as its Minister of Visitation on January 8, 1986.

Dad Crown was a great help and encouragement to me. Every Sunday he would tell me how great my sermon was. He had a heart for church growth and motivated the people to witness. He set the example in that department as well. He also seemed to focus his discipleship efforts on those that would respond. He especially worked on the Bolds brothers who were teenagers at the time. Bob Bolds would later go on to Baptist Bible College and Seminary and become a pastor at Dublin, Ohio.

Another one of dad Crown's disciples was a recovering alcoholic by the name of Mick Harden. Dad Crown patiently worked with Mick, who would later marry the girl he was living with, head up our own alcohol recovery ministry, and become a pastor in the hills of Kentucky. Dad Crown also worked on an employee at a local grocery store. The young man started to attend regularly and soon accepted Christ.

I believe dad Crown was on staff with me for five or six years before fully retiring. What a blessing to be able to work so closely with a man I loved and respected.

Pastor Dave Marion

By 1993 attendance was averaging around 300 and Dad Crown had retired. I needed another pastor on staff to help with the load. Almost since the beginning of the church I had been directing the choir and overseeing the music in the church with Nancy's help. She was also overseeing several of the children's ministries. The logical staff need seemed to be in the area of the music and children's ministries.

After checking with some Bible colleges one resume seemed to stand out. Pastor Dave, as he would be called, was a recent graduate of Baptist Bible College in Clarks Summit, Pennsylvania. His resume seemed to indicate that he might be the one we were looking for. So we asked him to come to visit the church with his new wife. After being interviewed by the deacons, singing a solo in church and directing the choir, he was called as our Music and Children's Pastor on September 19, 1993.

Pastor Dave had a sweet spirit and seemed to get along well with people for the most part. During his brief time with us he brought in several well known southern gospel groups for concerts, such as the Nelons, the Martins, Scott Fowler (who was singing with the Cathedral Quartet) and others.

But soon it became apparent that Pastor Dave was not working out as I had hoped. Nancy had told me that she had reservations about him before we hired him. She usually is right when it comes to sizing up people. To this day I do not know how she does that. Looking back on it, I know I did not follow good procedures when I hired him. We moved too quickly for one thing. In fairness to him and to us I wish I would have handled matters differently. But I would learn from my mistake.

I tried to help him musically. I could tell that he had an ear problem. He had trouble hearing each part separately and identifying the problem and solving it. I recommended that he listen to a recording of a choir following the musical score and train his ear to listen to each part (soprano, alto, tenor, and bass). That seemed to offend him. He was also struggling with the children's ministry. From my perspective his heart really wasn't in that ministry. So after a couple of years he resigned and took a ministry elsewhere.

Pastor Matt Otto

Another area that I needed help with was with our teens. I had become the youth director shortly after becoming pastor at Mount Vernon. After a few years I was able to find a couple to replace me by the name of Fred and BJ Gerling. But by 1987 or 1988 they resigned. At that point Nancy and I once again got involved in the youth ministry along with two other couples, Terry and Diane VanHouten, and Kevin and Barb Kidwell, who had teens in the youth group. Lori and Mark were in the youth group as well, and we felt we wanted to make sure the youth group was functioning well. Though our role was more as helpers, it was still time consuming and a challenge with all the other pastoral duties. During this era, we took the teens on summer trips to Myrtle Beach, the Wisconsin Dells, and other neat places.

By 1995 Mark was married to Andrea and had graduated from Cedarville. During his last year at Cedarville he had been a youth pastor in the Springfield, Ohio, area. I thought it would be great if my son could be on staff with me as our youth pastor. That had worked in some other churches that I had been aware of. But that was not to be in my case. Mark thought it best to make it on his own. I could understand that. He had a lot of me in him. Also when I presented the idea to our men, not everyone was excited about it. That greatly disappointed me and frustrated me. From their perspective, if there was ever a problem with one of us the chances were that they would lose both of us and that would not be good for the church.

After realizing that it was not going to be possible to have Mark on staff with me, I asked him if he knew of anyone who might be a good fit at Faith as the youth pastor. He immediately recommended that I contact one of his good friends and classmates, Matt Otto.

Pastor Matt, as we would call him, had recently married Krista, and was a native of Germany. His father was an executive with the Volkswagen car company. His father had moved his family to the Detroit area where they had found Christ and attended a Baptist Church in Taylor, Michigan. Matt had just graduated from Cedarville along with his wife, Krista, and felt that God wanted him to be a youth pastor.

Though I trusted Mark's judgment, I still wanted to be more cautious and thorough. So after having him complete a questionnaire that I prepared, Nancy and I met with him and Krista before having them meet anyone else in the church. After being impressed with Matt, I set up a meeting with the deacons and some appearances at the church. The church then called Pastor Matt as our Youth Pastor on February 1, 1995.

Shortly after he came, the Senior High was separated from the Junior High. Though he would oversee both groups, Terry and Diane VanHouten would directly work with the Junior High and would do so for many more years. Pastor Matt worked directly with the Senior High, planning missions' trips and other opportunities for growth and service.

I did not know when we called Pastor Matt that he had such a beautiful high tenor voice. The first time Nancy and I heard him sing we were amazed. We still love to hear him sing. Pastor Matt also had a heart for establishing a more contemporary style of worship music and is responsible for introducing that style to our church.

Being from the "old school" I was not in favor of that at first. On his own initiative he had started to use some of the drums and guitars on Sunday evening on occasion. But Lori and Mark by this time were into the more contemporary Christian music, and so was Phil. I realized that the church music was changing. Some churches were going through the "music wars", which was destroying them. I did not want that to happen at Faith.

About the same time we were maxing out our auditorium and parking space and had decided to go to two services. So we kept the early service as a "traditional" service using hymns and piano and organ, and had a "blended" second service using a blend of worship choruses and hymns. This worked well for us. It avoided the conflict some churches were having and allowed us to continue to grow.

Pastor Matt is still the Youth Pastor at Mount Vernon at this writing. He and Krista have raised their two children at Faith and involved them in their ministry. I remember hearing Pastor Matt talking to his parents in German on the phone in his office. I always accused him of speaking in tongues.

Nancy again

By the end of 1997 our membership was 407. Our kids by this time were out of the house. I had gone back to directing the choir, but really didn't have the time to put in that ministry that it required. Nancy, however, was very good at picking out the right music. She was, also, excellent at working with children. So on May 6, 1997, the church hired her as the Director of Music and Children's Ministries.

Nancy did an outstanding job at both. She prepared the children's Christmas programs, oversaw the children's Sunday school classes and curriculum, as well as the Wednesday night children's program and our VBS. In addition she picked out the choir music, which I directed, planned any church concerts, and set up the music schedules for special music. She also set in on our staff meetings which we held one a week. I have never had anyone do a better job in the areas of music and children than she did. She continued in that position until we moved to Michigan.

Vicki Duston

During the year 2000 we had been able to complete our new Family Center 22,000 square foot addition. Because of the layout of the office complex and Becky's expanded role, we needed a receptionist. After having a couple different girls fill that position Vikki Duston was hired on June 27, 2000. Vikki was saved several years earlier, when Evangelist Norm Sharbaugh held meetings at Faith. Later her husband Rick was saved as well. Vikki continues as the church receptionist at this writing.

Pastor Bob Veenhuis

Pastor Bob had graduated from Grand Rapids Baptist Seminary and been a pastor for several years in northeast Ohio. He had retired from the senior pastor position, and he and his wife, Elaine, had purchased property on a lake east of Mount Vernon, in the Apple Valley resort area. Shortly after attending Faith, Bob offered his help in the visitation and discipleship area. After thinking about it and discussing it with the deacons, Pastor Bob was called to fill those positions on April 25, 2001.

Pastor Bob not only oversaw our visitation and discipleship ministries, but also oversaw our custodians and our set up and tear down of the chairs and tables in our Family Center, which had to be done every Sunday. He recently retired from his position at Faith. By now he is probably in his 80s.

Everyone on the staff, including me, had our weaknesses. But each had their strengths as well. Without each of the ones on our staff Faith Baptist would not have become the outstanding church that it was.

CHAPTER 53

CELEBRATING MOM AND DAD'S 50th WEDDING ANNIVERSARY

After I graduated from seminary in 1970 it became more and more difficult to be with my parents. I was working hard at the ministry that God had given us. After dad sold his plumbing and heating business in 1967 they moved to Florida. They first moved to the Sarasota area where dad worked for a bottle gas company as a repairman. They then moved to Mulberry, Florida, to serve at Spurgeon Baptist Bible College. Dad was head of the maintenance department and mom oversaw the kitchen initially, but then took over the bookstore and library responsibilities. During their summers they would go up to Gitche Gumee Bible Camp to do similar work there. By this time Mel was the director of the camp. So the only time we saw them was when they were on their way to or from Florida unless we made a trip to Florida during the winter or to Gitche Gumee during the summer. I was so proud of my parents because of the way they gave their lives to serve the Lord.

In June of 1989 mom and dad celebrated their 50th wedding anniversary. So it was wonderful to have all our family together for the big event. By this time Keith had married Candy and had two children, Brian and Tiffany. Mel had married Carol and had three children, Nate, Susie, and Steve. And Marcia had married Gary Viegelahn, whom she had met up at Gitche Gumee. So we celebrated at our home church in Stanton to make it easier for dad and mom's siblings and friends to attend. Since all of the children were musical as well as Marcia, Mel, Keith and I, we did several musical numbers, which was fun. After the celebration at Stanton we had another celebration up at Gitche Gumee, which was more for our immediate family.

I had borrowed a video camera to try to record as much of the events as possible. We still have those tapes somewhere. I recorded Mark doing a funny scene about making coffee, as well as Mark and Phil arguing about lighting a sparkler.

It was during our week together that dad and I were able to go fishing together. I cherished those times because they were so rare, and because it was just the two of us doing something we both loved to do. Whenever Nancy, I, and the kids were up at Gitche Gumee, dad and I found time to go fishing. On this particular fishing outing we went to Lac La Belle. This was a fairly big lake that connected to Lake Superior, so presented an opportunity to catch some bigger fish. Dad had his favorite spot where he often caught perch, which was his favorite fish to catch. But those same places usually have Northern Pike, which is my favorite fish to catch. So it worked out great.

After we launched the boat we headed from the channel into the lake. I decided I would cast my lure behind the boat and fish, while dad motored to our fishing spot. All of a sudden I had a huge strike. A big fish had hit my lure. I really wasn't expecting that. Dad slowed the boat to a halt and let me fight the fish. When I finally got it in the landing net and into the boat, it was a huge forty one inch musky. That was by far the largest fish I had ever caught, and it happened while fishing with my dad. That was so special.

After getting home Mark and I made a funny video about catching the big fish out of the ditch near Garden City Road, but unfortunately I inadvertently taped over it and lost all the pictures of that fish. I was bummed about that. But mom did fix the fish for supper and it fed everyone there. That also was special to me. That week together with all of our families is a very precious memory to me.

CHAPTER 54

THE DIFFICULT MOVE TO APPLE VALLEY AND MOM'S PASSING

We had lived at the Upland Terrace address in Mount Vernon for sixteen years. It was adequate for our family and a wonderful location with great neighbors. At this point in our lives we believed we would retire in Mount Vernon. We had no reason to think otherwise.

Apple Valley was a resort housing area about five miles east of Mount Vernon. It was owned and run by the property owners, so it was totally private. It had a large lake, swimming pools, marina, club house, tennis courts, and even its own campground. We thought it would be the ideal area for us for our retirement, especially for our kids and grandkids. Several of our families lived in that area. One of the families had given us the keys to their pontoon boat, and said we could use it any time. When a couple of connecting lots, which offered a view of the lake, came up for sale at a great price (We paid $5500 total for the two of them), we purchased them and sold our house. We needed to have the house built, so we picked out the plan. Since our house on Upland Terrace had sold, we needed to live in a rented house until the construction on our new house located at 472 Baldwin Heights Circle was completed. Both lots were covered in nasty briers called multi-floral rose. So Phil and I had the huge job of clearing the land. I also hired one of his Mark's friends from the church, Scott Qualls, to help with that and the landscaping. When clearing the land I noticed with excitement that the deer had been using our lots for their bedroom. I couldn't hunt them in Apple Valley, but at least we would be able to see them.

As our two story house with a full basement was nearing completion, the owner of the house we were renting came to me on a Wednesday and said we needed to be out by Saturday since he had sold the house and the new owners were moving in. I was shocked, but prayed about it and told our builder that we needed to move in on Friday, and explained our situation.

Another situation, however, was totally occupying my mind. My mom had been diagnosed with terminal cancer in June and was in the last stages of her battle. The early 1990s had been a difficult period for our family. Mom Crown had passed away on August 23, 1990, at the Ohio State University hospital after a heart procedure failed. My sister, Marcia's husband (Gary) had passed away a year later of a massive heart attack while shoveling snow off of a trailer. It was now November, 1994. My brother, Mel, called me on Thursday and said that if I wanted to see Mom before she died, I'd better get up there. Mom and dad were living with my sister, Marcia, in the upper peninsula of Michigan in Lake Linden during mom's illness. I explained to Mel that we needed to move the next day, but that I would catch the first flight out of Columbus on Saturday morning. One of the families in our church somehow heard about my situation and had offered to pay for my flight.

So after a full day of moving on Friday and with little sleep, I drove to the Columbus airport Saturday morning. As I was walking to the gate preparing to board the plane, I was paged by the public address announcer and told to go to the airline counter. When I did, the person there told me that I had a phone call. It was Nancy, who told me that Mel had called and said that mom had passed away early that morning on November 12, 1994. After explaining the situation to the airline they refunded my money, and with the permission of the donor, used the money toward our driving the family up to mom's funeral, which was held at the First Baptist Church in Calumet, Michigan.

CHAPTER 55

LORI GROWS UP

Lori loved to sing almost when she learned to talk. So singing and music were a big part of her life when she was growing up and still is. When we moved to Mount Vernon, Lori was in the second grade. She adjusted quickly to her new school, the Pleasant Street Elementary School. I was very impressed with the teachers there. The school's music director put on a Christmas program that could have been put on in our church. I still remember the title: "The True Meaning Of Christmas". The child actors brought a big box wrapped in Christmas paper, but that was not the true meaning of Christmas. Santa Claus made an appearance, but that was not the true meaning of Christmas. I'm sure there were other things that were presented, but didn't answer the question. Finally children came out dressed in their robes and sat in front of a manger scene. The true meaning of Christmas was that God sent His son as a gift so we could have salvation. It was presented in a public school in 1978. How things have changed! But that was the kind of school that Lori and Mark attended in those days.

I have kept a file on each of our kids since they were young. When I was going through Lori's file in preparation for writing this I came across some really cool stuff. In the third grade Lori wrote the following story entitled, "My Cereal Bowl". At the bottom of her story she drew a picture of a cereal bowl.

"When I looked in my cereal bowl I saw something strange. It looked like a doorbell but it wasn't. I told my dad and he said it probably was just a piece of cereal. But I said it doesn't match the rest of the cereal. So I talked him into looking at it. But when my dad looked, he screamed. I said, what is it? He said it's a bug. Then I went, AAAHHHH!. The end."

I also came across the first song that Lori wrote when she was 10, entitled, "Do You Know Why?" I only have the words on a card, but there must have been a tune that she put to the lyrics, because it says, "Lyrics, Lori Jones. Music, Lori Jones."

"Do you know why?
I love him so.
Do you know why?
I love him so
For he Died on the
cross for me…
And I am so proud
To be … a Christian…
Through Jesus
Christ our Lord…"

Lori never had a problem getting up in front of people. She loved it. She was in a talent show every year at her school. In third grade she sang in a clown costume and came in third place. In fourth grade she played "Whirling Leaves" on the piano. In fifth grade she sang, "You Light up my Life", accompanied by her mom.

Her high school years continued to focus on music. She was in the high school choir all four years, sang in the "Show Choir" from her sophomore year through her senior year, and sang in the "Chamber Choir" her junior and senior years. During her senior year she was also the choir secretary and had the honor of being named, "Musician of the Year".

But what I am most proud of is that Lori used her talents for the Lord. She not only sang in concerts with Nancy, Mark, and me, but sang solos in church and sang in the church choir. She was developing an amazing voice.

During her sophomore year she entered a national competition called Talents for Christ. TFC was a competition for teens who were members of GARBC churches. There were several areas of competition such as Bible knowledge, writing, public speaking, and several musical areas including voice. If a teen won first place in the nation they won a year's scholarship to a GARBC approved college. That was huge. So Lori competed in the area of girl's voice. Though she did not place her sophomore year she gained a lot of experience. Her junior year she won second place at the state level. But to compete at the national level required winning first place in the state. But again she was learning and gaining experience. But she won first place in the state her senior year, which entitled her to compete in the national contest, which was held that year in Columbus, Ohio, not too far away. Lori won first place in the nation that year. Nancy and I were so proud of her. And I was thrilled that her first year of college tuition was paid!! Lori had already made up her mind that she was going to Cedarville College, which also thrilled us.

CHAPTER 56

MARK GROWS UP

At a very early age Mark displayed a heart that was sensitive to God. Mark had accepted the Lord as his Savior when he was 5 or 6. When I was asked to preach a week of evangelistic meetings at the Calvary Baptist Church of Coshocton, Mark wanted to go with me. After one of the services Mark came to me and wanted to talk with me. He had a very serious look on his face, so I knew he was really troubled about something. He was probably about age 7. He said he wasn't sure he was saved. I remember taking a quarter out of my pocket and put it in my hand. I then asked Mark to try to get it out of my fist. After struggling for a while, I showed him John 10:27-29. I told him that when he got saved Jesus took him into His hand. No one, not even Satan was stronger than Jesus. His salvation was as certain as the strength of Jesus, and was guaranteed by His mighty hand. That seemed to settle the matter.

Mark was always very expressive. I have lots of notes and drawings in his file that he gave to me. In one of his drawings at age 7 he drew a mail man and a mail truck, only he spelled mail, "male". Though he had a very tender heart he still struggled with his spelling. At age 9 he drew a picture of a cross with "Christ is Lord" written on it. When he was 11 he wrote the following note: "Dad I just want to tell you that I love you.
I think **you're** a great dad also. And DAD I think **you're** a great pastor. Go out there and preach tonight. I love you. P.S. Break a LEG tonight. Love, MARK Jones"

However, the classic note that Mark wrote was written when he was about 13:

"Dear Dad,

I'm really sorry that I got mad at you last night when I stubbed my toe. I guess I just had to get the pain out somehow. Dad, I really appreciate the things you do for me. I thank you for the love and care that you give to me. I hope you like this letter, because it has made me feel a lot better to get my feelings out.

Dad I really love you with all my heart and I don't go a day without thinking about you. I hope I didn't make you feel bad when I got mad at you last night. I just kept thinking about your feelings when I was in my bed. I hope you will forgive me for getting mad. I hope you like this poem on Fathers:

<u>Fathers</u>

Fathers are so loving,
Their kind, and tender caring
They care about your needs,
Their feelings they are showing.
MARK D. JONES

I hope you liked that poem I wrote. I meant it with all my heart. Well, gotta go! Your son, Mark. P.S. I Love You Dad!"

Mark loved sports. He loved to play catch, played colt football, and played basketball in the YMCA league. He could handle the basketball well, and had a really good shot, but didn't really like the contact part of it. He tried to like the things that he knew I enjoyed. I remember when he begged me to shoot my 20 gauge shotgun. He was probably 10 or 11. I finally gave in and agreed to allow him to shoot it. But I was really concerned that it might knock him down. So we went into the woods behind the church, and I had him sit down on the ground. I then had him pick out a tree to aim at. When he pulled the trigger, the kick of the gun knocked him on his back with his feet sticking straight up in the air. He hit exactly where he was aiming, but he never asked to shoot my gun again. That experience apparently satisfied that urge.

Another time he wanted to go hunt rabbits with me and some of the men in the church. When we got home I noticed that Mark quickly disappeared. After putting my gun away I found him in his room crying. After some prodding Mark finally blurted out, "I hate it". He hated hunting, but didn't want me to know that. After hugging him I assured him that he didn't have to like hunting in order for me to love him. We would find lots of other things to do together. That greatly relieved him.

Mark got a full dose of the Crown sense of humor. He loved to make us laugh, especially his mom. He would come home from school, open the door, and purposely trip over the step just to hear his mom laugh, which she did every time. Or he would get up on the hearth of the fireplace and tap dance. He usually had the funny parts in his high school plays. On one occasion he was playing the part of a fat man, which was a stretch for Mark since he was always pretty skinny. To make him look fat they had to stuff a pillow in his oversized pants. During one of the nights of the play Mark lost his pants on stage. Apparently he had forgotten his belt. Nancy had made him a pair of boxer shorts that had little ducks all over them. The crowd and everyone on the stage lost it. From that time on he was known as "ducky". Even the Mayor of Mount Vernon laughingly reminded me several years later about Mark's experience.

Music for Mark, like his sister, seemed to come easy to him. Though he took a few lessons, Mark pretty much taught himself to play the guitar. He had started singing with Lori and with our family almost since he learned to talk. But when he entered high school he began to make friends with the wrong crowd, primarily because they also played guitars. Soon they had formed their own rock band with Mark as their lead singer. Nancy and I were totally unaware of this.

Their rock band was scheduled to play during the intermission of the high school choir concert, which was held on a Thursday night. Mark didn't think I would be there since I always made visits for the church on Thursday nights. But I had planned to quit early that night, so I could at least catch the second half of the choir concert, since both Lori and Mark were in the choir. I walked i to the school lobby to see Mark with his rock band jamming. Our eyes locked. I could tell that Mark figured that his life was about to end abruptly. I was boiling inside, but didn't say anything to him that night. I didn't trust myself.

But the more I thought about it the next day, the more the Lord convicted me. Though I was concerned about the direction that Mark was heading, I knew I had not been discipling Mark as I should. So when Mark came home from school I took him downstairs to the family room to have a talk with him. I started out by apologizing to him for not being a very good father. I had not been helping him to grow spiritually as he should, but that was going to change. I then asked him if any of the friends he was running with were ready for heaven and if he had ever tried to tell them how to get to heaven? If they were really his friends, why hadn't he done that? Obviously heaven and hell were not very real to him. So we began a Bible study on heaven and hell with Mark having to memorize some verses on those subjects. I believe that study and confrontation was one of the things that changed the course of Mark's life.

When Mark was about 15 I bought a riding mower, weed eater, push mower, and trailer, so I could begin a mowing business with Mark. I thought it would help teach Mark responsibility, provide a good work ethic, and teach money management. Mark paid me back for half of the cost of the equipment out of his income. He did most of the work, although I helped him on some of the jobs. When he was old enough to drive, he drove himself to his mowing jobs. He did really well, was very responsible, and saved money towards college.

Mark continued to serve the Lord by singing in our family concerts, and running the sound system at church. His musical ability had won him the honor of being named "Musician of the Year" during his senior year of high school. He also entered the Talents for Christ contest. His first attempt was in the area of boy's public speaking. But during his senior year of high school he competed in boy's voice and one second place in the nation. In my mind he won first place, but for some reason that year the judges did not award a first place, only a second place. So Mark was the best contestant in that category that year. He also chose to use his scholarship to go to Cedarville College. By this time Mark already knew that God wanted him to serve in the ministry.

CHAPTER 57

PHIL GROWS UP

As stated earlier Philip always had an interest in art. I have a file full of his drawings. He often combined his art with his humor. At age 6 he cut out two paper hearts and gave one to me and one to Nancy after he apparently heard us arguing. At age 9 he gave me a valentine that was a drawing of a bee in the shape of a heart that read, "Bee my valentine, OR I'LL STING YOU". At age 10 on the first day of hunting season he gave me a picture of me shooting a buck with my crossbow. The title of the picture is, "You are a super Dad". He drew himself in the cartoon saying, "You did it. I love you". At age 10 Phil had his poem featured in the "Young Author's Corner" of his school paper. His poem was entitled, "Valentine's Day". It read: There's a Valentine sign outside the door. I dropped my Valentines all over the floor. I looked up and what did I see? I saw pretty blue eyes looking at me. It must be love as far as I can see!" At age 11 Phil made a birthday card for me. On the front of the card he drew a picture of a baker near his oven. The caption read, "I baked a cake just for you". Inside the card read, "but the cat ate it". Underneath the caption is a drawing of a cat lying on its back with its four legs sticking straight up. Underneath the cat is the caption, "Happy Birthday anyway. Love, Philip Jones."

The funniest card in my opinion was not written to me, but to Mark after he had gone to college. Philip wrote it as a church encouragement card when he was 12. Becky, knowing that I would want to see it, gave me the card and sent the message to Mark. The message on his card read: "How's it going DUDE! I'm using your wooden tape crate and your Michael Jordan bag. Dad's using your bedroom as his office. You better not mind. I got encyclopedias for my bedroom. Since you guys are gone mom doesn't have to spend as much on groceries so now she's buying all the good stuff. I'm probably going to start mowing Taylor and Mitchell. I can't wait! Mark, no matter how much I hate to admit it, I miss you! P.S. I love you. Your best blood, Philip Jones."

Phil's creativity with his art and humor occupied much of his time. He really didn't have much interest in playing sports and certainly had no interest in his school work. He got by in school but really didn't see doing school work as very important. I remember him telling me much later in life when he had to take some courses over in order to get his nursing degree, "Dad, if I could meet myself when I was 16, I would beat myself up." But Phil did love his art class and did very well in it. He also was in some school plays, though he really did not like to get up in front of people. One of my most prized art works from Phil was a pencil drawing he did on Father's Day when he was about 14. After coming home from church, Phil disappeared to the basement of our house in Apple Valley. After he returned he gave me a portrait of me that he had drawn from a picture and wished me happy Father's Day.

I made a wooden coaster cart for Phil and Mark that they used on the big Upland Terrace hill, until one of the neighbors called the cops. Apparently they thought that they might get hit by a car on the street. That ended that fun. Phil also made a friend with a boy up the street named PJ. PJ would try anything Phil or Mark suggested. He was a somewhat troubled child that had a bent toward getting into trouble. On one occasion that got Philip in trouble too when they took something from a local store. As far as I know that was the first and last time Phil ever did anything like that.

Though Phil had professed to receive Christ as his Savior at an early age, by the time he was in Junior High he was not showing any interest in spiritual things. He went to church with us, but I began to notice that his taste in music was very poor. He spent a lot of time in his room by himself. I wasn't sure where he was really at spiritually. I never saw him read his Bible nor did he initiate any spiritual conversation.

I believe it was the summer after Phil's freshman year in high school that everything came to a head. I had insisted that Phil go to camp at Skyview Ranch. He really didn't want to go, but I thought it would be helpful to him. I told him I would do all his mowing jobs for him. During that week on a Wednesday night after prayer meeting Pastor Dave said he needed to talk to me in my office. I could tell it was something huge, but I had no idea that it concerned Phil.

He told me that one of the teenage girls in the youth group had told him that Phil had been drinking and smoking among other things. My first reaction was disbelief. "How could anyone spread such gossip about my son?" I'm sure that had to be very hard for Pastor Dave to tell me. But something inside me told me that this might be true. At first I thought I should go to the camp and confront the girl that told Pastor Dave. But I thought better of it. After we got home I shared with Nancy what Pastor Dave had told me. We both cried and did not get any sleep that night.

I spent the next day praying throughout the day trying to do my job as a pastor and doing Phil's mowing jobs. I was at the church finishing mowing the church lawn, when I got a call from the camp director, Bill Rollof. He told me that Phil had gotten into trouble at camp and he planned to expel him from camp. When he approached Phil about it, Phil saw him coming and knew what it was about. Phil told him that he was guilty and knew he was royally messed up, and didn't believe he was saved. Bill then proceeded to lead Phil to repentance and to a genuine faith in the Savior. After Bill told me the above he put Phil on the phone. I then proceeded to ask Phil about what Pastor Dave had told me, and Phil told me that it was all true. He then proceeded to say, "But it's all going to be different now, dad". And it was, from then on. Phil came home completely changed. Praise the Lord! I learned later that there was an amazing revival that broke out at camp that week with several teens coming to know the Lord.

I couldn't wait to call Nancy and tell her. We both cried again over the phone. Then she asked me when I got the call and when Phil was saved. When I told her it must have been about 5:00 pm when Bill was confronting our son, Nancy started to cry again. When she composed herself she said that at 5:00 pm she had an overwhelming feeling that she needed to pray for Phil. So she stopped what she was doing and began to pray for Phil until the burden was lifted. Our God did that for our son!!!!

During the summer after Phil's sophomore year in high school he followed in the footsteps of Lori and Mark and entered the TFC competition. The only difference is that he competed in the category of Boy's Public Speaking. His speech was basically his testimony and pointed out the dangers of living a life of hypocrisy. He won first place at the state level, which allowed him to be in the national completion, which was to be held in Florida that year. Phil was one of the youngest competitors at the age of 15, but won first place. He really had a powerful message. Our family had the distinction of having all three of our children take first place in the nation in the TFC contest. I know of only one other family that had that distinction.

Phil took over the mowing business when Mark left for college. He also did well with it but was harder on the equipment than Mark. I remember catching him trying to make the tires squeal on the tractor. During Phil's sophomore year of high school he also began to take an interest in learning to play the guitar. He taught himself to play and began to excel at it.

When it came time to consider going to college Phil discovered that he had a problem. Unfortunately his grades were so poor that he could not get into most colleges. Cornerstone College in Grand Rapids accepted him on a probation basis, so he made plans to attend there, where his scholarship would be accepted.

CHAPTER   58

MINISTERING TO SOME FELLOW PASTORS

Ken Floyd

I'm not sure what year it was, but it was probably around 1993, when I received a call from a young pastor. He was in his first pastorate in the nearby town of Coshocton and was going through a rough time. I don't remember the nature of the problems, but I was glad to try to be of some help. I don't think I gave any outstanding advice, but I at least was someone he could talk to and pray with. Ken would later resign from that church and go on to have very successful ministries in Canton, Ohio, and Grand Rapids, Michigan. He is presently the respected director of the Michigan Association of Regular Baptist Churches, and is helping other struggling pastor's and churches. Ken's success I'm sure has had nothing to do with his visit with me, but has everything to do with his heart for God and his passion for people.

Carl Frank

Another young pastor that came to me for direction was a young pastor by the name of Carl Frank. Unlike Ken Floyd, I had never met Pastor Carl before. He was not in our fellowship of churches at the time, but was a pastor in a church with a different theology than Baptist. I think it might have been a Wesleyan Methodist church. At the time I was not sure what the meeting was about. He did not seem to be having a problem in his church. He seemed to be wanting to have a relationship, which was fine with me, but I had never had any pastor of that denomination seek me out for a relationship before.

What I learned later was that he was struggling with the theology to which his church held and was looking for God's direction. I wish I had been of more help to him than I was. Pastor Carl did eventually get the answers he was looking for, resigned his church, and began the very successful Genoa Baptist Church on the north side of Columbus. Ironically some of our good friends and former parishioners from both Faith Baptist of Defiance and Faith Baptist of Mount Vernon presently attend his church. He is a very loving and caring shepherd to them, for which I am very thankful.

CHAPTER   59

PRESIDENT RONALD REAGAN

In 1979 Pastor Jerry Falwell began an organization called the Moral Majority. It was designed to unite the vast number of Christians who were fed up with the immoral direction that many of our political leaders were taking our country. Pastor Falwell had met with Ronald Reagan, heard his testimony and passion for American and was convinced that he was a man conservative believers could get behind. As a result Ronald Reagan was elected to the presidency at least in part because of the efforts of the Moral Majority.

In April of 1984 Jerry Falwell and the Moral Majority held a huge rally for pastors. When I learned that President Reagan was to address that rally I planned to attend, since I had been a supporter of the President and his agenda on the moral and conservative issues and considered myself a part of the Moral Majority. I thought the rally was held at Liberty University, but it might have been held in Washington. Nancy and I had the privilege of hearing President Reagan address the huge crowd of 20,000 or so pastors. What an honor.

During his speech, however, some hecklers had somehow made it into the crowd, and began to yell and try to interrupt his speech. I remember thinking it was my duty to try to put them down, and started to move in their direction. But security and others much closer handled the problem and they were quickly removed.

But my privilege of seeing President Reagan reminded me of my great grandfather, Simon Cummins, who saw another president, Abraham Lincoln, while he served as a soldier during the Civil War. He wrote in one of his letters home about his experience of being in Washington DC., and "getting a squint" at President Lincoln when he addressed the troops.

CHAPTER 60

TAKING A 10% CUT IN SALARY

The southeastern part of Ohio is very hilly and rugged. Much of the ground contains a lot of shale rock and has produced some oil. Three of the families that were members of our church in Mount Vernon were in the oil business. Though I made it a point to never know who gave what in any of the churches I pastored, I suspected that those families were good givers. By 1980 oil prices had hit an all time high averaging $111.30 a barrel. That, of course, helped those families. But oil prices began to fall dramatically in the 1980s, which also affected those families and our church income.

By 1986 oil prices had dropped all the way to $9.85 a barrel. It became apparent that some serious changes had to be made in our budget in order to balance the books. Whenever there was a financial need, Dad Crown always told me to "tell God and tell the people", and God always seemed to meet the need. But in 1986 the deacons thought there needed to be some cuts made to the salaries, so a 10% cut was made to all salaries.

God had always met our family's needs, and I was sure He would do so again. I was also willing to take the cut, but inside I felt the deacons and other leaders should commit to giving more, so the sacrifice was equally shared. Though I struggled with that decision, I trusted God, and both our family's needs and the church's needs were met. I think the fact that I had taken a 10% pay cut encouraged others to give sacrificially. During this time Nancy and I continued to give sacrificially as we always had.

After a couple of years our salary was restored.

CHAPTER 61

ALMOST LEAVING

In 1988 I received a call from my friend Dr. Jim Phipps, who was chairman of the Communications Department at Cedarville. He had been also serving as the interim pastor for the Bethel Baptist Church in Toledo, Ohio. He wanted to know if I would be interested in filling the pulpit at Bethel with the possibility of becoming a candidate there. I had been struggling internally and questioning whether God wanted me to continue at Mount Vernon, so I said I would be willing to fill in and be interviewed by Bethel's pulpit committee.

Since I was only filling the pulpit and not officially candidating I did not tell the deacons how I was feeling. I preached in both the morning and evening services and Nancy and I sang. The pulpit committee interviewed me in the afternoon. Though that church was thriving at that time, something just didn't feel right. That whole experience actually made me realize that God had more for me to do at Mount Vernon. It must not have felt right for them either, because they did not ask me back to candidate.

CHAPTER   62

GOING WITH A.L. WILLIAMS

By 1990 I was turning 45. Lori was attending Cedarville University and Mark would be enrolling at Cedarville in another year. The reality of having two in college was beginning to hit me. Though Nancy and I sought to manage our money wisely, we just were not able to prepare financially for this. About this same time I was beginning to think about planning ahead for retirement. How could we possibly save money for that as well?

Not understanding anything about retirement plans or life insurance, I responded to an ad and an agent came to talk with me. He convinced me to transfer my existing life insurance policy into his universal life policy, because it would make me money toward my retirement. It sounded good.

About two months later I received a visit from one of our members, who I had led to Christ, Bill Drown. He was a former decorated Ohio State Patrol captain and post commander, who had begun to work for a company called A.L. Williams. I was sick when I learned from him that the life insurance policy that I had just taken out was a rip-off. I could take the same money I was spending, have a lot more life insurance coverage and still have money left over to invest in a real retirement program that would make a lot more money.

After changing my policy to go with A.L. Williams, Bill explained that the company was a multi-level marketing company for which I could work part time. The thought hit me that this might be the answer to my prayers concerning getting our kids through college. After getting the approval of the deacons to use my days off to work for A.L. Williams, I got trained and licensed to sell life insurance and securities and went to work.

I soon had three working under me and was becoming good at selling. But I began to realize that it was taking more time than I thought it would. At the same time the church was going through another growth spurt. I knew I could not do both. It just wasn't going to work. Although those above me in my A.L. Williams chain used the incentive of getting rich as a motivation, that wasn't what made me tick. I was a pastor who was just trying to make enough money to get his kids through college. I decided that I was called first to be a pastor and nothing should interfere with that. I would just have to trust God to get my kids through college, and drop out of A.L. Williams, which I did.

I do not regret at all my time with A.L. Williams. I really learned a lot about how money works, about insurances (both good and bad), and about mutual funds (securities). All of this would help me the rest of my life both personally and in my ministry to others. I probably would have been very successful selling life insurance and securities, but I would have missed God's best for me, and failed miserably when it comes to eternal blessings. God's grace was being poured out on me.

A couple of years later, thanks to the leadership of one of our members who worked for the Edward Jones Company (Fred Mankins), the church started a 403B retirement plan for me. They would match what I put into the program up to a certain amount. The church, also, allowed me to invest in the mutual fund of my choice. Thankfully that did well, which helps to supplement our Social Security checks today.

CHAPTER 63

MY BACK PROBLEM

I had had back problems to some degree going back to my teenage years. I had gotten hurt in football practice and went to see an Osteopathic Doctor. When he examined my back he told me that I should not be playing football with a back like mine. He never really explained why, so I ignored him and played football.

Another time when I was having some back problems in Defiance, I went to see a Chiropractic Doctor. I remember him saying that I had a back "like a snake", but I did not understand what he was trying to say either. But I did continue to see him and it helped.

But in 1992 I developed a severe problem in my lower back. The pain was going down my right leg to my ankle. Though I went to my chiropractor in Mount Vernon I was getting no relief. In fact, I seemed to be getting worse. It got so bad that I needed Nancy's help to get dressed in the morning. I could hardly get out of bed. Though I continued to preach I leaned on the pulpit, while I was preaching, and had trouble just getting to the pulpit. I could hardly use my right leg. In fact, I drove using my left leg. I was in bad shape and did not know what to do. My only option seemed to be surgery.

By the spring of 1993 I had almost resigned myself to live the rest of my life in extreme pain. Lori was to graduate from college at the end of May. I was not about to miss that huge event in my daughter's life, but I did not know how I was going to be able to handle the trip or all of the events. I talked to Dr. Dan Smith, who was a D.O. and a member of our church. He gave me some pain medicine that he said would help me. I was able to go to Lori's graduation and somehow made it through everything, but don't remember much. I think I smiled a lot.

All through this ordeal my neighbor, Mike Mickley kept telling me that I should go to his chiropractor, who really was not a doctor at all, but an Amish man named Toby. I kept brushing Mike's suggestion off. But I finally humbled myself to agree to go. What harm could it do? I was ready to try anything, even an Amish chiropractor named Toby.

Toby used a different approach on me. He did not try to "crack" my back, but was gentle using pressure in other ways. He also sold me some herbs that he said coated the nerves. He told me to stop using heat on my back. Though it made me feel better, it was causing the nerves to swell, putting more pressure on them and injuring them more. He said I should be putting ice on my back instead. I started taking the herbs, seeing him regularly, and following his instructions to a tee. Gradually I started to improve. I'm sure it did not help any that I continued to mow lawns, which sometimes required bouncing on a riding lawn mower.

Toby and I developed a wonderful relationship. I would talk to him about the Bible which he loved to do. He even went with me to make a visit in a nursing home. I ended up leading a man in the nursing home to the Lord. Toby never stopped talking about that. He had a lot of respect for me, and I thought a lot of him. Although we did not agree on everything, I really believe he was trusting Christ alone for his salvation.

Several months after meeting Toby I heard about a Christian chiropractor in Berlin, Ohio, who had been a big help to Pastor Bob.   One of the first things Dr. Winston Hall did was to take an x-ray of my back. For the first time in my life I began to learn what my problem was. I had scoliosis. I probably had it since I was a teen. I just didn't know it. My back curved the wrong way causing pressure on my lower vertebrae and the ones in my neck. If I wanted to get better I had to stop lifting any heavy weights, and be careful how I lifted any weights. I had not noticed until I saw that x-ray how my neck compensated, so my head would be straight and not tilted. It was like a light went on. It all began to make sense.

Dr. Hall treated me without charge. However, he would sometimes talk to me for 45 minutes or so about the Bible or family issues. Sometimes I felt bad when I went out to the exam room and saw a room filled with waiting patients. That never seemed to bother Dr. Hall or deter him from our conversations. I think we helped each other. I continued to see Dr. Hall and Toby until we moved to Michigan. I also began to do some lower back exercises recommended by a physical therapist.

I remember the first time I noticed that I was walking without pain. It was probably in 1994. I was at a gym walking on a treadmill. I remember stopping and bowing my head and thanking God. His grace had seen me through a very difficult period in my life. I was so thankful.

CHAPTER 64

MY TRIP TO RUSSIA

From 1945 until 1991 there existed what was called an "iron curtain" between Russia and free Europe. Travel to and from communist controlled Russian countries was restricted. Religious freedom was nonexistent in communist Russia. Though there were churches in Russia during that time they were controlled by the government. Christians who wanted to worship freely had to do so secretly in "underground" churches. These were usually in houses. Christians who met in these churches did so at extreme risk of fines or imprisonment. Bibles were scarce, although some organizations had a ministry of smuggling Bibles into Russia and other "closed" countries. Most of the pastors of the "underground" churches had no formal Bible training other than what they may had picked up from smuggled literature or Christian short wave radio programs.

In 1995 I was asked to be part of a team that would go to Russia to give some crash courses to pastors, most of whom had been part of the "underground" church movement. The team was being sponsored by a mission organization called Evangelical Baptist Mission, which had established connections in Russia. EBM's president was my good friend and former Cedarville roommate, Paul Jackson. The missionary who asked me to go and would lead the team was another friend from Cedarville, Byron Shearer. The subject he wanted me to teach was on church planting (starting churches).

I was excited and felt honored to be part of the team. I began to prepare the lessons, which required a lot of work. I would be speaking to the pastors three times a day for a week, and then the next week speak at a new Bible institute to a different group on the book of Philippians. The entire trip would take thirteen days.

I had never flown oversees, so I needed to purchase several things. I especially needed a voltage converter since the electrical outlets in Russia put out a lot more voltage then those in the U.S. I also needed luggage. I was told that luggage on wheels called a "Pullman" would be especially helpful.

About this same time Nancy and one of her friends, Carol Biggs, had discovered an Eddie Bauer Outlet on the west side of Columbus. This was not the usual Eddie Bauer Outlet. It was an outlet that sold returns and other overstocked items at a fraction of their original cost. I have always said, if there is a bargain within a 100 mile radius, Nancy will find it. I had to admit she did come home with some ridiculous deals. I stopped making fun of her when she came home with a pair of Eddie Bauer work shoes for me that she bought for $3.00. They only needed a little repair, which I was able to do for $2.00. So when she suggested that I go with her and Carol to the Eddie Bauer Outlet to find the things I needed for my trip to Russia, I agreed to go. I wasn't excited about standing in line to get into a store to shop, but the thought of finding everything I needed for a few bucks, overcame my reluctance.

By the time it was our turn to go into the store (the store could not hold all of the women who wanted to get in), I immediately saw women pulling suitcases, the exact kind that I needed. When I finally got to the back of the store where they seemed to be coming from, I saw a lady grab the last one right when I was reaching for it. And she seemed to have no remorse.

I was bummed. Then I heard someone say that they would be bringing more out later. So I made my way back to where it said "employees only" and stuck my head through the door. Sure enough, there was a whole stack of Pullman suitcases on a pallet, just like I wanted. So as inconspicuously as I could I waited near that door. I must have waited what seemed like an hour, when finally a man came though the double doors pulling the pallet stacked with Pullmans. I was all ready to implement my plan. All I needed to do was get directly behind that moving pallet and keep up.

But I discovered that I was not the only one who wanted one of those suitcases. They were selling them for $10.00, which was a tremendous bargain. There appeared to be fifty suitcases stacked at least eight feet high and wrapped tightly with shrink wrap to keep them in their stack. I was not prepared with how ruthless a bargain crazed woman can be. There was pushing and shoving and grabbing. Some of the women were breaking through the plastic wrap and grabbing them before the employee even got close to where he was planning to unload them.

Suddenly the man moving the pallet stopped and yelled at the women and said, "If you don't let me get these unloaded I will take them all back". That seemed to cool the ruckus for a few minutes. I kept my place behind the moving wall of suitcases trying to be as polite as I could and keep my Christian testimony.

Then it happened. A lady pushing a baby in a stroller next to me lost the wheel off of her stroller. My first thought was, "Lady, you should have known better than to bring an innocent baby into a madhouse like this". But she looked up at me with such pitiful eyes. So I bent down and as quickly as I could put the wheel back on her stroller.

I'm sure that only took a few seconds. But by then a very scary crowd was between me and the Pullmans. The employee had reached his destination and began throwing the suitcases on the huge table. But women were grabbing them before they even reached the table. Again the man yelled at the women, but this time they paid no attention to him. Finally, I think he feared for his life, he just walked away. By the time I finally could reach the table, every last suit case was gone. I couldn't believe it. I think I even said a quiet prayer, "Why Lord?"

Now I was really bummed. I had found everything else I needed for the trip, but really thought I should have been able to get a Pullman. It didn't seem fair. Some of the women had more than one. In fact, one woman, who was standing in the checkout with the only other man in the store, had **five** of them. I felt compelled to ask her as nicely as I knew how, "Mam, do you really need all five of those?" I thought my pitiful look might influence her to let me have one of hers. Her husband quickly came to her defense and with a look that seemed to be a fraction from a fist in my face assured me that I needed to back off.

But God is so merciful! A lady in another checkout line overheard my plea and took pity on me. She said, "Here, you can have one of mine", and she let me take one of her stash of three. I felt like kissing her hand. But I controlled myself and just thanked her profusely.

I left that Eddie Bauer Outlet that day a wiser man. I learned that bargains are not always worth it. I don't know how Nancy has survived all these years. I learned that those kinds of places are not intended for a man. I also left that day realizing that I needed a lot of time alone with God before I would be spiritually prepared to minister to Russian pastors.

Nancy was not in favor of me going to Russia. She was sure that the plane would crash or I would somehow be killed. Years earlier I had had another opportunity to fly to Brazil and speak at a missionary conference for my missionary friend, Mark Trimble. Though I had agreed to go, I had to call Mark and cancel because of Nancy's fears. I felt bad about that, but thought I should be sensitive to my God given wife. But this time it was different. I knew God wanted me to go and that God would help Nancy. Phil was still living at home at the time and was a very big help to her, and I called her from Russia more than once to assure her that I was ok.

All my teaching had to be done through an interpreter named Victor. He spoke English without an accent, but had a slight southern drawl. He said he studied English in Texas.

It wasn't long before I realized that all the lessons that I had prepared were not what the pastors were wanting. I had been misinformed. They did not need motivation or instruction on church planting. What they really wanted was instruction on how to disciple new believers. They knew how to lead people to the Lord, and how to start a church. But they needed material and help on how to help new believers to grow, so they could become useful helpers in their church. I had to change my lessons midstream.

I had written thirteen lessons just for that purpose in my church at Defiance, and continued to use them at Mount Vernon. And fortunately I had brought a copy of that lesson book with me to Russia. So I did the best I could helping them with what they needed. But I have always regretted that I did not leave that book with them, so it could have been translated into Russian. What was I thinking?

By the time I was done speaking to the pastors and preaching in one of the underground churches on Sunday, I was beginning to lose my voice. It was winter in Moscow at that time of year. I had grown up in the cold of Michigan, but their cold seemed so much colder for some reason. I spoke in the Bible Institute once or twice, but by then my voice was completely gone, so Byron finished the lessons for me.

After our teaching times were completed we had a day to sight see. I saw the huge Kremlin Building and the Red Square. I saw where some beheading had been done when the Czars ruled. I bought a Russian hat as a souvenir and a Russian Santa Claus for Nancy to add to her collection.

A few things stood out to me about my trip. **First,** I could not get over how depressing it was when I entered the Moscow airport. It was drab, and so unlike the airports in America. **Second**, I had never seen a real beggar before. I'm sure begging occurs in our country as well, but I had never seen it. I will never forget the image of an old man with a gunny sack over his shoulder going through a barrel of bones outside of a store as he tried to find something he could make soup out of. **Third**, I felt it was strange how reserved everyone was when they traveled on the trains. No one spoke to anyone. They trusted no one. They were still used to being under communism, though that restrictive oppression had been lifted. **Fourth**, I had the privilege of interviewing two pastors who had spent a total of 18 years in prison for their faith. I remember that one older gentleman's crime was baptizing a teenager. **Fifth**, the Russian Christians have the custom of greeting one another with a kiss including men with men. I had been told that they would not do that with us because that was not our custom.

Someone forgot to tell the older man that I interviewed. He came up to me and planted one right on my mouth. I was polite and hopefully did not show a negative reaction, but inside I had a lot going on. And it wasn't fireworks.

Finally, when we were getting ready to return home we had a problem. Something had gotten messed up with our visas. I'm not sure what the problem was, but Byron had to go somewhere and get the problem corrected. If he was unable to do so we might have to stay in Russia indefinitely. I really wanted to go home by this time, and was praying a lot. Added to the tension were a couple of Russian soldiers who kept following us and watching us closely. Russian soldiers seemed to be everywhere in Russia, especially around the trains and airport. When the visa problem was resolved and we were going through the final checkpoint, Byron slipped me a folder containing a few thousand dollars. I had already gone through the checkpoint but he had not. He slipped it to me when the guard wasn't looking. He explained later that taking out such a large amount of money would have caused a big problem. Somehow God was watching over me and I made it out of Russia ok.

I had borrowed a video camera for the trip so still have the interviews and highlights of the trip somewhere. It was a trip I will never forget. But I was very glad to come home, and so glad to be an American.

CHAPTER 65

ATTEMPTED CHURCH PLANT IN FREDERICKTOWN

Our church drew people from several towns in a twenty mile radius in central Ohio. Some drove to church from as far as Delaware, Ohio, which was about an hour drive. In 1998 we had at least three families coming from the town of Fredericktown. I was approached at that time by a young pastor who had a desire to start a new church in Fredericktown, named Nathan Pierpont. Another mature pastor had been attending our church, Pastor Bob Veenhuis, who also expressed interest in helping start the new church.

So in October of 1998 the new church plant in Fredericktown was launched in a rented school building. It showed some growth initially and was reaching people we would never reach. Thank the Lord some were saved through that effort. But after a couple of years the work reached a plateau and began to decline. It soon became obvious that the work was not going to survive, so we decided to close it down.

CHAPTER 66

THE MEN GIVE ME A GUN

I had always loved to shoot guns for as long as I can remember. One of my favorite things to do is to shoot clay pigeons, which are round disks made of clay and launched up into the air. I love the challenge of shooting them out of the air and seeing them turn to powder. I always shot at Skyview Ranch whenever I went with the men to the men's retreat. I continued to attend the retreats after moving to Mount Vernon. The men from Mount Vernon loved the retreats as the men from Defiance had. They also loved to out shoot me at the trap shoot or rifle completion. In a trap shoot the clay pigeons are thrown in front of the shooter from a thrower at ground level. In a competition the shooter usually shoots against four others each shooting at twenty-five "birds". I always tried to get a perfect score, but I don't believe I ever did. I think the best I did was twenty-four out of twenty-five.

Then men from Mount Vernon introduced me to a different twist on the trap shoot. It was called "sporting clays". It simulated more realistic hunting situations with the clays coming from all kinds of directions. Sometimes they would be going away from the shooter, sometimes toward him. Sometimes they would cross in front of him. Sometimes they would be coming two at a time, or sometimes one after another. They usually had one shooting station where they would bounce a clay pigeon on the ground simulating a running rabbit. Obviously sporting clays were a lot more challenging. I loved it, but did terrible at it the first time. I think I hit 13 out of 50. Sporting clays became an annual event for the men's ministry as an outreach event. Before we shot we had someone share their testimony and give the gospel.

One year after arriving at the sporting clays event I noticed that the twenty or thirty men had all gathered around a pick-up truck. Gary Fraley then came over to me and said they had something they wanted to show me. When I got to the pick-up there was a gun lying in the bed of the truck. I didn't understand what was going on. It was a gun I had borrowed a lot from Wes Crum. I loved that gun and had gotten pretty good with it. It was a Browning Citori over and under double barrel 12 gauge shotgun. It was a beautiful gun and probably worth about $2500.00. But Wes loved to have me shoot it. I think it was one of his favorite guns.

But Wes had had a stroke and didn't think he would be able to shoot with us anymore. I'm sure Wes had offered the gun to the men at a great price. The men had gone together and purchased the gun from Wes and presented it to me that day.

When they saw the puzzled look on my face they all laughed and said "it is now yours". I was floored. They had a camera there to take a picture of my shocked face. I still have those pictures and treasure that moment. Those men loved me! And I loved them! It was a moment I will never forget.

Earlier this year I received a call from Wes Jr. telling me that his father had passed away. I was so glad he thought to call me. A flood of memories came to my mind after that call. Among them was the evening I led Wes senior to the Lord and the day the men gave me that very special gun.

CHAPTER 67

THE STEVE FUNSTEN STORY

I had directed the choir almost from the beginning days of our church with a couple of exceptions. When we first came to Mount Vernon Ruth Agnew directed the choir. She was one of the most respected piano teachers in the county. But she was getting up in years and after a few months turned the job over to me. I was always looking for someone who could do the job. Not that I didn't enjoy it, but it took time to prepare, and I really needed to be able to focus only on my message on Sunday morning. But for about 20 years I directed the choir except for the two years that Pastor Dave was on staff and for a brief time when another man, Jim Frady directed it.

When the Funtsen family began to attend our church, I learned that Steve had a master's degree in music from Northwestern University. Both Steve and Gail joined our choir and read music very well. I had thought of asking Steve to see if he would be interested in directing the choir, but I was hesitant for a couple of reasons. Neither reason had anything to do with his musical qualifications. First, his degree of music was in instrumental music. He was an excellent French horn player and band director in a local school. But there is a big difference between directing a band and directing a choir primarily with how words are pronounced and phrased. My second, and major concern, had to do with Steve's personality. I loved Steve, and still do, but he could be direct and blunt at times. I was concerned that he might offend some in the choir in how he corrected them and lose them. So I did nothing.

About a year passed after Steve and Gail joined the choir when Steve asked me to come over to his house to talk over a matter. Probably after the first couple of opening sentences Steve, in his usual direct manner, asks, "Why haven't you asked me to direct the choir?" That question caught me off guard. I tried to think of a nice way to answer him without offending him. I'm sure I prayed to myself, "Lord, help me." What came out of my mouth surprised even me. "Steve, it's your personality".

 I waited for his bad reaction, but there was none. Instead he simply said, "Whew. I'm relieved. I thought you didn't think I was musically qualified." I assured him that I thought he was very qualified, and went on to express my concerns. During the conversation it became clear to me that God was in this. So I suggested to him that he try it for a few weeks and see how the choir responds. If all goes well he would be the new choir director.

He did amazingly well. He had the time to be so much more prepared than I was, and it showed. He continued to be direct but I could tell he was working on it. I think there was one choir member who didn't even give Steve a chance, but the rest all stayed and saw how well he did. Our choir grew and developed into a really great choir over the next several years that Nancy and I were in Mount Vernon.

I am so glad God had Steve in mind for our choir director. It certainly relieved me of a job I didn't need, and helped our choir and Steve to grow. God's grace is so awesome!

CHAPTER 68

AVOIDING THE "MUSIC WARS"

I was not raised on southern gospel music. I do remember as a teenager going to a Blackwood's Brother's Quartet concert at the Edmore High School and really enjoying it. Our musical training was formal, so I enjoyed classical music as well as listening to the pop songs on the radio.

In the 1990s a more contemporary sound was coming into the church. The instruments being used were changing as well, which include electric and bass guitars and drums. The younger generation thought the hymns were outdated and boring, and to them, so was the organ and piano. Some churches had changed totally and suddenly to the new music causing church splits. Some pastors did not handle the matter well as they attempted to force the new music on the older generation.

Lori, Mark, and Phil all liked the new music. Phil would eventually join a Gospel rock band called "Quietwiser" and travel the country making several recordings with that group. I, on the other hand, was dead set against it. In fact, I said privately that "we would have a set of drums in our church over my dead body." But Pastor Matt, our youth pastor, felt very differently. In fact, on his own initiative he started a small "praise band" on Sunday night using guitars and eventually a set of drums.

I could see that our congregation was divided on the issue. I needed to do something, but wasn't sure what to do. I decided to do a personal Bible study on the subject of worship. I also ordered a set of recordings on worship by renowned Pastor, Alistar Begg. The only solid argument I could see for the new kind of music had to do with their focus on expressing worship. Most of those songs were addressed to God or about God. Some hymns did that as well, but most were more about God or testimonials concerning one's relationship with God. But the hymns contained such great doctrinal truths that were a great way to teach people. I did not want to do away with them either.

As I began to study the Psalms especially, and other New Testament passages that had to do with congregational singing, I was surprised by what I learned. But when I came to Psalm 150 I was shocked, especially by the instruments God seemed to like. God said to praise Him with cymbals, even the "loud clanging" ones. I remember pausing and saying, "God, You can't mean that. You not only allow percussion instruments to praise You, but you command it." I began to mellow. God seemed to like something I didn't. His range of musical taste was obviously broader than mine.

About the same time that I was struggling internally with the music issue, we were out growing our building and parking area. We had discussed going to two services. It seemed like our only solution for the present. I did some research on it and got some material on how to go to two services. We made the decision to try it.

To prepare the people for the change, I preached a message on the necessity for going to two services. I then preached a series of messages on worship. We decided to have a traditional service in the early service using hymns accompanied by piano and organ. We would have a blended service in the second service using a keyboard, electric drum set and guitars and mix hymns and praise choruses. The instruments could all be mixed using the sound board, so none would over power the singers or each other. We felt the words were the most important part of the music. Worship is singing a message to God. That message can't be appreciated collectively if it is not distinguishable. We would avoid songs that were what I called "edgy" musically, and would use choruses that were easier to sing and had solid words.

The transition worked for us and did not cause division. When we built our new Family Center we held the second service there, which worked well. We continued to have an evening service which was also traditional. Our church continued to grow noticeably after going to the two services. I know other churches have been destroyed over the music issue. In my opinion much of that could have been avoided if minds and hearts on both sides of the issue would have been controlled by God's Spirit, not their own preferences, and put others ahead of themselves. I truly believe God's grace was being poured out on me once again through this whole matter.

CHAPTER 69

BUILDING OUR FAMILY CENTER

We had known for at least five years that we needed to expand our building. We had out grown every area of our building including our auditorium, nursery, kitchen and fellowship area, and our office area. Our teens needed a much better area they could call their own. Going to two services helped with our auditorium space and parking, but that was about all.

For three years prior to 1999 we had a special drive to pay off our debt on our first building. That went well and we were able to be debt free before launching another building project.

In 1998 we contacted a design/build company that specialized in building for growing churches. The McKnight Company president and leaders were all very nice to work with, and they saw our unique problem with expansion. Our property sloped so sharply down behind our existing building. They did not see any way to connect the new building with the old. We had already paid them a large sum of money for the plan they presented to us, but we were not happy with their plan. So we thanked them for their work, but parted with them.

I wasn't sure what to do next. I just prayed about it. Shortly after that, one of our members, who was in the construction business, Gary Fraley, suggested that we check out another design/build company from Delaware, Ohio, which was run by a man named Dean Fraker. Gary and I went to see one of the additions Dean had completed and were impressed. So we asked for Dean's help and suggestions as to how to solve our addition problem. He quickly had an idea as to how to attach the addition to our existing building. So we contracted with him to draw up the plans and build the addition.

I remember the terrible business meeting when the building committee presented the new building plans and cost to the congregation. I was not prepared for some of the opposition. To me it was so obvious. I was excited about the plan and was so certain that God was in it. But there were two ladies that had called some widows and stirred up some of the older folks against the project. I was hurt that they had not come to me first with their objections, and because of the scare tactics that they had used on the older people, saying that the debt would lead us to destruction. What hurt me, also, was that some of those leading the opposition had been charter members and so supportive of our first building project. I was devastated and discouraged.

But the vast majority of the congregation was very much supportive of the project and encouraged us to pursue it. When those opposed saw that they were not going to be able to stop the project, they unfortunately left the church. I think that involved perhaps four or five families.

Everyone else was so excited about the prospect of having our needs met. The project was huge. It was going to be a 28,000 square foot addition costing nearly two million dollars. Gulp! We had raised or would raise close to $700,000 of that. So our mortgage would be about 1.3 million dollars. With the help of one of our experienced financial planners, Fred Mankins, we were able to secure a loan with the First Merit Bank at a very good interest rate, which would allow the church to pay extra on the mortgage in the future.

For this project we hired a professional fundraising company to help us underwrite the mortgage with the additional giving from the people. We worked with a man who had formerly been a pastor, Larry Armentrout, who did an excellent job for us and was so easy to work with. We made sure that there was no pressure applied to the people and that all giving promises were kept confidential. The big rock that is still in front of the church today was Larry's idea and placed there as part of the stewardship campaign. It reads, "Upon this Rock we build", which refers to Jesus Christ.

The Ground Breaking Service for the new building was held on May 16, 1999. We had made an outline of the new addition using white paint and had the people all stand on the white line, making a human outline of the building. Our mayor and personal friend, Dick Mavis, joined us for that exciting service.

The work on the building was all done by the Delaware Building Systems people and their subcontractors except for the painting and finish work, which our men did. We spent a lot of late nights together. We had one of our ladies, Carol Biggs, who was a professional interior designer, make the decisions on the colors, furniture and decorations. Carol did an amazing job. We did not have one complaint about her choices. I had a couple of suggestions about maximizing the use of space, and I think Gary Fraley did as well.

When Gary suggested that we paint the ceiling in the gym black, I hesitated. I was not so sure about how that would look. But he assured me that it would save tons of money and the black would make the beams in the ceiling disappear when the lights were on. He was absolutely right. There were two or three that took turns spraying the black paint on the ceiling. They looked so funny when they smiled. All you could see was their teeth and eyes.

Everything about that addition was awesome. Our new office complex, the nursery area, the entrances and foyers…they all looked gorgeous. And it was all laid out so well and functional. After it was all done there was not one thing any of us wanted to change. God was so in it all. The only thing we forgot to do was to run a big conduit under the gym floor to connect the stage with the P.A. booth with sound cable. So we rented a lift, and I ran the huge cable through the steel rafters of the gym and down to the stage. I never really had a problem with heights. I thought it was fun.

The Family Center gym had a stage on one side under which we stored all the round tables. The chairs which were stacked had a designated room. Each side of the stage had stairs. One of the stairs went up to the nursery area and the other set of stairs went to the office complex. The connecting stairs were my idea. The new building involved three floors in order to accommodate the way the property sloped back so sharply, and to connect to the existing building properly. We incorporated an elevator that went to all three floors in order to help those who did not do stairs well. We also attached a carport to the main entrance of the new building to help in bad weather.

What a building God gave to us! His grace was truly poured out on us. Our first Sunday in our new building was in September of 2000, and the new building was dedicated a few weeks later on September 24, 2000.

CHAPTER   70

THE POWER TEAM

The story of our ministry at Mount Vernon would not be complete without telling about the Power Team.
Sometime early in 2001 Joann Kerr came to me about using the Power Team as an outreach to the community.
Joann worked for Knox County's Health Department and was a member of our church. Part of her role had to
do with working with teens in the area of sex education. Since she was a strong believer she was able to teach
abstinence to the teens. She believed the Power Team could help her in her ministry to the teens in the county.

The Power Team was a ministry composed of **extremely** strong men physically, who were also strong believers.
They would connect with a local church for the evening evangelistic meetings and do school assemblies in the
county during the day. In the schools they were not allowed to share the Gospel, but they taught abstinence, and
living drug and alcohol free lives among other things. They did feats of strength to get the kids attention and
respect before sharing truth with them. The kids really listened after they saw how strong they were. After the
team presented their assembly program they would tell the kids that they were also appearing nightly at the particular church with which they were working.

The Power Team had a wonderful reputation, and I loved their approach to evangelism. But I had a problem.
They all looked in their pictures like they were part of a TV wrestling show, which we all know is not real. I
was concerned about how we would be perceived as a church if we used this method of evangelism. Added to
my own concerns was the fact that Nancy was not supportive of the idea.

But the more I thought and prayed about it, the more I felt we should try it. When I presented the idea to the
deacons they were all supportive of it as was our pastoral staff. So the fall dates of October 3-7, 2001, were set
with the Power Team.

The preparation for the meetings was an enormous effort. The meetings required a huge stage crew with all
kinds of props including cement blocks to be broken, torches, fire extinguishers, phone books (to be ripped in
half) and a myriad of other things. The team needed drivers to take them to the school assemblies and help with
the props there. There would be five members of the team involved in our meetings. We needed personal
workers and follow-up literature. Preparing for the meetings was a big job!

But the meetings were a huge success. I had never seen anything like it. We had people come to the meetings
that we would never have had come to a "normal" evangelistic meeting. We had 271 salvation decisions and
165 other public decisions during those five nights for a total of 436 decisions. The last night of the meetings
was a Sunday night. We had 919 people attend that last night. We packed as many as we could into the Family
Center with the rest in the auditorium watching by means of closed circuit television.

One of the feats of strength involved rolling up a frying pan with one hand. I would not have believed it if I had
not seen it with my own eyes. The team member's name who did this particular feat was "Rock". He was built
like a rock. He shared his testimony of how he had found Christ while he was in prison. His arms were as big

as my legs or bigger. He took the frying pan and with one hand curled it up like a pretzel against his leg. After that meeting he gave me the frying pan which I still have. It is signed by all the members of the team.

The first night of the meetings the team announced that on the last night of the meetings they were going to do a special feat of strength that would involve the pastor. They were going to put a 600 pound block of ice on the pastor's chest and break it with a sledge hammer, while he was laying on a bed of nails. I was shocked when they made that announcement. They had never checked with about it. I had just gotten over some serious back problems. Nancy was not happy. When we got home she said, "There is no way you are going to do that". I tried to assure her it would be ok. There had to be some trick to it. But that didn't seem to help. I think she was mad at me for the next four days. But if it got people into our church to hear the Gospel, I would literally do whatever it took, even lay on a bed of nails with someone trying to hit me with a sledge hammer.

Finally Sunday night came. The news had spread through our community. There was standing room only in the Family Center, and we also packed the auditorium with people watching by means of closed circuit TV. They told me to wear a t-shirt and jokingly told me not to drink any water before the service (so I wouldn't leak). They had the bed of nails lying on a board about knee high. Hanging by a chain above the bed of nails was the huge 600 pound block of ice. There was a step ladder next to the block of ice so that the one using the sledge hammer could be high enough to break it.

The announcer took a pop can and struck it against the bed of nails to prove that they were really sharp. The pop can burst and sprayed pop all over. Then he called me to the stage and asked me if I was ready. He then did something that really shocked me. He asked if the pastor's wife were present and if she would come up to the stage. He had no way of knowing how much Nancy was against the whole thing they were about to do. But Nancy was put on the spot, and she had to come up to the stage. She was against what I was about to do, but at least she came to the meeting. After the crowd greeted Nancy warmly with a round of applause, he said, "Do you have any last words for your husband?" What she said next brought the house down. "Yes. Where's the insurance policy?" Everyone thought she was being funny. I knew differently. She was very serious.

They laid me on my back on the bed of nails, which were about a quarter of an inch apart. They were real nails, but I think because they were close enough together they did not hurt me. My legs bent down at the knees to the floor away from the audience. Just on the other side of my knees was a stack of blocks, which the audience could not see. The block of ice was then lowered with the front of the block on my chest, but most of the weight rested on the cement blocks. The team member who was to break the block of ice climbed the ladder (He was a former NFL player). He then hesitated and said, "Where's the sledge hammer?" They all acted as though they could not find it, while I was to act like I was in pain. What they did not know was that I really was in pain, a lot of pain. I had gotten a cramp in my leg and it was killing me, but I didn't want to ruin the moment. So I was the only one not acting. Finally they found the sledge hammer and broke the ice. They then picked me up off of the bed of nails and the crowd "went wild".

What a week! One of the men that was saved during the meetings was the father of one of our members, who was a professor at the Nazarene University down the road. He had been a big helper during the meetings and was able to get his father to attend. His father had recently retired from the Los Angeles police department, and had moved to the area. He really had no interest in the Gospel, but after hearing it, and the testimonies of the

Power Team members, God got a hold of his heart, and he surrendered his life to Christ. Just two months later he died of a heart attack. I had his funeral, which was attended by several of his friends on the police force from California, who attended in full uniform. He was apparently one of the most respected men on that force.

What if I hadn't had those meetings? What if I wasn't willing to get out of my comfort zone and do something that probably wasn't "politically correct" as far as some of my pastor friends were concerned? I am so glad that God impressed it enough on my heart to have the Power Team come. God's grace just kept pouring out on me.

CHAPTER 71

MINISTRIES THAT GREATLY IMPACTED OUR CHURCH

Discipleship Ministry

In 2001 we launched a discipleship ministry. I had always personally tried to disciple everyone I led to Christ using primarily material put out by The Navigators and by teaching a class for new believers using material that I wrote when I pastored in Defiance. I had used the Navigator material and taught my class for years. But what I had not done is trained believers on how to disciple others, and the Lord began to convict me about that.

Pastor Bob had heard of a church in New Philadelphia, Ohio, that had been training pastors in a local church oriented discipleship program. After Pastor Bob attended their training sessions, he recommended that I attend as well. After attending their training I was convinced that we needed to launch a training program for our own people and get serious about discipleship. Up to this point my philosophy of ministry had consisted of two Es: Evangelism and Edification (win the lost and build up the believers in the faith). But now I was adding a third E: "Equipping the believers for the work of the ministry".

In June of 2001 we had some leaders from the First Baptist Church of New Philadelphia give a discipleship training seminar. Later we taught training classes to our people with 34 completing the training and 20 people beginning to disciple someone. Pastor Bob became our Minister of Discipleship with this ministry impacting our church both in numerical growth and spiritual growth.

Upward Basketball

Another ministry that impacted our church was the Upward Basketball ministry. Nancy had somehow heard of this ministry, probably because she oversaw our Children's Ministry. She attended a presentation of the Upward Basketball ministry and came home totally sold on the idea of doing that ministry in our church. The Upward ministry had a DVD that I could watch. I was blown away by the possibility of using basketball to reach our community for Christ.

About the same time the First Church of the Nazarene in Mount Vernon had been using the Upward Ministry for just a few years. Their ministry had exploded to the extent that they had no more room for the kids that wanted to be involved. So they contacted us since we had a gym to see if we wanted to take part of the kids and have an Upward Basketball ministry. To me it was a no brainer.

The beauty of the program is that our coaches got to share Christ with their kids as part of the practice time. And during the half-time of the games one of our people would share their testimony with all who came to watch. During game day (Saturday) we would have about 1000 people come to watch their child or grandchild play basketball. Coaches were not allowed to put any kid down, and during the game, if a child committed a mistake after blowing his whistle the referee would explain the mistake to the child. It was a positive experience for each child, and the parents loved it.

The practices began in the month of December and the games were played in January and February. We were able to divide our gym in half, so two games could be played every hour at the same time. Games would start at 9:00 am and be played every hour until 3:00 or 4:00. In March an awards program was held where awards were given to every child with another opportunity to share the Gospel to about 2000 kids' parents and grandparents. This was usually held at the Nazarene University's auditorium since it was the only place large enough to hold that many people.

The lady who headed up this ministry for us was Susie Basista. She had been an outstanding basketball player at Mount Vernon high school, when she attended there and had a real burden to use that background for the Lord. She did an awesome job. We had a "Snack Shack" on Saturdays that served quickly prepared foods for those attending the games. We had people heading up that part of the ministry as well. Nancy and Susie had everything well organized.

I don't know how many people were saved through this ministry but I know that some were. I also know that it really helped our people get out of their comfort zone when they shared their testimony in front of a crowd at the games. It also helped put our church on the map in the community. As far as I know that ministry is still going on at Faith Baptist in Mount Vernon.

CHAPTER 72

MY TRIP TO ISRAEL

In 2005 I was contacted by Dr. Gary Candlish about having him come for some meetings at our church. I had known Dr. Candlish through my parents. He had been a professor of Bible at Spurgeon Baptist Bible College when mom and dad worked at that school in Mulberry, Florida. When Spurgeon closed its doors Dr. Candlish continued a Bible conference ministry in churches and launched a ministry to the Jews. Part of that ministry was taking Christians on tours to Israel.

When Dr. Candlish came to our church he presented to our people the opportunity of going on a trip to Israel.. He also wanted me to go. I had had an opportunity to go to Israel several years earlier, when Rev. Earl Umbaugh invited me to co-host a trip with him, when I was pastoring at Defiance. He said that if I got five people to go with me that I could go free. But I was concerned about leaving Nancy alone with our small children at the time and knew she would worry greatly about my safety, so I turned him down. But our situation was different now. The kids were all grown, and Nancy was getting somewhat used to me flying.

So I told Dr. Candlish about the deal that Rev. Umbaugh had offered me and wondered if that was a possibility. He told me that if I got seven people to go that I could go free. I was pretty sure I could do that. In fact when our members heard that I was going, several wanted to go. In addition, the deacons decided to pay the way for any pastor who wanted to go. I think we ended up with about twenty or so going from our church.

Since my way was being paid twice, in effect, I decided to see if I could take one of our kids. I knew Nancy did not want to go because of her fear of flying. My first choice was Mark, since he was in the ministry by this time. But he was preparing to go to Ireland as a missionary, so he couldn't go. I felt I needed to ask Phil next since we would be rooming together. After talking it over with his wife, Stacey, she also wanted to go and would pay her own way. Life was good! I was going to Israel, and sharing the experience with several of our members and my son and his wife.

But it would even get better. Though Stacey had been saved, she had never been baptized. She wanted to know if I would baptize her in the Jordan River. After talking it over with Gary Candlish, and securing the authority to do so from Phil and Stacey's church, the exciting plan was set in motion. But first we had to get to Israel.

All who were going on the trip were to meet at the Chicago airport and fly together through Turkey to Tel Aviv. I would be flying from Columbus to Chicago with our members and Phil and Stacey would be flying from Grand Rapids. We had no problem with our flight, but that was not the case with Phil and Stacy's. Because of a snow storm (we were leaving in March), their flight was delayed. Time was running out. Phil and Stacey still hadn't arrived. Our flight only had minutes before departure. I was praying hard.

I will never forget the look on Phil's face as he was coming down the steps of the O'Hare airport to where I was frantically waiting. He was dragging luggage and sort of dragging Stacey. She had taken some medicine to help her relax for the flight, and probably due to her small frame she was almost in "happy land". But somehow we all made it on the plane just in time. Thank you Lord!

The rest of the trip was indescribably awesome! We enjoyed every minute of it. A man by the name of Paul Karpenko, was our guide. He lived in Israel with his family in order to be a testimony of Christ's love to the Jews. He spoke several languages fluently including Russian (his native language), English, and Hebrew. We saw several Biblical sites during our ten day tour including the Valley of Elah, where David slew Goliath, the Sea of Galilee with its many Biblical towns, Jericho and its fallen walls, Bethlehem and the site of Jesus' birth, where I bought a manger scene carved from olive wood, and Jerusalem. We were also able to go into the country of Jordan and visit Petra, which may be the place where Israel will hide during the tribulation period. My two most favorite sites were the Garden Tomb where I had the privilege of giving a devotion to the tour group, and the Jordan River where I baptized Stacey.

From the Garden Tomb one could see the face of the cliff called Golgotha, which means "place of a skull". I could clearly see what looked like the shape of a skull carved into the cliff. It was special and sobering to know that I was looking at the place where Jesus had been crucified. A short walk from that location was the tomb, which we were able to go into a few at a time. I remember Dr. Candlish pointing out one of the spots in the tomb were it was obvious some additional chiseling had taken place. He suggested that since the tomb had been originally prepared for Joseph of Arimathea, that the last minute chiseling may have been done because Jesus was taller than Joseph. If so, we were looking at the exact spot where Jesus had been laid in that family tomb! It took my breath away.

When I saw the Jordan River it seemed much smaller than what I had envisioned it would be. The location where we went for Stacey's baptism was the "designated" baptismal location. I don't remember the name of the location on the river, but it was obviously a big tourist attraction for the purpose of baptizing. There were change rooms and robes available. Other groups were there doing what we were doing. The spot in the river where the baptisms took place had some kind of fencing or barricade going out into the river. I assumed that was to prevent people from going out to far into the river. I think there was another purpose as well.When it was our turn to baptize, I explained what the Bible said about baptism and baptized Stacey. That was so awesome. Shortly after her baptism we were walking back to the building to change when I noticed something floating in the river. It was a small alligator. Stacey had asked me earlier if I thought any alligators lived in the river. I honestly didn't think so, so I told her no way. Fortunately I don't think Stacey saw the alligator. That was obviously the other reason for the barricade.

I will never forget the trip to Israel. Everything about it was so amazing. The food was so great. The time together with Phil and Stacey was precious. Seeing so many places I had read about in the Bible had me so excited. I even had a brief opportunity to witness to a Jewish lady. We were at a hotel near Bethlehem waiting in the lobby. She actually initiated the conversation. She had come to live in Israel from New York, so she spoke perfect English. She said something about the Jewish religion being so much better than Christianity because they had over 700 laws. I asked her if she had kept them all, and what happened if she didn't? I also told her that Christianity was not a religion. It was a relationship with a real Person Who loved her and died for her on a cross not far from where we were. About that time a guard, who apparently had been overhearing our conversation, interrupted us and would not let us continue. I often wondered if she had thought about what I had said and pursued the truth.

The flight back was without incident, but I left knowing that one day my Savior would come to Jerusalem again riding through the Eastern Gate on a white horse to take the throne and rule the world. I took home with me some very precious memories – and over 700 pictures, some water from the Sea of Galilee, and five stones from the Valley of Elah, somewhere close to where David picked up his five.

CHAPTER   73

OTHER LEADERSHIP OPPORTUNITIES

While I was pastor at Mount Vernon God gave me several other opportunities to serve Him. I was an officer for the West Moriah Fellowship of Churches, which were the GARBC churches in the Columbus area. I continued to serve on the Skyview Ranch camp board in several capacities including secretary and chairman. I also served on the board of Baptist Mid-Missions for five years, which I really enjoyed.

Probably the ministry that I was most privileged to serve and probably helped the most was on the Council of 12 for the OARBC. The Council of 12 was a group of 12 pastors that were elected by the other pastors in the state of Ohio in the OARBC. The Council primarily oversaw all the activities and ministries of the OARBC. I served on the Council as secretary, treasure, vice-chairman, and finally as chairman.

I really learned a lot on the Council and had some very interesting experiences. I remember my first meeting as a Council member. It was actually very shocking. I was told that I had just "thrown my house keys into a pot". In other words, my house could possibly be taken from me. What I learned was that the OARBC was in big trouble.

For several years the OARBC fellowship of churches had provided a self funding health insurance plan to its pastors. Most of the pastors were in the plan, but it was not mandatory to use that plan. Because of that fact, the younger pastors were opting not to use it, but the older pastors did use it. As a result, the claims began to exceed the income. The insurance plan was going under. Since the 'buck" stopped with the Council of 12, we were ultimately responsible for what happened and how to fix the problem.

We did the only thing we could do and that was to tell the churches in the OARBC about the problem and to shut the insurance plan down. But the big problem was the several thousand dollars in claims that needed to be paid. If I remember correctly I think that figure was somewhere between $700,000 and $1,000,000. And we did not have the money to pay it. This problem was big enough to destroy the OARBC and to disintegrate it.

But God intervened. The Director of our fellowship at that time was Larry Fetzer, and the chairman of the Council was Tim Kenoyer. God used these men and others to steer us through some very rough waters. The Council made me the fund raiser to try to raise funds to pay off the claims. Larry Fetzer and others would call the doctors and hospitals, explain the situation and see if they would reduce their claims. The churches were encouraged to pray and do what they could to pay their pastor's claims. To God's glory we raised over $200,000, claims were reduced or forgiven, and all the claims were paid, and we ended up with some money left over, which we used to help start churches in the state of Ohio. Only God could have done that.

Though there were many other stories of dealing with serious problems while serving on the Council, I think I will mention two more. A few years after the insurance matter was settled I was elected treasurer of the Council. When I received the financial books from the previous treasure I noticed that something was not right. Our records showed that we should have $30,000 in the church planting fund, which was left over from the money we had raised to help pay off the insurance claims. But I did not see that money in any bank account.

When I asked the previous treasurer about it he at first said he had invested it in some securities. When he could not produce any records of that investment, I knew we had a problem. Finally he confessed before the Council that he had used the money for some personal purchases. I still don't know what he used the money for, but suspected that it was not good. He soon moved out of the state, and his father-in-law paid the Council the $30,000. Most of the churches in the state never knew about it.

The second major problem that I will mention had to do with an accident that occurred at Camp Patmos. Camp Patmos was one of three youth camps in fellowship with the OARBC churches. It was located on Kelly's Island in Lake Erie. The other two camps were Skyview Ranch, which was centrally located in the stated, and Scioto Hills Camp located in the southern part of Ohio. Camp Patmos up to this point had enjoyed a special relationship with the OARBC that the other two camps did not. It was technically owned by the OARBC. I had thought it best that the OARBC give the Camp Patmos to the Camp Patmos board, so all the camps would have the same relationship. Though that matter had been discussed, the founders of the camp were very much opposed to that idea, so the matter was dropped. They initially wanted to keep that special relationship to the OARBC.

But that was about to change. Though there were signs warning against it, a teenage girl dove into the pool on the shallow end and broke her neck. She would be a paraplegic the rest of her life. In order to pay the bills the parents sued the camp. But since the OARBC and all of its churches technically owned the camp, that law suit also threatened the entire fellowship of churches. All of us on the council and all the churches were praying about this very serious matter. Fortunately the lawsuit was settled and both the camp and the OARBC were saved. But after that incident everyone saw the wisdom of giving the camp to the Camp Patmos board, which was accomplished very quickly after the lawsuit was settled.

Before leaving Ohio I served as chairman of the Council. I really enjoyed the privilege of helping work though many issues and problems, but especially the fellowship with the other pastors who were leaders in the state.

CHAPTER   74

SUMMARY OF OUR MOUNT VERNON MINISTRY

God's grace was so wonderfully poured out on our ministry in Mount Vernon in so many different ways. Attendance and membership grew tremendously from the 42 original members in 1978 to 452 at the end of 2007. Morning worship attendance averaged nearly 400 during 2007. We had had Sunday morning attendances of over 600 and had our record attendance during the Power Team meetings of 919. At the celebration service, which the church had for us on July 27, 2008, they had divided our 30 year ministry into segments of ten. The back of the program for that service had the following statistics:

1978 - 1988
Salvation Decisions: 680
Other Decisions: 1,624
Baptisms: 229
Guests Recorded: 3,431

1989 - 1999
Salvation Decisions: 860
Other Decisions: 3,035
Baptisms: 216
Guests Recorded: 5,557

2000 – Present (July 2008)
Salvation Decisions: 905
Other Decisions: 2,770
Baptisms: 157
Guests Recorded: 3,349

What the above means is that, just like our ministry at Defiance, we averaged more than one soul per week being saved. That is just so awesome, and so much the grace of God! I believe we really impacted our community for Christ at Mount Vernon. I had established a wonderful friendship with the mayor of Mount Vernon, Dick Mavis, and our church was well respected.

During our ministry at Mount Vernon we also had several go out into full time ministry:
Our son, Mark, who pastors in Cincinnati
Bob Bolds, who pastors near Columbus, Ohio
Mick Harden, who pastored in Kentucky
Carry Plants, who served as a youth pastor in several churches
Bruce Butler, who pastored several churches.

Our staff grew to a total of three pastors plus a Director of Music and Children's Ministries, two secretaries and two custodians plus a multitude of volunteers. When I left our budget was around three quarters of a million dollars. Only God could have accomplished that!

PHASE VII

OUR MINISTRY AT OTSEGO

(2008-2015, Age 62-69)

Financial Changes

	2008	2015
Cost of Gasoline:	Peaked at $4.11	$2.40
Cost of a postage stamp:	41 cents	49 cents
Average cost of house:	$284,000	$228,000
Average annual income:	$52,029	$56,516

- Cost of Gasoline: Peaked at $4.11 / $2.40
- Cost of a postage stamp: 41 cents / 49 cents
- Average cost of house: $284,000 / $228,000
- Average annual income: $52,029 / $56,516
- Housing market crashes in 2008
- September 29,2008 stock market crashes. Dow fell 777.68 points, the largest drop in history.

Political Changes

- Barack Hussein Obama became president from 2009-2017 (First black president).

Social Changes

- Violence increase: First major school shooting was at Columbine High School in Colorado on April 20, 1999, with 15 deaths. On February 27, 2012, three students were shot at Chardon High School in Ohio. On December 14, 2012, 27 little school children were shot at the Sandy Hook Elementary School in Connecticut.
- Racial tension increases.
- The Supreme Court legalizes gay marriage in all 50 states on June 26, 2015.

CHAPTER 75

HOW GOD CALLED US TO OTSEGO

Moving for me was never easy. I like ruts. I like to be comfortable. Nancy, on the other hand, loves new things and variety. She had moved several times while her dad was a pastor. I had lived in the same place all my life until I went to college. I thought I would end my ministry years and retire in Mount Vernon. The thought of moving never crossed my mind since the 1980s.

But God began to place an uneasiness in my heart that I could not explain. We had talked about down-sizing from our big house in Apple Valley. Nancy had even mentioned that we needed to be careful about staying too long in one church as some pastors had done. But God was still blessing our church. We were still growing and seeing people saved. So why was I feeling the way I was?

In addition to how I was feeling, in 2007 I had received about a half a dozen letters from various churches looking for a pastor and wondering if I would be interested. It was not unusual to receive such a letter from time to time, but I had never had so many in such a short period of time. I had quickly responded to the letters saying that I was not interested. A couple of years earlier I had been contacted by a very large church in Grand Rapids. That one made me think a little. I even answered their questionnaire, but just did not feel I should mail it. But by the middle of 2007 I began to think that God might be trying to tell me something.

Nancy and I felt very strongly that if we ever did move, the Lord would want us near our twin grandsons, so we could be of spiritual help to them. They were born in July of 2007. Though Phil and Stacey were attending church, Stacey's parents were not believers. But another matter had to be considered. Nancy's dad had been diagnosed with the early stages of dementia, and I oversaw his care. At this time he was in an assisted living facility, but his money was gradually running out. Without any money I thought that the only solution for his care would be a veteran's nursing home. We had visited the one nearest to us in Sandusky, Ohio. But it was over two hours away, and we were not impressed with it. We also visited the one in Grand Rapids and thought it would be better for him. So if we were to move, all roads seemed to be pointing toward the Grand Rapids area. Nancy and I prayed about it.

In the fall of 2007 I was the speaker for the Senior Saints retreat at Gitche Gumee Bible Camp where my brother, Mel, was the director. During that week I was sharing with Mel what God was doing in our lives and told him that I thought God might be trying to move Nancy and me to another church. Mel assured me that he would pray about it.

One of Mel's best friends is Laird Wiley. Laird and his wife, Sandy, often helped at the camp in several capacities. On that day, when I was talking to Mel, Laird was in the office. I didn't think anything about it since that was common. But I am convinced that God had Laird there to hear our conversation. It "just so happened" that Laird and Sandy had recently moved south from the First Baptist Church in Otsego, Michigan, to another church not too far from the Indiana border. Their church was looking for a pastor. At that time they were being led by an interim pastor named Dan Gillette.

Laird must have told him about me, because Dan called me shortly after I had been at Gitche Gumee to see if I would consider coming to that church as pastor. I had known Dan for several years and always had a great deal of respect for him. So I was honored that he would even ask me to consider coming there to pastor. During the conversation I told him we had been considering leaving Mount Vernon, but thought we should get closer to Grand Rapids to better care for Dad Crown. Dan then said something that I had not heard before. He said, "If you are concerned about Dad Crown's money running out, he could always start receiving Medicaid which would pay for nursing home expenses no matter where you lived. You don't really have to live near Grand Rapids." Though we did not take his offer to go to that church, I had learned something very important.

In a couple of months Dad Crown's money did run out and we were able to get him into the Medicaid system in Ohio and move him to a nursing home in Mount Vernon. What a blessing! God's grace had struck again!

Sometime early in 2008 I received a call from the chairman of the pastoral search committee from the First Baptist Church of Otsego, John LaHuis. Since it was clear that I was not going to Laird's church in southern Michigan, John must have been told about me. He asked if he could send a questionnaire to me as well as a copy of their constitution and articles of faith. Otsego was only about 35 miles south of Grand Rapids. I said that would be fine.

After receiving the papers from the Otsego church I was sure that there was no way I could possibly go there as pastor. I saw a couple of things that were very wrong with their constitution. I could not conscientiously follow it. So, when John called me back, I told him that I could not follow through with the paperwork, and why. To John's credit, he simply said, "That is just why you are the man for us. We need someone who can help us get these matters straightened out." He went on to say that in the areas of my concern they had not been following their constitution. They needed someone who could help them rewrite it. I had done that both in Defiance and in Mount Vernon. So, following that explanation, I agreed to complete the paperwork and come and fill the pulpit for them with the possibility of becoming a candidate for their pastoral position.

About the same time Nancy and I had already planned to make a visit to Grand Rapids to visit our new grand-sons. So I told John that Nancy and I would plan to drive down to Otsego to meet him and see the church. When we arrived at the church we were met by John and Ken Doctor who gave Nancy and me a tour of the buildings. I could tell they needed help from the way their facilities were laid out. They also told me about their academy and its relationship to the church. I had some concerns about that, as well.

I preached for them in early May or late April I believe. After the service I was standing in the foyer greeting the people like I normally do. For some reason an overwhelming feeling came over me. There is no way I can explain it. But I knew without a doubt that I was going to be their pastor. I am not a very emotional person, but

I was so moved that tears had filled my eyes. At that point Nancy looked up at me and asked what was wrong. I told her that I would tell her later. When we were alone, I told her that I was certain that God wanted me to be their pastor. That very week they called and asked me to come back as an official candidate.

 Following that call I knew it was serious. It was time to let the deacons in Mount Vernon know what was going on, which I did at our next meeting. They were shocked. But after listening to me tell them how I knew that this is what God wanted, they understood and supported me fully. I told them that I still needed to candidate, and the Otsego church still had to vote on it. But in my heart I knew it was already settled.

After I was asked to candidate, two couples from the Otsego church came down to Mount Vernon to check out our ministry in order to hear me preach in that setting and see firsthand how our ministry functioned and how our relationship was with the people. That was actually a very good thing to do. After the service Nancy and I went out to eat with the two couples, John and Pam Lahuis and Cliff and Shirley Reber. The ladies said they were very nervous about being there, because they were afraid that if the people in the Mount Vernon church knew why they were there they might try to hurt them. I just laughed. While we were eating one of the families from the church came in to the restaurant, but they did not seem to think anything unusual about our eating with some strangers.

Candidating at Otsego

I had pastored two churches, but I had never candidated before, because I started those churches. So I was not sure what to expect. The weekend in early May that I officially candidated, I believe I met with the entire pastoral search committee, the deacons, and the trustees, all in separate meetings between Friday and Sunday morning. Each group had their own set of questions, which I answered as truthfully and directly as I knew how. After preaching on Sunday morning the church had a potluck dinner. After dinner we met back in the auditorium from about 1:00-3:00 so that the congregation could ask their questions. It was a very thorough process. Later that month the church voted to call me as their pastor, and I accepted their call. How could I not. God wanted me there.

CHAPTER 76

ANNOUNCING MY RESIGNATION

I knew that telling the people that we loved at Faith Baptist in Mount Vernon would be the hardest thing I had ever had to do. After accepting the call from the Otsego church I met with the deacons to let them know of my decision and to form a time table for telling the congregation and my final Sunday. I would tell the congregation verbally at the end of the second service on June 8th and would also send out a letter to everyone that week. I would end my ministry at Mount Vernon at the end of July. I was not expected to begin my ministry in Otsego until the first of September, which gave us a month to move and get settled.

During this stressful major change in our lives something else was going on that no one else knew about – something that concerned our daughter. Lori had developed a serious health problem.

That problem reached its peak the same day I was to announce my resignation. I received a call from the hospital Sunday morning letting me know she was in the emergency room and needed to be transferred to the Columbus hospital as soon as transportation could be arranged, which they thought would be around 1:00.

I can honestly say that I had never had so much on my shoulders as I was carrying that Sunday morning. In a way, the stress of announcing my resignation was "small potatoes" to the stress of concern about our daughter. Nancy and I prayed together and then went to church.   I preached about Abraham, who followed God's will, then had the people sit down after closing the invitation, and told them about how God had led Nancy and me to move to Otsego. I said nothing about what was going on with Lori.

As soon as we could get away gracefully from the church people Nancy and I made our way to the hospital to try to comfort our daughter before she had to be taken away. That was so hard.

That evening at church, I shared a little of what was going on with Lori. The people were so precious and understanding. They all loved Lori and would be praying for her and for Nancy and me.

Lori came home after a week in Columbus and was so much better.   For a year or two Lori was unable to sing at all after her health problem began. But, praise God, even though Lori continues to get some care, she is pretty much back to her old self again and able to sing again with Nancy and me. God's grace is so awesome!

CHAPTER 77

OUR BIG SEND OFF

The last Sunday of our ministry in Mount Vernon was July 27, 2008. The church had planned a special service for that evening to celebrate our thirty year ministry with them. It was such a special evening. It was held in our Family Center and kept rather informal, which I appreciated. The five hundred or so people all sat at the round tables, while three different men shared some of the stories during each of the ten years they were to talk about. I could not help but look out over the crowd and see the many lives that had been touched by God's amazing grace.

When the last man finished talking about the last ten years of our ministry he shouted, "O H". The crowd knew what to do next. In fact, any real Ohioan would know what to do next. The entire crowd shouted,"I O". That went on for awhile, followed by a lot of laughing and clapping. That was for my benefit, since I was moving to the state "up north".

All the people in the church knew that I was a Michigan fan and I "milked" that for all it was worth. The Sunday before the Ohio State/ Michigan game the guys in the sound booth would usually pull some kind of prank on me. Sometimes they would play the Ohio State fight song before I got up to preach. (I'm sure that prepared hearts for the message.) The last year, when I got up to give the announcements, they somehow put Pastor Matt (another Michigan fan) and me in Ohio State shirts up on the screen behind me. I finally figured out why the people were laughing, when I turned around and looked at the screens.

So this final night was their way of showing their special love for me, and they truly succeeded. And I loved it – and them.

CHAPTER   78

GETTING STARTED IN OTSEGO

The Move

We had lived thirty years in Mount Vernon, and had accumulated so much stuff. Even though Nancy and Lori had gotten rid of some of it, we still had – so much stuff! We end up giving some of it away. The rest we boxed and prepared for the move. The church in Otsego had a parsonage, which worked out perfectly for us, since we had not yet sold our house in Apple Valley. The parsonage was a lovely ranch style home with a full finished basement. The basement area was a perfect area for Lori. Very few churches have parsonages for their pastors anymore, but God knew just what we needed. His grace just kept pouring out on me. Being able to live in the parsonage kept us from having to make two house payments while we waited for our house to sell. I had no idea that it would be five years before our house in Mount Vernon would sell. But God knew, and took care of us.

The men from Otsego had rented moving trucks. When the day came for the move, we had lots of help from the people in our church in Mount Vernon, who helped us load the trucks. The men from Otsego then came to drive the trucks to our new home and we headed north. When we arrived at the parsonage there were lots of people there waiting to help us unload. It was amazing.

Somehow the word must have gotten out that I loved guns and loved to shoot. The men from Otsego really loved that since, many of them were hunters or at least loved to shoot. I will never forget the discussion I had with two of the men who were helping me unload in our new garage. Lew Roberts and Don Timlosky wanted to know how I felt about the issue of security for our church on Sunday. Their plan would involve someone with a sealed carry permit carrying a pistol at church. They wanted to be prepared in case some deranged person came into our church and started shooting. That has happened more than once in our country. When I told them I was all for it they seemed thrilled. I think I immediately made two new friends. In fact, Nancy and I soon made many new friends and felt right at home with the people at Otsego.

Helping the Church in Otsego

Just like people, churches can get depressed. At least, that's how it seemed the people appeared to me at the First Baptist Church in Otsego. There had been division in the church over the style of music to be used for worship on Sunday morning. In addition, the church had recently experienced some very bad "press" having to do with a previous school administrator. That situation had not been handled well which compounded the problem. They were hungry for solid Bible teaching and preaching. They had had a wonderful interim pastor, which had helped begin the healing process, but they were still hurting. They also had organizational and communication issues between the various parts of the church body. The lay couple that was working with the youth of the church had done a great job, but they were getting burned out. The church desperately needed a full time youth pastor. Their building layout was very disjointed. Though they had plenty of room, and a nice family center (gym), the layout of the overall building complex was not good. All of these problems needed to be addressed as soon as possible.

I began to address the issues as best I could. I met with the praise team soon after I arrived. The deacons had already addressed the issue of the style of music and had concluded that a service that used a blend of hymns and praise choruses would be best. While the hearts of those involved was good, the quality of the music needed help and the appearance of some of those involved was not good. Though they had enclosed the drum set behind a plastic wall, the drums dominated the sound. We were eventually able to get an electric drum set which greatly helped the mix. Dress standards were addressed. I also preached a series of messages on worship. I think all of these steps combined helped the church get passed the music issue.

The problems the academy had gone through effected how it was perceived in the community. There is not much one can do about that except the passing of time and winning people to Christ. I was making a lot of visits with the help of some of the people in the church, and we began to see souls saved and baptized. This was a great encouragement to the church. I started my New Beginners Sunday school class for the new believers helping the new converts grow.

I knew the church needed to have their constitution overhauled, and needed a policy guide, but I did not think I should begin that project right away. We did take other steps to improve the communication issues between the various parts of the church body, by creating liaisons to these and having reports from each in our deacons meetings. Later we improved this by having the chairmen of these major areas of the church submit their agendas to the deacons before their meetings, so we could know what was going to be discussed in order to prevent problems instead of fixing them after they occurred. We also prepared a membership questionnaire and set policies for bringing in members and dealing with inactive members.

I began to work on a plan to fix the building problems that would involve expanding the foyer and putting the offices and nursery on the main floor level making them easier to find. I even had my brother, Keith, who at that time owned his own engineering firm, help with some ideas. It was going to be a major project, but I believed I had a good plan. I posted it on the bulletin board. People could see that progress was happening. I also began the search for a youth pastor soon after I arrived. I was working hard, but I loved it. I could see God making a difference and using me. The spirit of the church was no longer depressed, but excited.

CHAPTER   79

DAD CROWN GOES TO HEAVEN

A couple years after mom Crown passed away on August 23, 1990, dad Crown met a wonderful Christian widow who lived in Mount Vernon, Clarine Burt. They were married on August 20, 1993. But by 2006 both of them had developed such serious health problems that they could no longer care for each other. Dad Crown moved in with Nancy and me at our house in Apple Valley, and Clarine moved in with her granddaughter in Mount Vernon. But in a month Clarine had to go to a nursing home where she died a few weeks later. Dad Crown then moved to an assisted living home. But by early 2008 his money had run out and we moved him to a nursing home in Mount Vernon.

I had told dad Crown about the possibility of moving to Otsego, Michigan, and asked him to pray for us about it. He was excited for us and very much supportive. As soon as our move was definite I let him know, and plans were made to move him with us. Nancy and I had looked around the Otsego area and decided that the Life Care Nursing Home in Plainwell would be best for him, since it was so close. So, after we had moved our things to the parsonage in Otsego, we moved dad Crown to his new home at the nursing home.

He was so happy at the new church for the few months he was there. People came to visit him and he loved coming to church. Bill Rose from the church especially went out of his way to make him feel welcome and visited him often. I took him out to eat every week, which he loved.

Dad Crown had some serious diabetes issues. He sometimes would have very low lows and would become disoriented. On December 7, 2008, dad Crown was not feeling well so did not come to church that morning. Nancy and I had planned to spend all day at the church that day because Nancy was setting up for the children's Christmas program, which was held that evening.

That afternoon dad Crown had one of his lows and they were not able to get him to come out of it. The nursing home had tried to get in touch with us, but they were unable to do so. In the meantime they had transported him to Borgess Hospital in Kalamazoo. When we finally got home we heard the message the nursing home left us on our answering machine. We immediately left for the hospital. We just made it there minutes before he passed away. He was eighty eight.

I lost my mentor and my good friend as well as my father-in-law that day. But I knew where he had gone, and knew that he was in a far better place. He had been such a godly and good example for me to follow.

We felt it was best to have his funeral service at the church in Mount Vernon, since he was going to be buried next to mom Crown at the cemetery there, and because he was better known there. I was able to preach his funeral, but only because God gave me the strength. Since our house had not sold yet, all of our family and Nancy's sisters and their families were able to stay at our house the few days before the funeral. The people from the Mount Vernon church graciously took care of us with plenty of food and support. Though it was a sad time, it was also a wonderful time together, remembering and enjoying being together.

CALLING PASTOR PAUL

I was certain that I knew what kind of an associate pastor the church needed. We needed a good male worship leader that could help the quality of our worship music. But we also needed a good youth pastor. So I began to search for someone with both skill sets. I read through dozens of resumes. While searching I did come across one resume that caught my attention. It was different from all the rest. It wasn't "canned". It seemed to be an honest story of who the person was. I liked the fact that he had a military background. But there was no mention of any musical ability, so I set it aside. But, for some reason, I could not forget about that resume from Paul Laborde.

At least a year and a half went by, and I just could not find the right one. A couple of times I thought I had the right guy only to discover a major problem in his character or the fact that he had taken a position in another church. By this time the Lord began to impress upon my heart that I should reconsider the kind of associate pastor that we needed.   The praise team was much improved by this time. That need did not seem to be as pressing. So I began to think about getting someone just as a pastor to our youth. Once I came to that conclusion, the name of Paul Laborde went to the top of my list to contact. I had had his resume for a long time, so I was sure by now he was already serving in another church somewhere, but I felt I should contact him anyway.

I called him late in November of 2009 to see if he was still interested in a position as a youth pastor and to see if I could send him a questionnaire. He seemed very glad to hear from me and was open to receiving a questionnaire and information about our church. I had no idea of the terrible agony he had gone through that year as he waited on the Lord to open a door of service for him. God was preparing him for Otsego, and He was preparing me and FBC of Otego for Pastor Paul. What an awesome God!

After I received and reviewed the completed questionnaire from Pastor Paul I was pretty sure he was the one God had for us. But after my next phone conversation with him I was sure of it. When I called him the second time in January of 2010, he mentioned that I might know his father-in-law, Pastor Tom Wright. I was shocked. Pastor Paul was the son-in-law of my good pastor friend from Ohio, Tom Wright. I had known Tom for well over 30 years. We had worked together many times on the Council of 12 for the OARBC. Tom was a highly respected pastor of the Memorial Baptist Church in Columbus, Ohio. I remembered Tom requesting prayer for his future son-in-law who was in Iraq in the army. Though I had not remembered his name, I had prayed for Pastor Paul several years earlier not knowing that I would be talking to him on the phone as a possible candidate for our youth pastor position. Now I knew that God was up to something, and I had better not mess it up. I just had to stay out of God's way and do what He wanted me to do.

I did check Pastor Paul's references and even called Tom. I made that call to Tom right after I hung up with Pastor Paul. But I already knew how it was going to play out. I knew Tom well enough to know that he would tell me the truth about his son-in-law. Tom basically said that if it would have been possible for him to hire Paul, I would not be getting him. That's all I needed to hear.

Even though I knew Pastor Paul was the one for us, the rest of the church did not. So we brought him and his wife, Beth, to Otsego to meet with the deacons and the church. At the July quarterly business meeting in 2010

Pastor Paul received a unanimous vote to become the youth pastor for the First Baptist Church of Otsego. A 100% vote doesn't happen very often in Baptist churches, especially when calling a pastor. But this young man with no youth pastor or preaching experience was God's choice. That's all that mattered.

I remember telling Pastor Paul two things that I wanted him to do or focus on. Many youth were attending the youth meetings but were not attending church. I wanted to see if we could strengthen the connection between the youth and the church. The second thing I encouraged him to do was to visit the shut-ins. I told him that they needed to know him so they could better pray for him. He needed a prayer team behind him.

He did visit all the shut-ins, and we also began to see teenagers baptized and attending the church. They were showing some spiritual depth. He was doing a great job! Through directing us to Pastor Paul God's grace was not only poured out on me, but also on FBC.

CHAPTER 80

JEREMY

I led several to Christ during my seven years as pastor at the First Baptist Church of Otsego. As in my previous churches, not all of those "panned out", but some did. One of those who did pan out at FBC was Jeremy Rogers and his wife Ruby. In November of 2009 I led our church in a "Friend Day". I had used this as an evangelistic outreach in Mount Vernon with great success, so thought it would work in Otsego. Though some did invite their unsaved friends, it wasn't as successful as it could have been.

I always tried to set an example. I would not ask the people to do something that I would not do myself. So I always tried to get someone well known in the community to attend like the mayor or sheriff. On this occasion the Otsego chief of police was glad to come for me. One of our members, Doug Fritz, also invited one of his co-workers, Jeremy Rogers. Jeremy did not get saved on Friend Day. In fact, he did not attend again for a few months. I thought the whole Friend Day attempt was pretty much a "bust".

Then in April of 2010 Jeremy attended again. This time he came with his wife, Ruby. After the service Jeremy and Ruby spoke to me as they were getting ready to leave the church. The question he asked was worded in such a way that it caught me somewhat off guard: "Can you help me get to God?" After I probably blinked a couple of times, I asked him if he wanted that help right now. I was prepared to take them aside and lead them to Christ right then. But he declined. But they did agree to have me come over the following Thursday evening and talk with them.

On Thursday evening they told me how they had just lost another baby because of a topical pregnancy and were very distraught. They had been able to have one boy, Allen, who at this time was four years old. But they had lost another baby before Allen was born. The doctor now told them that they probably would never be able to have any more children. I told them that I did not know what God's will was for them as far as having children was concerned, but I knew that God could solve their much bigger problem – how to get right with God. After sharing the Gospel with them that evening they both trusted Christ as Savior. A few weeks later they were baptized and added to the church membership.

Though both attended my new convert's class on Sundays, I began to disciple Jeremy in personal one on one meetings every week. He began to grow and memorize Scripture, which was hard for him. He shared how he had a smoking problem and felt God wanted him to get rid of it. He had smoked for several years and had tried to quit before without success. But I gave him some Scripture verses to memorize and told him I would pray for him. A few weeks later God gave him complete victory and took that habit away.

Jeremy and Ruby have had their struggles, but they have remained faithful and growing. On top of everything our great God did enable Ruby to become pregnant and give birth to a healthy baby girl, Ceanna. Both children show every evidence of having hearts for God as well. Only God's grace could do that.

CHAPTER 81

AMAZING GIFTS GIVEN TO ME

I have been so blessed to have been the pastor of some very loving and giving people. I mentioned about the man who taught me the grace of receiving from the Defiance church, Gale Yenser. He was always giving to us. The men in Mount Vernon gave me a very wonderful and expensive shotgun. I continued to be blessed at Otsego.

One man in particular was so gracious and giving to both Nancy and me. He and his wife often took us out to eat. They let us use their condominium for a getaway. He gave me several guns and hunting clothes and helped us buy a car after ours was totaled. He just loves to give. But it isn't just to me. He is doing the same for Pastor Paul now and to Pastor Steve, our new youth pastor. I'm sure God will truly reward him. He has no idea how he has encouraged us in the ministry.

Another man also truly encouraged me. In 2011 Mark Kleinbrink approached me and asked if I would be interested in going with him out to Wyoming to hunt mule deer in 2012 for his pastor appreciation gift. Wow! What a way to show appreciation for your pastor. I could not get, "Yes, I'll go" out fast enough.

I did not know that I would have heart problems in May of 2012 (which I will talk about later), but I quickly recovered and prepared for the hunt of a lifetime. I practiced shooting long distance shots all summer with my 30-06 that I had been given by the gentleman referred to above. I could shoot a good 4 inch group at 200 yards and put the bullets in a pie plate at 300 yards, but hoped I would not have to shoot at those distances.

The hunting trip with Mark in Wyoming will be a memory I will always treasure. I could share a lot more of the interesting experiences we had, but that would go beyond the scope of this book. We both were able to get nice mule deer. My deer was only out about 120 yards so it was a rather easy shot. It wasn't so easy getting to that spot to shoot it, though. Since it was the largest deer I have ever shot or probably ever will, I had it mounted. On the way to get into position to see my deer we kicked out a cougar. That was another first for me.

You would think that getting a huge buck would be the highlight of that trip for me. But there was something that even topped that. I was able to lead one of the other hunters to the Lord. Since he had gotten his elk early and I had gotten my buck early, we were left at the camp by ourselves all day. That gave me a great chance to talk to him about the Lord and lead him to the Savior. We maintained contact for several years after that.

CHAPTER 82

BLESSED WITH OPPORTUNITIES TO HUNT

Deer hunting for me was an outlet. Some pastors golf and others fish. But when I am out in the woods sitting in a tree or hunting shack, I forget about everything else. It is both relaxing and exciting at the same time. I always read my Bible before I go hunting in the morning and pray when I get to my hunting spot before day light. There has always been something special about that to me. To have opportunities to hunt after we moved back to Michigan was important to me – almost essential.

One of the members at FBC invited me to come out to his place to hunt. Dick Simmons was fast becoming a great friend to me. I enjoyed hunting at Dick's place. He had built a platform up in a huge tree in the northwest corner of his field next to his woods. Every hunting season he covered the wood platform with a piece of carpet and enclosed it all with a hunting tent. Inside he put a comfortable desk chair that swiveled. I called it the Taj Mahal.   I have gotten more than one deer out of that location.

I remember on one occasion when I was hunting there with my crossbow. Dick must have been watching me with his binoculars, when he saw a buck come out of the woods and come near where I was hunting. But all of a sudden he could not see the deer. Soon he was on his golf cart coming out to me to see what had happened. What actually had happened is that I had shot the deer and it had dropped immediately to the ground, so it had gone out of his sight. While Dick was preparing to come to see me, I had gotten down from the tree, gone to the deer and finished him off. I then was going back up to the hunting tent to retrieve the rest of my hunting gear, when Dick arrived. He asked me if I had seen the deer, and where it went. I told him that I did indeed see it, and it was lying "over there in the field".

 I think Dick was happier than I was. He loaded me up in his golf cart and took me back to his barn where he could get his tractor with the front-end loader. After I put my gear in my vehicle, we went back and rolled the deer into the bucket on the front of his tractor and took it back to a big tree near his barn and stung it up, where we "gutted" it. I can honestly say that I have never field dressed a deer and brought it in with as much ease as I did that day. Wow!

Another hunting location that was made available to me was at my cousin, Jerry's. I had not seen Jerry for probably fifty years. Our paths just had not crossed. His dad was my Uncle Merton, who I mentioned earlier. Jerry and I were born a day apart, but he lived near the Detroit area while we were growing up, so we did not see each other that much. But when I moved back to Michigan we were able to reconnect. He invited me to come over to his place in Charlotte, Michigan, to hunt. He had purchased a 40 acre farm primarily for the purpose of hunting. I have gone over there to hunt every year, and have taken some nice deer there.

I think it may have been my first year hunting with Jerry, when I took a nice 7 point buck. Traditionally every opening day of gun season some of those hunting with him drive a swale, which usually pushes out some deer. On this occasion I was placed in a woods across the field from the swale. Jerry and his friend, Rick, were to my right in the same woods about 100 yards apart from each other. Jerry's son-in-law, Joel, and grandson, Tommy, then drove the swale. I soon saw a doe run out moving across the field to my left. I really should not have shot at a running deer at that distance of probably 150 yards, but did anyway. I missed her completely, of course. But when I looked back toward the swale, I saw another deer, which had come out, but was not running. It was standing in the field to the left of the swale. I could tell that it was a nice buck, and that it was standing broadside looking toward the doe that had just run out. I leaned my gun against a tree, took careful aim, and pulled the trigger. The deer dropped immediately to the ground and never moved. The other guys could not get over that I had dropped that deer with a shot gun slug with open sights at that distance. Jerry, of course, brought up the fact that I had extra help from above since I was a pastor. I didn't disagree with him. He was so right. I would never have gotten that deer without God's help.

But God also provided another hunting location that has been a real blessing to me. I had grown up hunting small game with Dave Wickes on his parent's farm about four miles north of my home town of Stanton. After Dave's parents passed on to heaven he began farming their land as well as several other properties, which totaled around 700 acres. During my years in Ohio I had not seen my friend, Dave, for a long time. But we were able to reconnect after moving back, and he invited me to hunt on his property.

When we were growing up in the Stanton area we rarely ever saw a deer, though there was lots of small game. Today the opposite is true. Small game is rare, but the deer herd is very plentiful. In fact, Dave was happy to have me take some "corn eaters" as he calls them. The first year that I went up to Stanton to hunt I went by myself thinking that Dave might be hunting, also. But that time of year is the time of harvest and not a good time for a farmer to be taking time off. So I hunted by myself. But with Dave's permission I have been able to take my friend, Cliff Reber, and others up there to hunt. We tried to use the time to get next to some of the men in our church. Pastor Paul Laborde has also gone with us and taken some nice deer. We usually meet Dave at lunch time, so it has been fun for me to be able to reminisce with Dave about the past and enjoy the fellowship with the men from FBC Otsego at the same time. I have been able to take several deer up at Dave's. Probably the most enjoyable was being able to take some deer with my dad's old 30-40 Krag rifle.

CHAPTER 83

GOD TOTALLY REDIRECTING MY LIFE

I have been blessed with fairly good health all of my life, which has allowed me to work hard. When at Mount Vernon I preached the two morning services on Sunday, taught my Sunday School class between those services, sang at choir practice in late afternoon, and preached the evening service plus attending all the other meetings during the week. I was used to averaging over seventy hours a week and dealing with all of the stress related matters that a pastor faces. Though I did not have some of those tasks at Otsego, I continued to work hard and pour my life into God's work. That was my life, and I was happy with it. I was doing God's work and being used of God to change lives forever. It doesn't get any better than that.

In the spring of 2012 I had a "wake up call". Nancy and I had gone to a "55 Alive" (Senior Saints) party at church. I was hesitant to go since I was not feeling well, but decided I would go anyway. After about an hour I told Nancy that I thought I'd better go home. She said she would find a ride home and come home later.

After I got home I kept feeling worse. I thought for sure I had pneumonia. I felt pressure on my chest and was having some trouble breathing. I was still dressed and sitting on the edge of the bed when Nancy came in. Before she came home I was debating on whether I should go to the emergency room. When she looked at me she said, "You need to go to the hospital". I told her I could drive myself. I thought they would give me an antibiotic and send me home.

After x-raying my chest the doctor told me that my chest was clear. I did not have pneumonia. I was shocked. What else could it be? He went on to say I had a "funky" heart beat and they were going to transport me to Borgess Hospital in Kalamazoo. I called Nancy to tell her, but told her not to worry.

The next day after almost losing me during a chemical stress test, they did a heart catheterization and discovered that I had an artery that was over 90% blocked. After putting a stent in the artery the doctor told me that all went well and that I was very "lucky". He called the artery that was blocked the "widow maker". Apparently that was an artery that usually causes fatal heart attacks.

With physical therapy and medication I recovered rather quickly. I actually felt better than I had felt for some time. I'm sure that my recovery was partly motivated by my desire to not miss my fall hunting trip with Mark.

I went quickly back into the same work routine that I had always kept. I turned 67 in the fall and thought I would keep going as a pastor for several more years. But in the spring of 2013 I had some more heart problems that would totally redirect my thinking.

I went to our church's men's retreat with my cousin Jerry. Since Jerry only lived about an hour from Otsego, he came over to go to the retreat with me. After I went to bed on that Friday night I got sick and was sick off and on all night. In the morning I told Jerry that I probably should go home. After taking me home, he and Nancy talked me into going to the hospital. Again, I thought I just had a "bug" of some kind.

After doing another heart catheterization they found another blockage in the same artery. Though the doctor tried to put another stent in, he could not do so because the blockage was between the heart and the other stent. So they did the "balloon" thing.

My recovery from this second episode was much different. Even though I did the physical therapy, I just had no energy. I tried to preach a couple weeks after being in the hospital. After the service I had to sit down. I was exhausted. The deacons then did something that was absolutely amazing. They gave me the entire summer off with pay in order to recover. That was so loving and gracious of them. And I really needed it. I had never been off of work that long. But it gave me time to think and pray.

I began to get what God was trying to tell me, and I finally surrendered to His will. I told Him that He had my attention, and I was willing to retire. That was big for me. I did not know life without work. I did not know what that would look like, or how I would handle it. But I knew without a doubt that that is what God wanted for me. I really didn't have a choice.

Nancy was very much in favor of me resigning from being pastor at Otsego and retiring. She was concerned about me and didn't want to lose me. She also wanted to be able to spend our future years doing things together. I started to draw social security at age 66 and a half. With that "extra" money we were able to purchase a much needed pick-up truck and get it paid off and pay off our camper. Though we were able to eventually sell our house, we really didn't end up with much equity because we had to sell it at such a reduced price. We knew we would have to buy a house, but I also knew that somehow God would provide for us. Nancy was just looking forward to doing a lot of camping and traveling together. We did do a lot of that the summer I had off and we both loved it.

I started back in the pastor routine in September of 2013, but was still struggling to have enough energy. By mid October I had made my decision. I needed to retire.

CHAPTER 84

GOD'S GRACE ENABLING ME TO HELP FBC PREPARE FOR THE FUTURE

After making the decision to retire Nancy and I set up a meeting early in November with Pastor Paul and Beth in order to let them know of what was going on. After telling them that I did not think that I could keep pastoring much longer and needed to retire, Pastor Paul informed me that he thought that God wanted him to be a senior pastor. You need to understand that when Pastor Paul first came to Otsego, he had absolutely no interest in preaching. In fact, he really did not want to preach, though he was willing to do so. But Pastor Paul had done a lot of preaching for me when I had the summer off.   At the same time that God was convincing me that I needed to slow down, God was convincing Pastor Paul that he needed to preach more. The timing could not have been any better, of course, because God had orchestrated it all.

Up until that meeting I had no idea that Pastor Paul was thinking that God wanted him to be a senior pastor. In a moment, the lights went on in my head, and I realized that God had brought Pastor Paul to Otsego to become the next senior pastor. After I shared my thoughts with them about that, we decided to pray about it and discuss it with the chairman of the deacons, John Lahuis, after the first of the year. But I would give Pastor Paul more opportunities to preach in 2014. I also told him that I would try to get the church ready for him by launching the small group ministry, completing the policy guide, and rewriting the constitution. I was just hoping the Lord with give me the strength to be able to do all of that.

In January of 2014 we had a meeting with John Lahuis to inform him of our plans. John also saw the hand of God in it all and was very helpful and supportive. Together we laid out a plan for informing the deacons, then the church, with my retirement officially beginning at the end of May in 2015. That meant we had a year and a half to train the small group leaders, prepare the policy guide, and rewrite the constitution.

I had already been working on writing the training manual for the small group leaders. I was able to finish the manual and get the leaders trained, and launch the small group ministry with four small groups. That ministry was successful and is still going strong. I thought that ministry would be helpful to the stability and growth of the church for years to come.

Pastor Paul, John, and I had several meetings as we worked through the policy guide. The deacons had already passed several policies, but they were not in a book that was easy to use. About the only deacon that knew what those policies were, was John. There were policies about other matters that needed to be made as well. Clear job descriptions needed to be written and as well as policies concerning the staff. I thought if these were put in place, it would really help Pastor Paul as well as the entire church. Some items that had been in the old constitution really needed to be just in the policy guide, so it was necessary to do the policy guide first. I had written a policy guide for the Mount Vernon church before leaving there, so was able to use some of that material as a guide. That document ended up being nearly a hundred pages. After it was completed it needed to be reviewed and approved by the deacons. This was accomplished in the summer and fall of 2014.

In August of 2014 the deacons were informed of my retirement plans and the possibility of Pastor Paul becoming the next senior pastor. The men were very understanding of why I needed to retire, and every man was very much in favor of pursuing the possibility of presenting Pastor Paul to the congregation as a candidate for the senior pastor position.

Pastor Paul, John, and I then began to work on the constitution. Some of the election procedures held at the annual meeting were cumbersome and needed tweaking. The wording was also very outdated. After a few months that work was finally completed and reviewed and approved by the deacons. It was then presented to the congregation for review and then approved by the congregation at the church's annual meeting in April of 2015.

In January of 2015 the congregation had been informed of my plans for retirement at the end of May. They were also informed of the plan to have Pastor Paul be the interim pastor while a search committee moved forward in search for the next senior pastor. They were also informed that the committee planned to begin by looking at Pastor Paul first. If the committee was favorable, Pastor Paul would be presented to the congregation as the first candidate and voted on at a July business meeting. The congregation would approve of my resignation at the April meeting.

There was absolute unity through it all. In fact, many wondered why we needed to have a search committee. "Let's just call Pastor Paul". But the deacons wisely felt that due process should be followed, and it was. At the April business meeting in 2015 my resignation was approved, as was the constitution. In July Pastor Paul received a 98% vote to become the next senior pastor of the First Baptist Church of Otsego. The church was set for the next several years with a policy guide, up to date constitution, a small group ministry, and a great young senior pastor. God had graciously given me the strength to continue to pastor the church until I could help them through these much needed changes. In early June the church held a wonderful retirement celebration for me. It was wonderful being able to have our family all together at that celebration as well as my brothers and sister.

CHAPTER 85

SUMMARY OF OUR MINISTRY IN OTSEGO

Although I was not able to get done all that I wanted to do in Otsego, I believe I was able to help the church as I mentioned above. I would have liked to have built the church up to the point where we would have gone to two services and then gone through a building program, but that was not in God's plan for me.

We did see the church grow during our ministry there and saw many come to know the Savior. The morning service was averaging around 150 in attendance the year before I came. By 2013 by God's grace the average attendance had peaked at 223. My last year, 2015, the morning attendance dropped to an average of 211. We saw a total of 320 recorded salvation decisions in our various ministries between 2008 and 2015. This amounts to an average of nearly 46 per year, which falls slightly short of one per week. We added 112 members and baptized 73 during my seven years as pastor in Otsego. My last two years I was just not able to do as much, which is reflected in the attendance average drop the last two years as well as the decline in souls saved and baptized. But I praise God for what He did through me.

In summary, I believe God used me to help prepare the church to function better by creating a policy guide and by updating their constitution. I believe the greatest help I gave the church was to bring in their next pastor, Pastor Paul, and to facilitate the transition to his leadership.

We loved the people at FBC of Otsego and still do. I trust it will always remain true to God's Word and His ministry of reaching the lost and building the saints.

CHAPTER 86

DAD GOES TO HEAVEN

After mom died in November of 1994, dad decided to move permanently from Florida back to Michigan. So in January of 1995 I borrowed a box truck and drove down to Florida, where I met my brother Mel and his wife Carol as well as dad at dad and mom's place on the campus of Spurgeon Baptist Bible College in Mulberry, Florida. We loaded everything dad wanted to take and made the trip back to the U.P. of Michigan. I was very nervous about driving a borrowed tuck in the middle of winter in the U.P., but everything went well and I was able to get the truck back to Mount Vernon with no problems, but very tired. I had traveled over 3000 miles in less than one week.

Dad lived with Marcia for several years after that until he fell and broke his back. He then moved in with Mel and Carol. Dad recovered from his fall and continued to do maintenance at Gitche Gumee well into his nineties. His dedication to service and positive spirit was absolutely amazing. One of the funniest memories I have of dad is when I was standing in the Gitche Gumee camp office. Mel said, "Come here, you've got to see this' '. Dad, in his nineties, had his hat on backwards and was riding on his maintenance four-wheeler, flying across the campgrounds heading off to fix something. It was classic dad. But it was hilarious.

When dad turned 100 in March of 2013 we had two huge celebrations for him. The first one was at our home church of First Baptist of Stanton. What a reunion that was. We saw relatives and friends we hadn't seen in years. Dad loved it. We then went back up to Gitche Gumee and had a celebration of dad's friends up there. Dad loved all the cards he received. And even though he was very soft spoken and not out going, I think he really loved all the special attention.

For the last several years, I had always gone up to celebrate dad's birthday along with my brothers and sister. My brother Keith would usually fly into Grand Rapids from his home in Boise, and we would ride up together. That gave us a wonderful time to fellowship together. Keith's wife, Candy, had battled cancer for over ten years, which, of course, was so hard on Keith. Those ten hour rides up to see dad gave me some time to listen to my brother and try to encourage him. Candy was very ill when we celebrated dad's 100th birthday, but she was determined not to miss it. In fact she was doing her usual thing of helping in the kitchen when she could. Candy finally was promoted to glory on June 21, 2014. I was honored that my brother asked me to have her funeral.

Dad loved to see the deer go by the window at Mel's house during the winter. He loved for me to share hunting stories with him. He often would say, "I think I could still go hunting if I could get out to a spot somewhere". At that point in his life he had a lot of difficulty walking. He also frequently would say to me, "I don't know why the Lord still leaves me here". He had wanted to go to heaven for several years. He missed mom and all his friends.

By January of 2015 dad was rapidly declining. He passed away quickly on January 22, 2015. Probably one of the more difficult things I have had to do as a minister was to preach his funeral on January 31st, which was held at the First Baptist Church of Calumet. Though part of me wasn't looking forward to it, another part of me couldn't wait to talk about my dad and his love for Jesus. He was not one to get up in front of people, although he could do that, he was a wonderful, and perhaps the best ever example of what a servant of God should be like. I am so looking forward to future chats with dad.

PHASE   VIII

OUR RETIREMENT YEARS

(2015- Present)

CHAPTER 87

GOD PROVIDES A HOUSE

Because we had lost most of our equity in our house in Mount Vernon due to the crash in the housing market, I thought we would either have to buy property and build with the help of the men in the church, or buy a fixer upper. After I retired in May of 2015 the church graciously allowed us to continue to live in the parsonage while we looked for our own place to live. We, together with the deacons, had tentatively set the date for being out of the parsonage at the end of 2015, but we had actually begun our search for a house in 2014. But we were not doing well with finding the right house for us. Either it needed too much work, was not in a good location, or it was just too expensive. We believed it would help the transition to Pastor Paul if we continued to attend FBC in Otsego, so we wanted to be in the Otsego area.

Our Christian realtor was working hard for us. We had pretty much given up on the idea of buying property and building. By the time we put in the well, septic, and landscaping, the house would be well above what we could afford, even if we had volunteer labor. And with that volunteer labor, the construction would no doubt drag out much longer than the end of 2015 when we really thought we should be out of the parsonage. Nancy and I were faithfully praying hard, since it was already getting into late fall of 2015.

One day our realtor called and said she had another fixer upper to show us on Douglas Road south of Plainwell. It was a stately old farm house with a lot of charm and some out buildings. But after carefully looking it over, it was apparent that it would take a lot of work and time to get it into a livable condition. We were getting discouraged. The realtor then mentioned that she had just talked to a lady who had lost her husband and needed to sell, but the house was not yet on the market. It was not a fixer upper, but she thought the house itself fit the description of what we were looking for.

We left the old farm house and followed our realtor out east of Plainwell to the house she had in mind. The house was located just east of Plainwell on M-89 on ten acres. The moment we walked into the house we knew it was the right one. In fact the floor plan was almost identical to the one I had drawn up when we were thinking of building. It was perfect for us. It had a room on the right just inside the front door that would be perfect as a studio for Nancy to teach piano lessons. It had a full basement that we could finish. It also had an attached garage as well as another garage big enough for me to have a work bench and process deer. It even had a small woods behind the house where I could go hunting!! The seller's price was affordable for us. In fact we thought it was a very good deal. We quickly closed the deal, bought the house, and moved in at the very end of December of 2015. We have taken turkey every year since purchasing the house, and so far one buck. God provided in such a wonderful way. He not only provided for our need of housing, but He provided even for our dream place for both Nancy and me. His grace is just so amazing!

CHAPTER 88

UPDATE ON OUR KIDS

Lori

I have already told some of Lori's story. But God's grace has been so good to Lori, too. Lori got married after we moved to Michigan in 2008. She met Ken Wall Jr. at the First Baptist Church of Otsego. His family had attended that church since before "Kenny" was born. So he had grown up in that church and had trusted Christ as his Savior when he was a boy. They were both very shy so needed help from a wonderful couple in our church, Cliff and Shirley Reber. Kenny was also coached by his sister, Tina. He e-mailed Lori and asked her out on a date. He even brought her flowers on their first date. They soon got engaged and were married on October 23, 2010. When the dear folks at Mount Vernon heard about the wedding the put together a whole bus load and came up for the wedding. I'm sure Becky Durbin had a lot to do with that. That was such a blessing to Lori.

After a few months of marriage God provided a bank owned house for them just a few blocks from the church, which they were able to purchase for the amazing price of just $35,000 with money that Kenny had been able to save. Kenny and Lori attend Otsego Baptist, where Lori continues to use her vocal talent, and Kenny serves with a non-profit organization called Handymen for Christ. They seem happy together for which Nancy and I are so extremely thankful.

Mark

Mark attended Cedarville University from 1991-1995. While traveling with his sister, Lori, for Cedarville in a musical group called the Sword Bearers, he got to know Andrea Gordon. Andrea had grown up in Brazil since her parents were career missionaries with Baptist Mid Missions. I remember the first time I met Andrea. Before Mark was dating her she had come to our church in Mount Vernon as part of the Sword Bearers group to minister to our teens in an "all-nighter" event. Nancy and I were still working with the teens at that time so we were involved that night. We were playing basketball with some of the teens and Andrea and I were on opposing teams. I remember saying to myself, "Wow, she is a scrappy competitive ball player." Phil, who was still in the youth group at the time, became friends with Andrea that night.

When Mark was home during Christmas break in 1993, he said he wanted to talk to Nancy and me. I remember him asking us to go back to our bedroom and asking us to sit down. I began to think the worst. I knew he was dating Andrea at the time. I trusted Mark, and I knew she was a wonderful young godly woman. But I also knew that in a weak moment bad decisions can be made. So I honestly thought Mark was going to tell Nancy and me that Andrea was pregnant. I prepared myself for the blow. Instead, Mark began his prepared speech to try to convince us that it was a good idea for him to get married that summer before he graduated from college. He even used the fact that Nancy and I had gotten married before I graduated as one of his arguments. When he finished, I was so relieved that I simply gave him my blessing. I think Mark was shocked. He had no idea why the battle for which he had prepared never happened. So Mark was engaged on Valentine's Day, February 14, 1994, and married Andrea in August of that year.

Mark served as the youth pastor at Cornerstone Baptist Church in Springfield, Ohio, from 1994-1999, and was the youth pastor at Calvary Baptist Church in Covington, Kentucky, from 1999-2006. In 2007 Mark and his family went to Ireland as missionaries, and came back to the states in 2009. After working for a Christian cleaning business for two and a half years, he started the Living Church in the Cincinnati area, which he still pastors. Mark and Andrea have four children: Grant, born on May 30, 1999, Luke, born on November 21, 2001, Aislinn, born April 25, 2006, and Kate, born in Ireland on July 7, 2008. They also had a miscarriage a month or two after arriving in Ireland.

Phil

Phil attended Cornerstone University in Grand Rapids, Michigan, from 1997-1998. While there he became part of a Christian rock band called Quietwiser and performed several concerts all over the nation and made several recordings with them. His interest in the band overshadowed by far his interest in academics at that time in his life. Though he dropped out of school after his first year, he continued with the band until 2005.

Nancy and I honestly did not "get" the music style that Phil loved, but we loved our son and were thankful that he wanted to use his band to bring others to Jesus. So Nancy and I actually attended one of his concerts when they were releasing a new recording. The concert was held at the Grand Rapids Seminary auditorium. We innocently made a very bad seating choice. We wanted our son to know how much we supported him, so we sat near the front – directly in front of one of the speakers. It was so loud it hurt. I tried to protect my ears. As discretely as I knew how I slipped my fingers up the side of my face and into my ears. Our ears survived, and we were proud of our son.

Phil met Stacey Vroma at a music store where she worked. They became fast friends because of their shared interest in their musical taste. They were married on August 16, 2003. On July 7, 2007, fraternal twin sons were born to Phil and Stacey (Jackson and Brayden). Unfortunately during that same pregnancy Phil and Stacey lost a third baby, a little girl, due to a topical pregnancy. Phil and Stacey would, unfortunately, get divorced in 2013.

Phil worked for a cell phone accessory business until he bought the business in 2005. His business involved having kiosks in four malls. From 2007-2009 he was a store manager for Blockbuster Video. In 2009 he changed careers and became a nurse tech. He continued in that capacity until 2014 when he graduated from nursing school and became a licensed RN. He continues to work as an RN in Spectrum Health in Grand Rapids at this writing. He loves his job and sees it as a ministry as he brings physical and spiritual help to others.

When Phil began studying for his new nursing career, he called me on the phone somewhat discouraged. He discovered that he had to take some courses over that he had already taken in high school because he had not gotten good enough grades on those courses. I remember so well what Phil told me: "Dad, if I could meet myself when I was back in high school at 16, I would beat myself up." Phil got excellent grades while attending nursing school and passed his state license board exams on his first try.

CHAPTER 89

GOD'S GRACE TO US IN OUR RETIREMENT YEARS

God has continued to allow us to help churches and pastors in our retirement years. I believe I have been able to be an encouragement to Pastor Paul at the church in Otsego. Nancy and I have been able to use our music at the church in Otsego as well as at other churches in the area. I have been especially blessed to be able to help my home church in Stanton, Michigan, while they were without a pastor by filling in some and helping the deacons through the process of calling another pastor. It has been encouraging to see that church get back on its feet. I have, also, filled in for some pastors in the area, helped some churches prepare for a new pastor, preached at Gitche Gumee Bible Camp, and held Bible conferences. At this stage of my life I am just happy whenever God gives me an opportunity to serve Him.

I am really looking forward to going to heaven. I think it would really be cool to be one of those caught up in the rapture.   I know that it will happen so fast that I won't have the sensation of flying, but it would still be really cool. I, also, know that God may choose to take me home by means of the "valley of the shadow of death". I have thought about what it will be like to see Jesus face to face. I don't think I will freak out. I think the God, Who has given me grace all my life, will give me grace for that moment as well. I just hope he gives me the grace that would allow me to kiss His feet.

CONCLUSION

There can be no doubt that God has extremely blessed my life. His grace has truly been poured out on me. But what about you? Where are you at in your relationship with God? Everyone is in one of three spiritual conditions:

Perhaps you have trusted Jesus as your Savior and have made Him the Lord of your life. You have given him the right to steer your life. This is the place of blessing. That doesn't mean that you will not have problems in life, but it does mean that you will have God's help through those problems, and His guidance, even when you don't know what to do (Psalm 1).

The second possible condition is that you have trusted Christ as your Savior, but you are not in fellowship with Him. You are trying to run your own life, and making decisions that you know would not be approved by God. If that is your situation you have got to be miserable, or you soon will be. God will bring circumstances into your life to bring you to a place of surrender to Him. That is His promise to you in Hebrews 12:6-8, "Whom the Lord loves He chastens...." The passage goes on to say that if you are not living for the Lord and are not getting "spanked" by Him, you are not saved. That is serious! That's not because God is mean, it is because He loves you and knows what is best for you. Get on your knees and confess your sin to Him (I John 1:9). Start going to church regularly (Hebrews 10:25), and getting to know Him by reading your Bible daily (I Peter 2:2). That is what turned my life around. I am so glad I finally gave in to God and surrendered the controls back to Him.

Thirdly, it may be that you are not saved. Maybe you thought you were saved at one time, but now you are not so sure. This is nothing to fool with. You must make sure. Heaven is real, but so is hell. And once you die, it is too late to be saved then. Allow me to share some simple truths that will help you make the right decision.

1. **First, you need to see your need to be saved.**

   The reason you need a Savior is because of your sin. Sin is disobeying God, the Creator of all that is. And that very God says we all have sinned. Romans 3:23 says it: "All have sinned...." Think about some of the ways you have sinned: lying, swearing, cheating, etc. The list could go on and on. You can even sin in your thoughts. God's Word says that sexual lust is sin (Matthew 5:28), and coveting what someone else has is sin (Exodus 20:17). You can even sin by not doing anything! God has given us a list of things to do such as read His Word, Pray, go to church, etc. And when we don't do what He tells us to do, that is also sin. So how many sins do you think you commit in a day after seeing all the ways it is possible to sin?

   Let's suppose you only committed three sins a day on average over your lifetime. In my opinion that would be a pretty good person. That would be over 1000 sins a year. Now multiply that by your age. Let's suppose you are thirty. That would be 30,000 sins that would have accumulated. What do you think a local judge would do with you if you came before him with 30,000 counts of crime on your record? I'm sure you would agree that you would never again see the light of day. You will one day go before The Judge, almighty God, Who knows all about you. The bottom line is that you are in big trouble – trouble that effects your eternal destiny.

But just when you think the situation couldn't get any worse, you need to realize some things about this God. Not only does He know every word you have ever spoken and every thought you have ever had (Psalm 139), He is also perfectly holy. What this means is that He can't let sin or a sinner into His heaven. Revelation 21:27 says that nothing that "defiles or causes an abomination or a lie" can enter heaven. The question isn't how could a good God send anyone to hell? The question is, how could a good God allow anyone into heaven, since we are all sinners?

But, perhaps, you think you can fix this problem yourself? Maybe you feel you can change, and start living a better life? God's Word makes it clear that we just can't do that. Ephesians 2:8&9 states: "For by grace are you saved through faith, and that not of yourselves. It is the gift of God. **Not of works**, lest anyone should boast." No one can be good enough to get into heaven. We would have to be perfect – without any sin. And our good deeds do not erase our bad deeds. Trying to get into heaven by being good enough is like trying to jump across the Grand Canyon. It just doesn't work.

But this leads us to the second truth you need to know. There is some very good news for you.

2. **God, Himself, has provided a way for you to get to heaven.**

One of the most well known verses in the Bible states: For God so loved the world (that includes you) that He gave His only begotten son, that whoever believes in Him (that includes you), shall not perish (go to hell), but have everlasting life (go to heaven) (John 3:16).

God exists in three persons, Father, Son, and Holy Spirit. That is hard to understand, but think of it something like you having a body, soul, and spirit. There is only one of you, but at death you are in two places at once. Your body is laid to rest in the ground, but your spirit and soul go to a place of torment, if you are not saved, or a place called heaven if you are saved. God sent His Son down to this earth to become a man (John 1:14), so He could live the sinless life you and I could not live.

Because he became a man, he could take your place and be your substitute before a holy God. Because Jesus was still God, He could pay the **infinite** sin debt for **every** person. That is exactly what Jesus did when He died on the cross. God the Father poured out all the hell you had coming to you on His own Son. Jesus paid your sin debt for you. That's what I Peter 2:24 states: "Who His own self (Jesus) bore our sins in His own body on the tree, that we being dead to sin might live unto righteousness...." Because He was without sin, His sacrifice for you and for me was acceptable before the Father.

This leads us to the third truth you need to know to be saved.

3. **You need to repent of your sin and place your trust in Jesus as your personal Savior.**

Remember what John 3:16 says, "whoever **believes** on Him...." God doesn't force His salvation on anyone. You have to want to be saved and take His offer in order to be saved. To **believe** on Him, means that you **receive** Him. John 1:12 states: "But as many as **received** Him, to them He gives the power to become the sons of God...." To receive Him, also, means that you turn from your sins and claim God's gift of salvation, by asking Jesus to save you. Another verse tells us how to do that. Jesus said, "Behold I stand at the door and knock. If anyone hears my voice and opens the door I will come into him" (Revelation 3:20). The door mentioned is this verse is the door of your heart. By inviting Jesus into your heart you are receiving Him as your Savior.

Suppose this is Christmas time, and there is a gift under the tree with your name on it. Someone goes and gets your gift and presents it to you. What do you have to do before that gift becomes yours? Remember it is already bought and paid for. You just have to take it!! That is the way it is with salvation. You trust God, that He has provided the gift of salvation for you, and you take what He offers.

Let's review. Do you know that you are a sinner and in big trouble with God? Do you believe that God, Himself, provided the way for you to be forgiven and cleansed from all your sin, by sending His own Son to come down to this earth and pay your sin debt? Do you believe Him, when He says He will save you if you open your hearts door to Him, and invite Him into your heart as your Savior? If you answered yes to those questions, then let's do just that. Let's talk to God and invite Him to be your Savior.

Here is a prayer to help you do that: "Dear Lord Jesus, I know that I am a sinner and deserve to go to hell. I believe you died on the cross for me as my substitute. Please come into my heart. I now receive you as my Savior. Please forgive me of all my sins, and help me to live for you. And take me to heaven some day. Thank you, Jesus. Amen."

Did you just pray that prayer and mean it. God does not lie. So if He said He would come into your heart, what did He do? That's right, He came in. And if He came into your heart, you are now going to heaven. Listen to what 1 John 5:12 says, "He that has the Son has life…" (eternal life).

If you just asked Jesus to save you, please let me know. I want to pray for you and help you get growing in your Christian life. You can call me on my personal cell phone number at 269-532-2684, or e-mail me at pastormejones@gmail.com. See you in heaven!!